River Otter

FIRST EDITION

Authoritative Guide
For Rafters, Kayakers, Canoeists

RiveR OtteR

Handbook For Trip Planning

Maria Eschen

anotter press, LLC

BOISE, IDAHO USA

River Otter

Handbook for Trip Planning

Published by: Anotter Press, LLC
115 Provident Drive
Boise, ID 83706-4017
http://www.anotterpress.com

Cover photograph by Todd Swanson. Back cover and all others (unless otherwise noted) are from the Eschen family collection.

Front cover design and line illustrations by Joshua Hindson.

Back cover design, typography, and layout art by Margaret Parker.

Lyric to "Brokedown Palace," by Robert Hunter, copyright Ice Nine Publishing Company. Used with permission.

Publisher's Cataloging-in-Publication
(Provided by Quality Books, Inc.)

Eschen, Maria.
    River otter : handbook for trip planning :
authoritative guide for rafters, kayakers, canoeists /
Maria Eschen. -- 1st ed.
    p. cm.
    Includes bibliographical references and index.
    LCCN 2003092099
    ISBN 0-9740046-0-X

    1. Canoes and canoeing. 2. Kayaking. 3. Rafting.
4. Travel--Planning. I. Title.

GV783.E83 2003   797.1'21
                    QBI33-1299

The paper used in this book is acid-free and recycled.
Printed in the United States of America

Dedication

For friends of the rivers: may our passion for river running always be fired by our desire to treat all precious watersheds with respect, so generations of river otters who follow us will enjoy the pleasures we have known.

Contents

LIST OF TABLES

APPENDIX TABLES

MEALS:

SHOPPING:

PACKING:

LIST OF ILLUSTRATIONS

Foreword

By Bill Sedivy

I remember the launch of my first multiday river trip as if it were yesterday.

There were six of us – all fairly experienced paddlers, but novices in the world of river expeditions – preparing to embark on a five-day journey through Desolation and Gray Canyons on Eastern Utah's Green River. It wasn't a pretty scene at the Sand Wash put-in.

More than a dozen dry bags lay scattered around the beach. Cases of beer baked in the hot sun. There were bags of potato chips everywhere. Everyone, it seemed, had brought along a lifetime supply of Lays. Lying loose in the dirt were ropes, straps, carabiners, and cargo nets. Being safety conscious, we had extra paddles, and throw bags, plus climbing rope, plus clothesline for securing odds and ends.

Now ordinarily, I'm a pretty easy-going guy. But on the day of our launch, at the start of my first-ever river expedition, my temper was as stormy as the winds that must have blown all that gear around the put-in. First, all of our supplies had to fit in one, 14-foot self-bailing raft, which I was rowing. No way. Second, it was 90 degrees by 10 a.m. But, the bottom line was that we had no idea what we were doing.

Before long, I began to snap at my traveling companions.

"Geez, Doug," I bellowed. "We said one bag each. What in the hell are you going to do with all this stuff! A wetsuit! You're kidding. It's a hundred degrees out here! What are we going to do if I pin this boat? It's a barge! Isn't there anything we can leave in the trucks?"

Eventually, my companions – and worst of all, my wife Maryl – began to snap back.

For the first mile or so, I doubted we would make it out of the canyons alive – much less make 15 miles to our planned destination for the day. Being an eastern paddle-raft guide, I was used to barking orders at my crew to line up for drops on rivers with current, rivers like the New and the Gauley in West Virginia. Left to my own oars, no real current and no crew to bark at, I couldn't seem to make the damn boat go straight – even in that placid flatwater.

Finally, I was able to make the boat go straight. Then, ever so gradually, I seemed to get in sync with the flow of the river. The canyon deepened and the miles slid by.

The remainder of that first expedition went fairly smoothly. Oh sure, we ran out of beer on day two, crushed chips, and had to deal with Maryl's scary allergic reaction to the wrong sunscreen.

In the end though, we had a ball. We saw new species of birds, deer and other wildlife. We saw pictographs drawn by ancient natives and deep, beautiful canyon walls bathed in the rosy light of early morning. Then there were the stars at night...and the marvelous quiet...quiet that is only experienced in the wilderness.

Looking back, that trip – dramas at the put in and all – changed my life.

River trips became an essential part of my being. Rivers became highways, taking me and my friends to places of quiet solitude. Rivers have taken me to places where I could forget about the day-to-day stresses of life. Rivers have transported me through new, spectacular landscapes...and rivers have shown me Mother Nature at her best.

In time, I realized the importance of protecting our rivers and streams from development, pollution, dams, diversion, and inappropriate mining and logging. That realization led me to the board of directors of American Whitewater. And today I work as executive director of Idaho Rivers United, a nonprofit advocacy group dedicated to helping river lovers protect the wild rivers and streams of Idaho.

But because that initial launch was such a disaster, my life could have turned out very differently. Yes, that Green River expedition could have been ruinous. My marriage, my friendships, and my river-running career could have ended on that hot, July day had the River gods not smiled on me. Only dumb luck, I'm sure, kept Maryl from leaving me after that first trip.

That is why I urge you to go forward now – novices and experienced river rats alike – and read Maria Eschen's book.

A veteran river trip planner and participant, a clear and entertaining writer, Maria has put together for us the Koran of coolers, the Torah of teamwork, and the New Testament of timetables, trip logistics, and multiday meal planning.

In these pages you'll also find worthwhile tips on safety, first aid, food handling, communication, and conservation – taking care of the rivers we float.

Ah...if only I'd had this book to guide me before that chaotic Green River launch. If only I'd had access to Maria's chapter on dividing trip chores...on menu planning...on packing the raft. It wouldn't have been the same, I guess – but Day 1 would have been way more fun.

So, novice floaters, read on and benefit from Maria's wisdom and experience. And you, river trip veterans – read on and add to your own store of knowledge.

Read this book, then have a good laugh the next time you see me at the put in – searching frantically for that missing kayak paddle or that AWOL life jacket. Go ahead and laugh as I stuff those extra cases of beer back in the truck.

And by the way, have a nice trip. If you read this book, and don't forget to review your checklist before you leave the house, you probably will.

Photo: Russ Krump

River Chef Bill Sedivy in Camp: former American Whitewater Board member, author of River's End: A Collection of Bedtime Stories for Paddlers, *and current Executive Director of Idaho Rivers United.*

Heads up!

Ask any otter: river running is a high-risk sport that can cause severe injury or death.

When you choose to organize or participate in a river trip, you are accepting full responsibility for your own safety. No book, manual, or video is a substitute for paddlesport skills learned and practiced under the watchful eyes of experienced boaters. This book cannot predict all the avoidable (and unavoidable) life-threatening hazards found on rivers or prevent all the possible pickles you might get yourself into.

River Otter: Handbook for Trip Planning is designed to provide you with ideas, but not a brain transplant.

This book offers descriptions of procedures and techniques that assume the reader has a basic level of knowledge and good sense. It cannot make an expert out of a novice. The lists, recipes, and examples herein grew by trial and error using information gained from readings, classes, discussions, and experience. These have worked for us up to this point. Use this handbook as one more source in your lifelong pursuit of river knowledge.

Read broadly, join paddling clubs or organizations, and practice new skills and techniques in the safety of your kitchen, backyard, and easy water close to home. Take short, simple outings on rivers of graduated difficulty. Always include experienced boaters on your multiday trips. Take first aid, CPR, and river rescue classes. Stay current and informed.

Above all, be honest with yourself about your and limitations. Rivers have ways of keeping us humble.

Introduction

River Otter — *Lutra canadensis*

Habits: Aquatic, but may travel several miles over land to reach another stream or lake. A sociable animal, usually 2 or more travel together.

—BURT AND GROSSENHEIDER; ROGER TORY PETERSON, ED. *A FIELD GUIDE TO THE MAMMALS*

One sunny day you choose to be a river otter.

Day jobs, day care, and day-to-day problems lie behind you. No hired guides, just you and your raft, canoe, or kayak, some friends, some grub – and off you go. Independent.

Ahead, the current whispers your name. Swirling images of congenial river camping with your self-outfitted group tease up memories of childhood campfires. Huck and Tom, *Wind in the Willows*, freedom from the humdrum. The scent of seep-spring monkey flowers, the antics of mayflies and trout. Yes, you fantasize, a noncommercial, multiday float trip. In the wilds. A spontaneous success. Ah, for the fun-loving otter's life – part playing and part surviving!

This book is for recreational river runners, professional outdoor educators, and river managers who want to learn how to spend more time playing and less time struggling. My purpose is to keep the otter's spirit alive on the river with a handbook for planning and executing multiday, self-outfitted trips that are fun, safe, and ecologically sensitive. The down-to-earth advice I offer you was born on the river … watching friends and their river families organize … rubbing paddles with Canadians, Alaskans, Austrians, and Grand Canyon folks. I've tried to capture the essence of what has to be done and how to do it.

Planning makes any trip better, for trip leaders and group members, novices and experienced boaters, great cooks and great eaters. The goal is a hassle-reduced trip with the forces of nature and chance as the main challenges. This handbook will be especially useful for anyone who would like to organize a "leave-no-trace" trip on a regulated river.

Otters have lived for millennia on the river and have passed their learning from generation to generation. This book passes on practical information I've learned from twenty-four years of canoeing and twelve more kayaking. My philosophy is simple: river runners want to be otters. But here's the problem. *Lutra canadensis* has spent its whole life hanging around rivers. It's rare for humans to have the otter's river experience and skills, no matter how much gear we have or what we paid for our nonmotorized boat. And very few river runners can let their trips happen pell-mell, like otters sliding down a riverbank.

The river otter icon – – will appear throughout this text with reminders: to focus on why we're floating rivers, to lighten up, to offer helpful facts and hints. From time to time while writing this book, I'd feel things getting heavy – flashbacks of river accidents and near misses. Then I'd picture the otter, and I'd have to smile. I'm a competent Class III-IV kayaker, but am getting more cautious with age, especially when novices are with us. Our river trips no longer meander in the channel of least resistance as they did when we'd throw the kids in the canoe along with sacks of ramen noodles. Maybe I like planning my fun more now because I've discovered it prevents worries and gives me free time on the river and in camp … time to sing otter songs.

My tips and hints are the result of trial and error, seasoned with some of the negative stress that you'll read about in my adventures. But paddling rivers in a group is usually a positive stress. The experience of meeting unanticipated challenges together and handling the consequences builds self-esteem, skills, and life-long friendships. Lack of preparation increases the likelihood that bands of human river otters will squabble, degrade sensitive river corridor ecology, and, let's face it, endanger their lives.

I've floated Idaho's permitted Middle Fork, Main Salmon, and Hell's Canyon on the Snake, as well as less regulated river stretches of Class II-IV whitewater in vacation wonderlands. I've made my share of mistakes and learned from the river. Will I ever forget canoe-camping with my husband Barry and our two-year-old son on the Buffalo in Arkansas and kayak-camping with them twenty-plus years later when I turned fifty on Oregon's Owyhee River? Whether it was Colorado's Upper Rio Grande, New York's Erie Canal, California's Nacimiento, or Oklahoma's Glover and Mountain Fork, river travel has created peak life experiences for our family, along with some close calls.

These pages came to life because two veteran river runners in our group, Keith Taylor and Mike Norell, friends of the late kayak legend Walt Blackadar, urged me to write down the organizing methods our group uses.

"Boring," I said to them.

"Not at all – it's important stuff. And, you know, we're not going to be around forever."

"I bet someone's done this already," I said.

"Quit your grumbling and get busy," one of the silver foxes told me.

I dug into river literature. My shelves and those in our public library are full of many useful river handbooks. Among the best are Kesselheim's *Wilderness Paddler's Handbook*, Huser's *River Running*, Bechdel & Ray's *River Rescue*, Mill's *Rocky Mountain Kettle Cuisine*, and Gill's *Wilderness First Aid*. The Internet is loaded with private and commercial webpages, providing hours of browsing pleasure. My research, however, turned up no books or sites devoted solely to river trip planning. No sources talked about how group dynamics, leadership, health, safety, sanitation, and good food fit together to make a great mixed-craft trip. Unlike learning to paddle or raft, I couldn't find a how-to book on organizing and pulling off a self-outfitted trip, despite the popularity of river running.

Old-timers may grumble at the explosion of paddlesports and the growth of government controls on American and Canadian rivers, but regulations function to protect water quality, river flora and fauna, and "the wilderness experience" from hordes of river runners. Just compare river camps near you to what they were a few years ago, and you'll know what I mean. Thousands of visitors annually could wreak havoc on your favorite pristine river unless everyone follows basic river etiquette. The Bureau of Land Management, U.S. Forest Service, National Park Service, and local authorities issue lottery or on-request permits to monitor the demand and enforce preservation policies. This handbook offers tech-

Take a look at what's happening!

- The National Park Service reports the waiting list for a private boater permit on the Colorado River in the Grand Canyon now exceeds twelve years.

- The U.S. Forest Service reports applications to float Idaho's four permit-required rivers increased twenty-four percent (24%) in five years (1996-2001). The ratio of success for applicants for Middle Fork of the Salmon River permits went from one in twenty (1:20) to one in thirty (1:30) during that same period.

niques I've learned for dealing with river regulations and etiquette so you and your great-grandkids (and mine too) can have enjoyable trips through river otter country.

HERE ARE THE HIGHLIGHTS:

PART ONE – PRELIMINARIES. Essential "pre-logistics" concerns are covered in-depth:

- river options
- commercial or noncommercial trip style
- paddling party selection
- lottery and on-request permits
- river authority regulations on group size and conduct
- river etiquette

Important formal regulations and informal ethics are reviewed with an eye on what's necessary to keep our rivers healthy and a joy to visit.

PART TWO – PLANNING. Learn how to set up a timetable, evaluate your group's abilities and skills, communicate clearly and openly, and set a good meeting agenda.

Photo: Todd Swanson

PART THREE – ORGANIZATION. Explore in-depth the team approach strategy for delegating daily camp duties:
- meal preparation
- clean-up
- providing for sanitation and water requirements
- assisting with raft loading and unloading.

PART FOUR – RESPONSIBILITIES. Discover how to divide the major responsibilities (leadership, finances, gear, supplies, medical, safety, transportation, food, and fun activities) into manageable chunks. Look here for complete sample gear and equipment assembly lists that have helped organize our multiday trips for three to twenty-four participants.

PART FIVE – MASTERING RIVER MEALS. Adapt the real-life tables for menu planning, shopping, and packing to your party size. Tinker with them until they fit your style.

PART SIX – PACKING PUZZLES. "How's all this gonna fit?" Learn how to stage your packing to prevent forgotten gear.

PART SEVEN – POST TRIP. These duties include what we all hate to deal with (the chores) and what we love to do (partying, sharing photos, and planning for the future). Explore how to wrap up a successful adventure on the best note possible.

Twelve **appendices** are included. Appropriate sections can be shared with trip members at the first planning meeting.

- Appendix 1 – "river safety talk" is geared toward novices on a crew, but is a good annual review for any boater.

- Appendix 2 – "copy ready versions of tables" includes practical examples of menu sheets and corresponding shopping and packing lists, all ready to pass out to trip members.

- Appendices 3-10 are full of down-to-earth details on group cooking, designed to avert a headache or two for trip food planners and camp cooks.

- Appendix 11 – "contacts for river trip permit applications" lists updated contacts and websites.

- Appendix 12 – "resource contacts" lists important river-running information about conservation groups, sources of education and training, maps, and key water-user data to link you up for fun and adventure.

- The **bibliography** offers an opportunity for readers to further explore details of river running and trip organization after finishing this book.

- The **index** is designed for rapidly finding what readers need.

In summary, this handbook is designed to provide ideas for you. It does not propose to make experts out of novices. Gain experience either by including experienced river travelers in your party or by starting out with simple short trips.

So, will this handbook save time, money, and energy?

Yes. More river runners will meet the goal of enjoying multiday trips like so many river otters enjoying life on rivers.

- You'll sleep better.

- Your friends will love you.

- Your trip will have a greater chance of being a dream come true, rather than a nightmare.

Too much? Over the top? Well, let's begin with a real-life vignette.

Part One:
Preliminaries

A kayaking couple on a commercial trip with a professional guide, running Idaho's Lower Salmon River for their anniversary. Note the cataraft's metal floor, rocket storage boxes, and well-packed load.

CHAPTER ONE

A True Story

Do you have anything for a headache?

—TRIP LEADER ON THE EVE OF DEPARTURE

A dozen friends have gathered in a home the evening before your launch date on a wilderness river. Sacks of food fill every kitchen counter. You just tripped over a case of beer on the floor and barked your shin on an empty military rocket-box. Your river pals are snacking on tortilla chips – the ones you bought for the taco salad on the last night in camp. If you're the trip leader, you keep hearing your name … so often you'd like to change it. If you're a group member, you try to help, offer your thoughts along with the others:

"Hey Trip Leader! Where should I pack the frozen chicken – it's thawing out!"

"What d'ya mean there's gonna be no decaf … cocoa … diet pop … salt substitute?"

"I don't think all this junk can fit in my raft's drybox. What am I, a Sherpa?"

"We don't have enough beer!"

Dogs bark and babies cry.

"Would people just shut up for two minutes," the leader yells. "I'm going crazy!"

Yep. Suddenly, you realize you won't be able to stand the sight of these people for seven long days on a river. Your stomach's in knots and you're one worried boater. In fact, you feel so grouchy you don't laugh when someone says there's one advantage to all this pandemonium: you could offer *Paddler* magazine an article on "River Trips from Hell."

Ah, but there's a better way.

Pre-Logistics Checklist

Before charging into the mind-numbing details of trip planning, sit down a moment and dream. Find a riverbank or a cozy chair and imagine your ideal river trip. Ask:

- Who? Who are your favorite paddlers and their significant others? Who else has good abilities and experience to assure a safe trip?

- What? What kind of a trip is best for you – high, medium, or low difficulty: fighting rapids, floating currents, or fishing flat-water? What kind of craft will make the ideal trip?

- Where? Where's the ideal spot for that kind of trip? Where is the best practical choice?

- When? When's the best time to take the trip? Consider personal and river dynamics.

- Why? Why are you going? Will others share these expectations?

- How? How can you and your ideal group slog through the pre-trip hurdles – regulations and organizing – and have fun doing it?

    Read on ...

Photo: Todd Swanson

U.S. Forest Service River Ranger Sara (left) assembles a group for their pre-launch trip talk and distribution of boat registration tags.

CHAPTER TWO

River Manager Riddles

What walks on four legs in the morning, two at noon, and three in the evening?

– THE SPHINX'S RIDDLE FOR OEDIPUS

WHO RUNS THE RIVERS?

The easy answer is boaters.

- Millions of people float down rivers in nonmotorized craft annually.

- An estimated 24.8 million people kayak, canoe, or raft in America, a number predicted to grow at least 5% per year (Jeffrey Yeager of the American Canoe Association [ACA], 1999).

- Forty-five thousand individuals belong to the ACA, which trains 100,000 students a year and sanctions more than 700 events.

- Every year 22,000 river-runners float down the Colorado River in the Grand Canyon, and about 7,600 others wait for their names to be chosen. And that's only one river.

- America Outdoors,® representing 500 professional outfitters, serves 2.5 million a year.

- The website Boatertalk.com boasted 23,791 registered members in March, 2003.

- River-running is a *multi*-million dollar industry.

Boaters rule, right?

Yes, but you're only half right if your riddle answer guessed it's boaters who run rivers.

Running rivers also means controlling them. And government authorities control America's and Canada's best multiday trip rivers. These local, territorial, county, provincial, state, and federal employees run complex operations to protect rivers by issuing permits and enforcing regulations.

They wear different agency hats: U.S. Forest Service district rangers and river managers, U.S. National Park Service employees, Bureau of Land Management officers, U.S. Fish and Wildlife Service personnel, and a variety of cooperating governmental employees in the Canadian Heritage Rivers System.

It is hard to find a river with multiday trip potential that hasn't been touched by the hand of river managers. On a hundred sixty Wild and Scenic Rivers and hundreds more protected river segments, including thirty-nine of Canada's best rivers, these managers enforce policies written in statutes, rules, and regulations. They process permit applications and assure legal compliance with fines and even jail time. Appendix 11 lists websites to access more information about hundreds of multiday trip options on protected U.S. and Canadian rivers.

HOW DO RIVER MANAGERS MANAGE US?

River authorities categorize river runners according to their type of craft (motorized or nonmotorized) and their purpose (commercial or non-commercial). They govern boaters by using permits that are issued to recreational and for-profit applicants. The 1989 Colorado River Management Plan (CRMP) of the U.S. National Park Service is the granddaddy of all river planning regulations. Its definition for noncommercial (private boater) river trips has become the model for other regulated wilderness rivers in Idaho, Oregon, Utah, and beyond:

> A non-commercial river trip must be participatory in nature. Trip preparation (including logistics, food purchases, equipment assembly, transportation, and vehicle shuttle) and conduct of the trip (including food preparation and sanitation) must be shared by members of the group.

> (CRMP, Appendix VI, section D. A. I, 1989)

The regulations clearly require that the plethora of duties must be shared on a self-outfitted trip. If river runners want to float the Grand Canyon or other similarly permitted rivers, we have two choices: 1. pay licensed outfitters and guides to take us down on their commercial trips; or 2. win a noncommercial boater permit and self-outfit using the participatory model – everyone helps and no one's compensated for outfitting or guiding. Float trips on unregulated rivers offer the same choices: hire a licensed guide or do it ourselves.

Let's use an example from one of the original eight Wild and Scenic Rivers, designated by Congress in 1968. The Middle Fork of the Salmon River in Idaho's Frank Church River of No Return Wilderness requires a permit. It is a river with many rules to follow, such as a prohibition on motorized craft and a limit to group size. The private permit-holder must also affirm in writing that the trip meets the following Forest Service District definition:

> *A trip is noncommercial if there is a bona fide sharing of costs where no part of the fees are collected in excess of actual costs of the activity, for salary or financial gain in any manner for any of the group, its leaders or sponsors or for capital increase or amortization of the major equipment. Noncommercial trips include the genuine 'do-it-yourselfers' who get together to participate in river trips. Group leaders may not be paid in any manner.*

(U.S. Forest Service, Four Rivers Lottery
System Information, 2002)

River authorities don't ask if our private groups might be better off on a commercial trip. They expect we understand the International Scale of River Difficulty (Class I-VI, see Appendix 1) and have assessed the skill level of our group to run these rapids. They trust us to know our abilities to provide for the well being of our group of "do-it-yourselfers."

Now, assume you've weighed the advantages of each type of trip and you decide to be a legal, noncommercial group on the Middle Fork. Four important steps are ahead:

1. **STEP ONE – OBTAIN A PERMIT.** In the case of the Middle Fork of the Salmon, a boater can float the first seven miles of the Middle Fork without a permit (from its birth in the confluence of Bear Valley and Marsh Creeks

advantages of Commercial and noncommercial Trips

- Outfitters treat you like guests. They transport you and your gear, set up your tent, prepare scrumptious meals and beverages. Your chance of a bad meal are slim to none. They'll tell you stories, even teach you yoga and history lessons on specialty trips. You can rest assured that licensed outfitters and guides will keep you safe and happy on rivers that you might not otherwise be able to travel because of hard-to-obtain permits or river difficulty.

- A self-outfitted trip costs less, approximately one quarter the cost of a commercial trip. You treat yourself like a guest on the river and tell your own stories. You structure your trip around your group's style of river running/camping. You reap the benefits of your own work.

Self-contained trips allow boaters to experience remote river and spectacular scenery.

until the Boundary Creek Campground). From there on, every group needs a permit to complete the next ninety-eight miles, obtained by lottery for summer trips and on a first-come-first-served basis during the off-season. Application procedures for other permitted rivers are highly variable. The Rogue River in Oregon, for example, has contracted the process to a private company, yet Oregon's Owyhee River has the BLM issuing on-demand permits. Know your river – you may not need any kind of permit or permission to run it. Consult Appendix 11 for how to choose the right river for your trip.

2. STEP TWO – SHARE EXPENSES. The easy part is roughing out a budget and requiring all participants to share the expenses equally. Of course, this means no trip member can be paid to conduct the trip. The trickier part comes after the money's in the trip account.

3. STEP THREE – TRIP PARTICIPATION. Once I knew a permit-holder who shared trip expenses, but acted like a professional outfitter, while his group members sat back. He told them to stay out of his kitchen and they did. He wasn't paid, but his "my way or the highway" attitude put the otter's fun spirit in jeopardy. Needless to say, I stayed out of his kitchen and off his trip list. How will participation be shared as equally as the trip funding?

- "The team approach" is the answer to completing daily river camping chores. The details of this concept are in Part Three. This is the same teamwork we learned as kids in baseball, yet that's what often makes it so hard for boaters. Many of us are *individual*-sport, not *team*-sport, oriented. Democratic leadership is the goal, but anarchy threatens when we're in a group. Decision making is often piece-meal and free-floating. Yet we all know certain decisions aren't amenable to the democratic process (like whether or not to pack the toilet paper in a thin plastic trash sack). The "team duty roster" offers a practical method of organizing that makes a trip smooth. Key tasks on the roster are: water/sanitation, food (planning, packing, and preparation), and clean-up. Gear tables in check-off format will help readers plan and pack with the most efficient lists available.

- "Key responsibility assignments" is the answer to not leaving important leadership duties to chance. Individuals contribute specialized skills and take responsibility for the tasks I'll explore in Part Four. Self-supported trips need willing and capable individuals to meet such group needs as health and safety interventions, in addition to the on-going work of the river camping teams.

4. STEP FOUR – USE YOUR RIVER MANAGERS. River authorities provide information and guidance for us on how to conduct our trips so as to maximize conservation and recreational values as defined by their agency. They publish printed materials, answer inquiries, conduct riverside ranger talks, and even serve as floating river encyclopedias as they monitor their river. It's a big job that merits a closer look.

DOES A RIVER COME WITH OPERATING INSTRUCTIONS?

Rest assured, the river managers will send permit-holders lots of "guidance" before you launch. Read it all or risk losing your permit. For example, one year our permit-holder didn't read the instructions to confirm acceptance in writing by a deadline. I was among sixteen people with long faces when our trip was forfeited. We had to call the Forest Service every day for a couple weeks to see if anyone had cancelled and we could take their spot.

Here are some examples of information sent to us by the Middle Fork Ranger District in the *2000 Boater Information* publication:

- "Before making a final decision on the items you plan to take ... pack all gear in your inflated boat ...."

- "Patching equipment for major repairs should be present in each boat ...."

- "We recommend that your food supply contain as many non-perishable items as possible ...."

- "A first-aid kit designed for wilderness survival ...."

- "Boats should not be overloaded ...."

- "A float trip is very strenuous activity ...."

- "The guards will check your required equipment before you launch ...."

"What is all this?" you mutter while reading the pages in your info packet. "Isn't a river trip supposed to be fun? This sounds like a military expedition."

The time invested up front in effective preparation will make your trip fun and less problematic. Planning can be fun, too! When you have followed the suggestions of these river managers, who are experienced boaters and outdoor recreation specialists, you will feel prepared. A co-worker once told me our party looked like we could take over a small country, we were so prepared.

Consider these two important steps as required logistics homework:

1. Sit down and read the specific river manager materials pertinent to your river. What you learn about hazards, safety, and equipment will pay off when you're on the water and enjoying life in camp.

2. Review the written guidance with an eye toward the composition of your river party. Try to choose your trip members as carefully as you'd choose your line down a rapid. Match the difficulty of the river and the skill of your team.

Eric Hermann summarized how to do this in *Paddler* magazine (March-April, 2000): "The first step is enlisting a core of committed paddlers …. If the journey demands a certain skill level, be candid enough to exclude paddlers with questionable skills." Whether you are a trip leader or a group member, you now may be pondering the question of appropriate trip members and how to make your crew click.

Some major answers can be found in good trip organization and a careful review of trip responsibilities.

America Outdoors®

If you realize now that self-outfitting is only going to put you one step closer to a heart attack, stop reading here. Contact http://www.americaoutdoors.org – "the national voice of America's outfitters and guides" – an international non-profit association of professional companies who provide outdoor recreation services. In order to protect the public, outfitter members of America Outdoors® must hold the permits required by river authorities. An example of one of their state affiliates is the business trade organization, Idaho Outfitters and Guides Association (208-342-1438 or www.ioga.org). These groups can provide river-specific lists of professionals who can offer you a commercial trip where you are treated as a guest on the motorized or nonmotorized craft of your choice.

Part Two:
Trip Planning

Relaxing in an inflatable kayak between rapids keeps Andrea in sync with the river's tempo.

CHAPTER THREE

Your Crew and Capacities

No gale that blew dismayed her crew
Or troubled the Captain's mind.

—CHARLES CARRYL: *A NAUTICAL BALLAD*

If you are the permit-holder or trip leader (or if you can influence them), begin the process of choosing trip members with river authority information. If you don't have specifics, consult a guidebook, Appendix 11, or the Leave No Trace Center for Outdoor Ethics literature (the National Outdoor Leadership School – NOLS – was a founding partner). Their philosophy is that modern river runners seek beauty, excitement, and solitude in wild rivers; planning is necessary to help us protect those valuable qualities.

> *Adequate planning and preparation is the first step in protecting the area you will visit. Plan ahead by considering your goals and those of your group. Prepare by gathering information, communicating expectations, and acquiring the technical skills, first aid knowledge, and equipment to do the trip right.*
>
> (Leave No Trace Center for Outdoor
> Ethics: *Western River Corridors*, 2001)

Better mull over who exactly your group (crew) is and whether they have the abilities and experience (capacities) to meet your parameters for a safe and fun trip on your chosen river.

If you're a hardshell kayaker, you know that almost any river suitable for a multiday float party can be run self-contained by skilled paddlers. Assume, however, that not everyone who wants to go on your trip will be a skilled boater. For your river, raft support may be the answer.

Raft support makes a river trip sing and compliments the scouting/safety-boating services of kayakers. Throw in a few canoeists and the orchestra strikes up: a variety of craft taking a harmonious and fun trip.

Let the search begin. Who has river knowledge, first aid experience, and gear? Who'd be fun? Compatible crew members are usually found among

Photo: Todd Swanson

Hardshell kayakers like Christian can't carry much gear, but they're invaluable safety boaters whose antics in rapids are surefire crowd pleasers.

your friends from day trips close to home. Size up your future trip buddies ahead of seeing them for a week of mornings before you've had your coffee.

As a sample, let's use the *2000 Boater Information* from the Middle Fork of the Salmon River Ranger District. Be honest as you evaluate ranger guidance in light of your prospective trip member alternatives.

- *Those who do have problems and are forced to walk or fly out are usually: Parties that were ill prepared because of sub-standard boats, poor equipment or poor judgement; OR Parties that attempted to run whitewater far beyond the skills, knowledge or capabilities of the boatman.*

Think about whether it's safe to invite Clarence Couchpotato and his army-surplus pontoon boat. Maybe he'd like to try an inflatable kayak. Perhaps you should ask Carly Catarafter to provide raft support instead; she has solid equipment and skills.

- *Life jackets should be worn at all times on the river.*

Think about overhearing Macho Matt Monkeybiz say, "I swim better without a bunch of padding weighing me down – no jacket for me." Think about Staircase Steve who has swum the tough stuff and survived thanks to his PFD (personal floatation device). These two should talk.

- *Your camp gear should be sturdy enough to withstand the rigors of the river travel and light enough to avoid overloading your boat.*

You know the upper stretch is a rigorous and rocky. Thurgood T. Tweedy, a classy rafter, calls you. The first thing out of his mouth is how he'll bring four cases of his home microbrew in glass bottles, "which should last us until The Flying B." Does he know the hazards of drinking while paddling, not to mention the dangers of glass on the river? Maybe you should invite Ala Nonymous to the planning meeting – the old canoeist who once said "Anything I can do, I can do better sober." And speaking of overloading, what's your childhood friend, Gary Gearhead, going to say about having to leave his collapsible kitchen sink-table contraption and his canvas tent and cot at home?

- *One of the following human waste pack-out systems is required....*

Think of Ellie Engineer who has designed an ergonomic seat for portable toilets. She needs to chat with your cousin Connie Cowgirl who spurns outhouses and such "cuz hikers and packhorses do their business wherever they please."

- *All personal items should be placed in waterproof bags and secured to the boat.*

This doesn't mean the same thing to everyone. Aimee Surplus's idea of a waterproof gearbag is a black plastic garbage sack. But she's new to river camping ... you have an extra waterproof bag ... and she's a great wilderness cook.

- *Overboard: If you become separated from your boat....*

Good grief, your godfather Uncle Ulysses can't swim a stroke and would panic if a raft flipped. You realize a nice commercial trip's for him and contact America Outdoors®.

- *Be alert for rattlesnakes, falling rocks, poison ivy, ticks, wasps, bees and yellowjackets, black bears, and other various wildlife.*

You know Beatrix Beesting will need to have an epinephrine pen along; maybe others have allergies too. Jot this down on your agenda for group discussion. Consider whether your sister-in-law Hampton Hallie would be happy camping out for seven nights, because she hasn't camped since Girl Scouts. "Wildlife"? Have a plan for when Tina Teenybopper and friends want to paddle the inflatable kayaks off at night to meet "hotties" in a neighboring camp.

- *We recommend treating the water you drink because it is always subject to contamination ... filter or boil all drinking water prior to consumption.*

You wonder how many water bottles Billie Jean Backpacker's pocket filter really can fill before noon each day. Maybe it's time to buy an expedition-size pump and filter system if the trip maxes out at twenty-four.

- *Build fires only in safe locations within a fire pan ... Do not build fire rings.*

The s'more-lovers will have to toast them on something smaller than a bonfire; you'll have to control Freddy Fireball's passion for pruning camp trees to make an inferno. You rest easy knowing Samantha Smokejumper will be along to arm-wrestle him into controlling his urges.

- *Picking up all garbage ... cigarette butts....*

Will Joey Camel, Jr. comply, or will you have to hassle him, even clean up after him? You remember Nancy Neatnik, RN, not only sets up a good kitchen protocol, but will ride herd on Joey if need be.

- *The Antiquities Act prohibits the casual collection of artifacts....*

Bad news for Arrowhead Abe who wants to add to his collection. Good news for Sylvia Safetyboater who is majoring in anthropology and would add interesting information on the Native American culture in the river corridor.

- *Use any soap products well above the high water mark.*

Sid Skinnydipper won't like hearing that salon products are among those prohibited in the river and in the hotsprings. You can solve that problem by bringing along a solar shower or bucket for bathing away from water sources.

Tired from all this?

Yes, choosing a crew is brain-wracking. Only you can judge your comfort level with other boaters and passengers on the trip. If the permit-holder wants an all-kayak trip and is prepared to "go light," but you aren't – then find another trip. The opposite extreme is a group that operates with a carved-in-stone formula of one raft per two people – one to row, a passenger, and unlimited cooler capacity. There are almost as many crew/capacity combinations as there are rivers, but two stand out.

1. Number one is the ability and experience level of your river party relative to the difficulty of your river.

[A] Proficient rafters, familiar with the stretch of river, are the best insurance you can have. They'll share opinions on trip numbers and let you know how much gear they are willing to carry: "What d'ya mean we only got two rafts and fourteen kayaks!" Cranky rafters get that way because a river trip is supposed to be a vacation for them, too. Nine personal gearbags, two coolers, two dryboxes, and miscellaneous porta-potties, buckets, chairs, and other containers of food and fuel would make even Santa grouchy.

A small river running crew with more than 100 years of combined experience assured this expedition was safe as well as fun.

[B] Kayakers who refuse to self-contain any of their personal items tend to widen the rift between themselves and the rafters. They earn the reputation of play-boaters in the rafters' eyes. Child-parent behavior patterns can emerge – a river trip can turn into "Ferris Bueller's Day Off." Be on the lookout for sarcasm from the martyred rafters (calling kayakers "river maggots") and adolescent cracks from kayakers (calling raft passengers "hood ornaments"). Some joking is normal nonetheless, because, as Travis Emerizy once said: "Rafters are the goalies of River Folk; what they do is completely different than kayaking."

[C] The high maintenance members of the crew tend to be inexperienced members (possibly beginner inflatable kayakers and raft passengers). This is especially true if they are poor swimmers or new to camping. Provide them information and be prepared for "teachable moments." Be sure they listen to the river safety talk (Appendix 1), as they need to learn what a mistake on their part can do to the trip and to themselves. Any member of your trip, however, can get hypothermia and sunstroke, foot and leg injuries, and exhaustion. I've been on trips when: a Grand Canyon rafter only brought shorts and T-shirt for the first frosty night; highly educated professionals got hypothermia, heatstroke disorientation, and burned feet; and I've been grateful someone recognized I was pooped and needed to stop for a rest and food.

Consider this humor yardstick to measure spirit:

Rafters are on a beach making chukar calls. A passing kayaker says loudly, "Must be trying to make contact with some form of higher intelligence." Your rafters may chuckle, splash the kayaker with an oar stroke, or get nasty – refusing to share gorp or water. Keep your ears open for intra-group conflicts that undermine the otter's spirit and think about ways to help your crew establish healthy communications.

2. Number two in capacity and crew considerations is group spirit – the "All for One and One for All" type of spirit.

If your crew is composed of friendly, considerate team players, you can probably accommodate a few more "newbies." But, if your dead-weight is a selfish prima donna teen who naps while everyone else makes dinner and adds nothing to camp life but a new hue of nail polish, you may decide against inviting him (aha, caught you, didn't I?).

Many a good navigator and excellent campfire story-teller has come from the ranks of the "newbies." Just because a person is "only a passenger" or is new to river running, don't exclude them out of hand. Think about it. You had your first river trip with someone who was kind enough to think you'd like it and you came back for more. If you don't know how someone will do on your multiday trip, take a one- or two-day overnight trip with them. Camp out on the riverside and see how it goes.

CHAPTER FOUR

Communication

No pleasure is fully delightsome without communication....

—MONTAIGNE: ESSAYS, III, I

On an extended trip, particularly in the wilderness, your party must be able to communicate clearly. It may save a life.

A trip leader can set the example in the way potential party members are approached and kept informed. Then, at the planning meetings the leader can promote open communications as the trip standard. However, getting issues out on the table diplomatically is both a gift and a developed skill. We all know people we don't like to be around. Assess whether or not certain personality types should be invited on your trip, and, if they are, how you plan to deal with potential conflict. The river's a great place to get close to people as well as nature. Try not to let communication problems fester and blow up.

First, just say "HALTT!" Problems can stem from group members who are suffering from HALT (Hungry, Angry, Lonely, or Tired – I've added Thirsty as the additional "T"). Usually just getting some water/food into them is all that's necessary for a behavior change.

River trips do come with built-in stress:

> Many natural hazards exist and conditions can change at any time, such as high and low water, named and unnamed rapids, sudden weather changes, blocked river channels, falling rocks and trees, fire, wildlife, plants, insects, avalanches, land slides, blowouts, cliffs, large boulders, jagged rocks, water currents and temperature, ledge hydraulics, holes, eddies, whirlpools, strainers, exposed or submerged undercut rocks, boulder sieves, standing waves, etc.

(Middle Fork Ranger District:
2000 Boater Information)

Indeed. Any part of that list may put a trip member over the edge. The result is that now the group needs to deal with a human problem as well as a natural one. What preventive techniques can be used to assure a good supportive environment for effective communication?

A trip leader or member should step in when they hear *judging* (criticizing, name-calling) or *control-freaking* (ordering, threatening, moralizing). Remind them that we all make mistakes, and we were all beginners at one time. No one should ever try to cajole river runners out of their careful decisions to portage around a rapid. Use judgment in deciding whether to take someone to the woodshed or discuss the issue in a group meeting. Always deal frankly with concerns before they blow up, especially these:

DOMINANCE CONFLICTS: "BOSSY AIN'T ONLY A COW."

If the leader treats trip members like supervised workers, the crew may mutiny. Bossy boaters upset the otter's friendly spirit and need to be reminded of the independent nature of river tripping. Being able to arrive at mutually determined decisions will assure that group members enjoy the trip. For example, make compromises about daily rise 'n' shine and launch times. Negotiating skills creating a win-win situation come in handy. Try also to reach decisions by consensus rather than voting. Reaching consensus takes longer, but voting almost always means someone loses. Make sure your members are willing to compromise. A trip member who is unwilling to compromise for the good of the group should be left at home.

A large crew poses after packing 20 boats for 21 boaters and gear for an eight-day expedition.

PASSIVE-AGGRESSIVE DISPLAYS: "WHADYA MEAN THE BEST DEFENSE ISN'T A GOOD OFFENSE?"

In the animal kingdom an aggressive behavior may spring from insecurity over territory or other fears. We're no different. On the river many challenges face us, from gnarly boat-eating holes clearly labeled on the map to unanticipated problems like bears invading camp at night. Some trip members may react to stress by turning on their friends, counter-productive as that may seem. Understanding this dynamic has helped me not to bite back and take outbursts personally. Even the cutest river otter can turn snarly when afraid, hungry, or exhausted.

HONESTY ISSUES: "THERE'S SOMETHING ABOUT THE RIVER THAT KEEPS US HONEST."

Multiday river running is a demanding sport, one where we have the opportunity to face our boating strengths and weaknesses honestly. I've developed a terrific respect for the sheer force of moving water and subscribe to the belief that there are only two kinds of boaters: those who have swum and those who will. None of us has the ability to always outmaneuver the force of the river. Remember: "it is challenging to run with a herd of elephants," Tim Delaney said in *On the Eddyline* (1997, vol. 102). He compared a thousand cubic feet per second (1,000 cfs) river flow to the weight of six elephants passing a given point *per second*. Imagine watching a river at 5,000 cfs for a minute. You'd see 1,800 elephants per minute thundering by! Honesty means facing the river humbly.

Sticky issues should be faced in a forthright manner. Constructive trip members watch, listen, and respect their intuition. They speak up before a situation gets worse. Not that it's easy to tell a slightly irrational friend that you think she's become dehydrated or hypothermic … yet, easier than dealing with a sicker victim later.

Imagine a blistering hot afternoon on a long river day with lots of slack water. A skilled kayaker keeps hanging back alone, trying to catch tiny surf waves. She flips. You're surprised she can't get her roll. She pretends not to hear you as you urge her to keep up with the group. Finally, you catch the party and tell them to wait on a shady beach for her. When she arrives, there are no apologies. She just sits in the full sun in lotus position, closes her eyes to meditate, and promptly keels over. Dehydration and salt loss were the problems. You'd missed the clues.

Some trips like this one are heavy on the kayakers who count on raft support. (Note dissembled raft frames being loaded into the trailer.)

DEALING WITH THE QUIRKY: "WHAT? YOU TALKIN' ABOUT ME?"

Your private party on the river is likely to contain a non-team player or two. Most folks will come around with frank discussion of the group nature of the experience. However, you may be faced with a genuine problem group member. Perhaps a narcissist, or an invalidator of the "nasty person" sort (you know, the guy who tries to make you feel like doggie-do if he doesn't get his way). Maybe a person with a phobia. Possibly someone with a drug or alcohol or other mental health problem. Remember, even if you're a therapist, stick to trying to resolve barriers in good group communications and leave the couch for the professionals back home.

CHAPTER FIVE

Timetable

Gather ye rosebuds while ye may, Old Time is still a-flying;
And this same flower that smiles to-day, To-morrow will
be dying.

—HERRICK: TO THE VIRGINS, TO MAKE MUCH OF TIME

One method of adding structure to decisions about your crew, capacities, and communication is to set a trip timetable. Usually our studded snowtires are still on the car when we decide to go on a summer river trip. We gaze out the frosty windows and look forward to sunny, warm days, swirling currents, and camping fun. The problem with daydreaming is that time slips through our fingers faster than summer sand sneaks into a sleeping bag.

Suddenly it's spring already. I've had many a last minute scramble as a permit-holder for additional trip members, gear, and shuttle drivers. It's tough to learn that a favorite friend is unable to get time off from work unless she has several months lead-time. It's also bad news to find out that the extra raft (inflatable kayak, drybox) our trip counted on renting had been booked by another party and isn't available. Where did the time go?

We've learned to get our calendars out early and work backwards from the day after we get home. That's right, the clean-out-the-coolers day. Years ago, I decided I didn't like to scrub out coolers, dryboxes, and 5-gallon buckets all by myself. Planning to have some of the party help with group item take-down, return, and clean-up improves any trip leader's happiness quotient. If you are a task-oriented leader or group member – one who has a "do it yourself if you want it done right" attitude – then group participation and delegation skills will be a stretch for you. Remember, stretching makes you flexible! And the stretch of delegation assures you will have a participatory trip. How about a real-river example of a trip planning timetable?

Consider using a schedule like the one we used for one summer trip. We launched on August 2nd and ended on the 9th, with clean-up on the 10th. We used the trip calendar as a communication aid for the party members in making travel arrangements and planning vacation times. Plenty of lead-time means more time for fun later. Our planning schedule looked like this chronologically:

JANUARY – PERMIT APPLICATION DEADLINE.

1. Talk to friends about mutually satisfying dates, party size, and other potential members.

2. Pledge to invite them on your trip if you are awarded a permit for the agreed dates, and vice versa. This is a code of honor thing – it's called "putting in together."

3. Be clear about who's in your put-in group. Decide if the eventual permit-holder/trip leader is free to include buddies, their extended family members, etc.

4. Encourage spouses and significant others to make an application. Otherwise, your vision of a small trip will change the day you pull a permit. All it takes is for your best rafter to say he expected he could bring his wife and four kids, their cousins and parents as part of the deal. You are now up to eighteen and running a floating daycare center.

5. Make a list and send it out in writing. When in doubt, particularly about trip size, talk it out – the earlier, the better!

FEBRUARY 15 – FIRST COMMUNICATION TO YOUR PRIORITY LIST OF POTENTIAL CREW MEMBERS.

1. Soon after you receive your permit date notification (or choose your unregulated river and trip length), send out via e-mail or letter: "You are cordially invited on my river trip … and here's a list of those included so far."

2. Describe tentative dates for put-in and take-out; ask for verification of name, address, phone numbers, e-mails, faxes.

Trip leader Pete points to launch day at a trip planning meeting.

3. Invite suggestions for a waiting list, but acknowledge that being wait-listed is no guarantee of a place on the trip. That will begin to shake out at the first meeting of those officially in your group – those who had "put in" for the agreed-upon dates, but weren't chosen in the lottery.

4. If two or more members of your group have pulled permits, they'll need to meet and sort through the advantages and disadvantages of breaking the trip into two smaller ones and which group members wish to go on each trip. Perhaps one permit-holder wants to give up a permit so that another trip member can snap up the cancellation. The topic will contribute to a lively group meeting later, I assure you.

MARCH 1 – TIME TO COMMIT LETTER TO THE PRIORITY LIST.

1. Select trip treasurer (maybe someone who'd rather do the budget than shop for groceries) and begin accounting for all deposits and reimbursements.

2. Work out your reservation deposit system (the dollar amount and deadlines to reserve a seat on your trip) with the treasurer.

3. Describe the deposit system and the tentative timetable in another written correspondence, including travel time to the put-in and home from the take-out.

4 Avoid scheduling surprises like the one we had once on an 8-day trip. Someone on Day 6 figured out she had to be home for her babysitter within 24 hours.

APRIL 1 – PRELIMINARY TRIP MEETING AND DEPOSIT DUE (TO HOLD YOUR PLACE ON THE LIST).

1. Invite your current list of party members to a short river trip planning meeting. After work on a weeknight works for us, especially if everyone brings a snack or hors d'oeuvre.

2. Attach a copy of the most current party list to the invitation. Include boaters on your waiting list if you wish.

3. Draft a meeting agenda to discuss key items (see Chapter 6 for a sample agenda).

4. Begin the meeting with self-introductions and move on to discuss "trip business," like evaluating the number of rafts, kayaks, and raft passengers and the skill level of each individual.

5. Be open to making new friends. For a band of kayakers, eligible rafters are often as sought after as a hotspring campground. For an all-raft group an expert may speak up and note that "we need a skilled kayaker

as a safety-boater." If you're lucky like we were in our novice years, you may make a valuable new friend – that's how we met kayaking legend Mike Norell and his son David.

6. Finish off with discussing potential trip add-ons and waiting list rules (a capable rafter may take priority over a kayaker, even if the kayaker was wait-listed first, for example).

JUNE 15 – LAST DAY TO CANCEL AND HAVE DEPOSIT REFUNDED.

1. Send out the trip treasurer's report of reservation deposits received to date.

2. Attach an updated list of party members to this group – those who have confirmed by deposit.

3. Work with the young boater who'd make a great trip member, but is having financial trouble.

JUNE 20 – RIVER TRIP POTLUCK AND ORGANIZATIONAL MEETING.

1. Notify trip members that this is a very important meeting and work hard to schedule it when all can attend.

2. Ask members to think about what leadership role they'd be interested in: safety/rescue, meal planning, food purchasing, advance food prep, medical/first aid, supplies and equipment, guidebook/map ordering, sanitation/water, shuttle (details are described in Part Four). If you want help with something, don't wait until someone volunteers, just add it to your agenda for discussion. Group process is great for dividing up work fairly. Trust it.

3. Invite folks to bring a favorite river recipe with notes on quantities needed for preparation.

JULY 1 – FINAL PORTION OF TRIP DEPOSIT DUE TO TREASURER.

JULY 5 – SECOND RIVER TRIP POTLUCK AND ORGANIZATIONAL MEETING.

1. Require trip members to bring their final deposit, *or else*.

2. Ask folks to bring any gear that needs to be compared or evaluated (like propane connecting hoses for the second stove, gearbags, cooking pots, etc.).

3. Make final assignments for lead organizers according to the skill pool in your group.

4. Pass around a sign-up list (see Part Four, Table 15-1, "Group Gear List") for major gear items. Encourage candid discussion of the condition of

the gear. Test out whether one person's drybox will fit on another's raft by planning a trial run on a nearby river.

5. Pass out a sign-up list for advance food prep items, like Table 23-1 in Part Five.

6. Throw in a mandatory river safety video session for first-timers, or schedule it for another day (*Heads UP!* is excellent – available from the American Canoe Association, featuring Les Bechdel, co-author of *River Rescue*). Add extreme whitewater videos if they fit your group (*Broke, Hungry and Happy* by David Norell ©2003, for example).

JULY 15 – DEPOSIT DEADLINE AND FINAL CONFIRMATION OF GROUP TO RIVER AUTHORITY.

For the Middle Fork of the Salmon, this was our red-letter deadline for the Forest Service to receive *(not postmark)* the names and deposits of our party with a put-in date of August 2nd.

JULY 29-30 – SHOPPING AND PRELIMINARY PACKING DAYS.

1. Give shoppers purchase lists by categories (e.g., meat, bulk-bin, dairy case, etc.) or by store.

2. Deliver purchases to staging area.

3. Sort items by river days into boxes (e.g., "Day 2 – Dinner") or label for freezer or refrigerator.

4. Double-check the advance-prep frozen items for labels and double zipper bags.

5. Segregate miscellaneous stuff like fresh-picked box of plums; label and handle appropriately.

JULY 31 – PACKING DAY AND 8 P.M. PIZZA PARTY.

1. Tell the crew to come to the staging area once they have all personal gear packed.

2. Ask them to help finish group packing and loading.

3. Then, celebrate with pizza.

4. Have a brief meeting to go over last-minute needs and arrangements such transportation.

AUGUST 1 – TRAVEL DAY AND CAMPING AT THE LAUNCH SITE.

1. To make Put-in Day (River Day 1) less tense, plan a travel day and a night of camping at the launch site camp.

2. Give your group time for last-minute cooler packing, checking gear lists, and settling into travel vehicles with sack lunches to eat on the road.

3. Find a nice campsite at the launch camp; check in with the river ranger, if one's available.

4. Get the rafts in the water; check mooring lines and tube pressures.

5. Have a fun group dinner and a good night's sleep.

AUGUST 2-AUGUST 8 – PUT-IN DAY, PLUS THE NUMBER OF NIGHTS YOU PLAN TO SPEND RIVER CAMPING.

Many permitted rivers have a maximum number of days and nights. In this example, the trip was for eight days and seven nights, important numbers for all to know and agree to.

AUGUST 9 – TAKE-OUT DAY.

Say goodbye to your last river campsite, paddle a few miles to the take-out, pack the cars, and drive home. In the case of most backcountry rivers, you may not be back home the same day you take out. To minimize disagreements, particularly when you're tired, be sure pre-trip to get consensus on post-trip meals, accommodation plans, and who will pay for them.

AUGUST 10 – CLEAN UP, RETURN, PUT-AWAY DAY.

If each member of the party spends an hour or two helping, no one is stuck with clean-up.

AUGUST 17 – PICTURE PARTY POTLUCK.

1. This is the wrap for a perfect trip – photos and stories are shared and lost gear is returned.

2. Take a few notes about what worked and didn't, most and least favorite meals, etc.

3. You may want to distribute the leftover food and supplies using some kind of a game or the routine of the holiday gift exchanges that allow a limited number of "swipings" after choices are made. Our favorite is to ask an unsuspecting person to pick a random date. Then the line forms in order of successive birthdays. Each person chooses an item in turn and the line circles until all the leftovers are taken.

4. Plan the next trip.

CHAPTER SIX

Sample River Meeting Agenda

Hey! You got some kinda agenda or sometin'?

—AL PACINO-TYPE RAFTER TO TRIP LEADER, FIRST
ORGANIZATIONAL MEETING

1. Chow down on a Scrumptious Potluck and Get to Know Each Other

2 Start the Meeting with Introductions, including review of past experience on the chosen river. Invite participation, encourage openness to suggestions, kindness and respect for all ideas, and favor group consensus over voting on controversial issues

3. Review Schedule, using a flipchart with a big calendar of the trip month

4. Assign Tasks, including assistants and helpers to each of these:

   • Trip leader (a permit-holder cannot delegate the permit, but may choose to delegate the role of leader) and Assistants

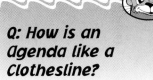

Q: How is an Agenda like a Clothesline?

A: Because it gives you a way to hang your ideas out in the sunshine.

One way a permit-holder or trip leader can guarantee important issues are clearly communicated is to put them on a meeting agenda — either handouts or written on a flipchart.

Here's a sample agenda (items in order of importance, natch).

• Raft Captain (to fairly distribute gear and coordinate borrowed or rented craft and gear)

• Safety and River Rescue Leader (ideally someone who's taken a river rescue course)

• Quartermaster (the person who makes sure all equipment and supplies are good to go)

• Transportation Coordinator (includes shuttle arrangements, trailers, vehicles)

- Trip Treasurer (honest, not afraid of numbers)
- Medical/First Aid Coordinator (could be anyone with a recent CPR certificate)
- Meal Planning Guru (includes menus and food purchasing/packaging)
- Photographer(s)
- Volunteer for Processing Group Guidebook/Map Purchasing Orders
- Chair of Spontaneity, Games, Songs, and Suds (or any one of these)

4. Discuss major equipment and supply items, using gear list handouts

5. Sensitive issues for this and future mtg.:
   - trip goals – expected daily launch times, average miles per day, traveling as a group
   - tents – number, type, and who sleeps with whom
   - amount of personal gear
   - alcohol and other recreational drugs
   - nudity
   - allergies/health conditions
   - food preferences

Dryboxes, coolers, five-gallon buckets, and mesh bags of rescue gear accumulate in preparation for packing day.

- partial (or non-) payment of deposits, drop-dead deadline to hold your reservation
- estimate of total trip costs, including review of major expense items
- waiting list priorities
- reimbursement for broken oars, bear-chewed coolers, or other damaged personal gear used by the group (not your lost sunglasses).

Sample Agenda for Last Organizational Meeting before Launch:

1. On the way into the meeting, participants stop off first in the garage and then in the kitchen. They drop off extra gear for sharing (like drybags for newbies), plus assigned items from quartermaster's list. After the meeting everyone will review the gear. Then they put a scrumptious potluck item in the kitchen and proceed to the meeting room.

2. General meeting: re-introduce participants; give brief update on final number going; appoint "work group leaders" to lead discussion groups (raft captains, safety & rescue, shoppers & packers, medical & first aid, transportation/shuttle, etc.); assign everyone to a work group.

3. Enjoy a potluck dinner with fellow work group members and discuss the tasks ahead, making assignments as appropriate.

4. Reconvene as a large group; work group leaders give reports and timetables if pertinent.

5. Final announcements and reports from visitors if any. Having a guest from another recent trip talk about flow conditions, hazards, and necessary portages is a helpful complement to such updates as expected weather conditions and e-mail postings about bear alerts. Re-emphasize loading and departure times.

6. Adjourn to gear drop-off area in the garage or yard to size up gear and the fit of shared equipment (e.g., coolers and raft-frames, cooking pots, propane hoses – check if the fittings are compatible with Jim's stove and Mindy's lantern tree). Also, check the fit of any clothes items that are borrowed, like jackets or booties before taking them home to pack in personal gear. If food isn't to be packed at this site, send the coolers/dryboxes home with appropriate people.

One of the positive results of good trip planning: a fair distribution of group gear so everyone can enjoy running gnarly rapids like John in his cataraft.

Part Three:
Trip Organization

Trip organization has layers, just like this Dutch oven lasagne. The team approach to camp duties increases the fun quotient by sharing chores.

CHAPTER SEVEN

The Team Approach

We've got spirit, yes we do. We've got the team for
me and you.

—HEARD (LOUD!) AT AN EAST JUNIOR HIGH
FOOTBALL GAME, 1984

Two kinds of people have inspired the Team Approach to organizing camp duties. One is the L'il Abner type who always chooses mattress-testing as his job. The other is the St. Mary-Martyr character who gives everyone a guilt complex. Neither type of trip member is fun to be around for a whole week. So, what to do to assure the work is shared fairly?

Let's say you're an expert river runner, you could go on a small-sized (less than eight) trip with other expert boaters. If you know each other well, it is possible that true democratic leadership could happen spontaneously. No member would be a slacker or a victim. Mutual respect and friendship would reign and you'd sing the chorus: "This is the dawning of the Age of Aquarius." In reality, however, most trips divide camp chores using leadership principles.

Les Bechdel and Slim Ray, the godfathers of river rescue, have summarized the duties of a leader in their book, *River Rescue:* "to *observe, organize,* and *direct* the efforts of the entire rescue team" (Appalachian Mountain Club Books). That list of duties might also apply to the river trip permit-holder. An efficient leader helps others accomplish tasks. An inefficient leader tries to do everything alone. Remember, no one person has to have all the answers or shoulder every job – that's what the river trip team is for.

Float trip camping on a noncommercial trip means there are no guides to cook and clean for you; there's lots of responsibility to go around. What often baffles folks is how to distribute the tasks that need to be done every day. Developed on the Grand Canyon, where trips can be three to four weeks long, the Team Approach identifies four major activities: 1. Meal preparation; 2. Clean-up; 3. Water pumping, Privy set-up/take-down, and Raft loading/unloading; and 4. the "Off!" day for R & R fun.

Usually the permit-holder leads a discussion of team duties before anyone puts paddle or row to water. On trips that have a base camp the night before

Photo: Todd Swanson

Demonstrating water filter filtration techniques for the Water-Privy-Loading Team.

the launch day, a good time is after everyone's had dinner and socialized a bit. At the after-dinner trip meeting the permit-holder shares information from the river ranger, such as launch details, downriver camp assignments, miles per day, etc. On trips that launch without camp time together, set up a riverside meeting, regardless how anxious the gang is to launch. Talking about teamwork fits in logically because most group members are excited about making the adventure a success.

How does it work out?

First, begin by dividing the total trip membership by four to determine the size of the Teams (we call them A, B, C, D). You're in luck if you have a trip of twelve – four teams of three each. If you have an uneven number, some teams will just have one person more or less. It's no big deal. Explain that there are four major "duty" groupings that rotate every day. On a four-day trip, for example, each team has the opportunity to be "on" for one day at each job, on an eight- day trip each team will do a job twice.

Second, ask the group how they wish to sort themselves out and what team letter they want to be. Family units may want to stay together and such, but consider alternatives and even encourage family units to break apart. This promotes new friendships and experiences, especially for young boaters. I remember a fun trip where I was the only adult on a team with three teenaged girls. I told them I had three sisters and they enjoyed picking which one they'd be as I told them about adventures the four of us had as kids. Each

THE TEAM APPROACH 57

team does need at least one experienced person. Imagine trusting an all-novice team with the propane stove, the Katadyn water filter, the portable toilet, the cooking detail (heaven forbid!) – and you'll know what I mean.

Third, give team members a duty schedule to follow like the example in Table 7-1.

Teams form the rows, and the columns are the river days by number – from launch day to take-out day. Teams can jot down the sequence or you can pass out three-by-five cards printed with the table below. One year we had a techie in the group who used his color printer and laminated cards for everyone. They worked great. We've found if each boater has a copy, they don't keep asking what their job is. This is especially true for pre-teen paddlers, senile boaters, and most of us in between. The logical pattern of chores – Meals, Clean-up, Privy, etc, and Off! – soon becomes second nature. Wait to pass out the roster until the teams are chosen and named by letter. Doing this keeps some people from obsessing over the sequence of duties.

Team members need to know a few details about kicking the system into gear. Begin sequencing jobs *when you land at camp everyday*. Thus, put-in (launch) camp duties are an example of the teamless approach: everyone pitches in on dinner, clean-up, and privy duty – ditto launch camp breakfast and packing rafts and the lunch cooler for Day 1. Experiencing this teamless confusion makes everyone ready for organized teamwork when you reach camp on River Day 1 (also River Night 1 for food packing and prep organization).

Here's how it goes, job by job.

TABLE 7-1: **TEAM DUTY ROSTER**

River	Day 1	2	3	4	5	6	7	8
Team A	Meals	Cleanup	H$_2$O/Pv/Load	Off!	Meals	Cleanup	H$_2$O/Pv/Load	Off!
Team B	Off!	Meals	Cleanup	H$_2$O/Pv/Load	Off!	Meals	Cleanup	H$_2$O/Pv/Load
Team C	H$_2$O/Pv Load	Off!	Meals	Cleanup	H$_2$O/Pv/Load	Off!	Meals	Cleanup
Team D	Cleanup	H$_2$O/Pv/Load	Off!	Meals	Cleanup	H$_2$O/Pv/Load	Off!	Meals

Tending the coals takes patience. Note raised firepan and detachable grill sit on fireproof blanket, as do the Dutches.

CHAPTER EIGHT
Meals

An army marches on its stomach.

—ATTRIBUTED TO NAPOLEON BONAPARTE

Using the duty roster, Team A is in charge of "Meals" and begins by setting up the kitchen at the first campsite, keeping in mind this counsel:

> *Use care when selecting a kitchen site. Just like in your home, people tend to congregate in the kitchen. On river trips, this area experiences the most impact. A large sandy beach is an ideal kitchen spot.... Consider using a kitchen floor tarp made of open-weave scrim cloth to catch small food scraps and other 'micro-trash.'*
>
> (Leave No Trace: *Western River Corridors, Skills & Ethics*, pp. 9-10)

Team A is responsible for keeping the kitchen clean and organized, preparing dinner on Day 1, breakfast on Day 2, and packing the lunch cooler on Day 2. "Meals" are handed off to Team B when the second campsite is reached on Night 2.

Some tips that we've used to get Team A started off right are:

- Have a handwashing and rinsing bucket available, even at lunch.

  1. Require anyone handling food to use it.

  2. Indelicate as it sounds, discuss the need to exclude anyone with diarrhea from food prep and handling clean kitchenware.

  3. Require everyone to wash hands before going through the food line.

- Set up a separate "pre-wash" bucket for soaking utensils and dishes until the clean-up crew is ready to wash (5-gallon bucket of river water with two tablespoons of bleach to sanitize).

  1. Keep dirty dishes from sitting around, becoming harder to wash.

  2. Remind cooks that if they are mindful of not dirtying all items in the kitchen, the clean-up team will be kind to them in turn. On one trip we actually had two teams making a game of who could make the biggest clean-up mess for the team on clean-up. This bickering chased the river otter's spirit from our camp.

- Use of propane stoves and charcoal briquets cuts down on ash residue and keeps campsites from being denuded of natural down wood (refer to Appendix 8).

  1. Elevate your firepan on rocks – or better yet, invest in one with legs to prevent scorching the ground and sterilizing the soil. In high fire danger areas, use a 3' by 3' fireproof blanket underneath it.

  2. Don't burn trash in the firepan – toxins are released into the air and ash residue multiplies. Pack it out instead.

  3. For ash residue, use a watertight ashcan (gallon paint cans or metal Army-surplus ammo/telegraph boxes work well).

  4. Beware of heated sand under a hot firepan. Even if you move the firepan, the sand can stay hot enough to burn the skin off someone's feet fifteen minutes later. Once on a two-week trip my husband blistered toes and soles after stepping in hot sand.

  5. Remember that synthetic clothing can melt on your skin with sufficient heat. The resulting burns our friend Madonna Lengerich sustained from boiling potato water sloshed onto her poly socks put her on an evacuation jetboat down the Main Salmon.

- Going light not only helps the rafts stay light, but cuts down on packaging waste.

- Advance prep and freezing entire menu items in plastic zipper bags cuts down on in-camp preparation time and dishes to wash. This contributes to trip members getting to know each other before the trip. One Hell's Canyon trip we had a cook-a-thon at a couple's home and learned how to use a device to heat-seal the main courses.

- Easy hors d'oeuvres packed at the top of each night's food bucket can stave off the munchies and keep non-meal team members out of the kitchen.

Are you a ravishingly hungry river otter?

If so, and you can't wait, skip directly to Part Five, "Mastering River Meals" where you'll find the nitty-gritty on mastering river cookery. Or check out the appendices: they're full of hints for hungry boaters so your favorite recipe can go with you on the river.

CHAPTER NINE
Clean-Up

I heard the water lapping on the crag,
And the long ripple washing in the reeds.

– TENNYSON: IDYLLS OF THE KING

On Day 1 Team D does the dishes from dinner. On Day 2 they clean-up after breakfast. Everyone pitches in on lunch clean-up.

Once on the first day of a long trip into the wilderness, we had lots of hands opening and closing the lunch cooler. Our trip mojo hadn't kicked in yet and the lid wasn't closed properly while folks ate and swam in the eddy. When Gary Payne opened it later that night some six miles down the river, he let out a yell that startled us all. A chipmunk sprang out of the cooler right into his crotch, then scurried down his leg. The cool little guy – the chipmunk, that is – could have been killed in there with all that cheese and salami. Lucky for him, he lived. Although his separation from home and family upriver was sad, "Stowaway Chipmunk" taught us a lesson in ice conservation and cooler management, and made a great theme for the group's epic trip poem.

Lots of little jobs make for a good clean-up:

- making sure all food is put away and not left to attract bears or camp critters and bugs

- smashing cans for recycling and compacting other garbage to decrease volume

- wiping down cooking surfaces, with an eye to keeping the micro-trash on the scrim groundcloth and then in the garbage sack.

What about the big job? The job no one likes, except the otter who wants the cleanest claws in camp – *dishwashing*.

For dishwashing in a small or self-contained kayak trip we use a variant of the three-bucket method – our cooking pots. On a raft-supported trip, we might have a collapsible bucket or two, but the empty 5-gallon, screw-top, gasketed buckets that contained food work great. Sometimes we even throw in a small dishpan if there's room.

1. *The Pre-Soak Bucket of river water conserves fuel and elbow grease.* If folks scrape their own plates right after eating (using a rubber spatula), then plop them into the pre-soak, less hot water will be necessary for washing.

2. *Bucket Two is for washing with heated river water* (no sense in wasting filtered water when sanitizing rinses follow). Use gloves and as little biodegradable soap as possible. Wash mugs, cutlery, and plates first, saving cooking pots and utensils for last. Use scrubbers, brushes and muscle. Remember never to soap up Dutch ovens – use soaking, scraping, and hot water to preserve the seasoning of cast iron. Aluminum Dutch ovens are a little more tolerant of soap, but I treat them like cast iron to increase their nonstick quality.

3. *Bucket Three is for the first rinse.* Five gallons of river water that have been allowed to sit 15 minutes with $1/8$ to $1/4$ cup of household bleach makes a good sanitizing rinse and will rinse better if warm water is used. Check the effectiveness of the chlorine by using litmus papers available at

Use the Scrim Cloth (or a tarp) to cover your Food Scrimmage Area:

Team D's last job on their first night of clean-up is demonstrating the big advantage of the scrim cloth ground cover. You can buy this lightweight netting material at fabric stores in a yard and a half width (four and a half feet). A five-yard length (fifteen feet) can be cut in half and the seven and a half foot pieces sewn together to make a rectangle seven and a half by nine feet. That's perfect to put under a fold-up lunch table or in front of your dinner cooking table to catch crumbs and micro-litter and let spills drain through. After the meal the clean-up team just gathers it up and shakes it directly into the trash. Not having to pick up micro-litter and food particles by hand gives them more time for post-dinner activities and for packing up in the morning. This keeps riverbank camps clean and prevents infestations of ants and wasps from taking over camp areas.

No scrim cloth? Use a tarp or ground-cloth.

In some areas of Idaho, yellow-jackets and farmer bees are ferocious enough to chase you downriver. Once they chased us from a popular lunch spot as soon as we opened the first can of tuna and mixed up the Gatorade®. Several sets of lips got their wrinkles removed in the process of competing with the thirsty stinging insects for a drink out of Gatorade® bottles. Like bears in food-littered camps, bothersome insects know where the grub is served.

pool/spa stores. Chlorine residual should be between 50-100 ppm to pass health department specifications for a sanitizing rinse.

4. *Bucket Four is the final hot rinse in water you've boiled hard* for at least a minute to kill viruses and cysts. Leave some water on the stove for after-dinner tea and cocoa drinkers.

Two rinses plus air-drying will reduce the incidence of camper diarrheas due to nasty microorganisms and soap/detergent residue. Yes, soap can be the cause of "campers' runs" as well as micro-critters. We use a small, cheap mesh hammock for drip-drying large items and a tight-weave mesh sack for drying utensils.

Whatever river you float, wastewater (graywater) from all the dishwashing buckets must be filtered before disposal. We've used a kid's sandbox strainer covered with a nylon stocking or a kitchen strainer. The clean-up team must deal with wastewater according to the ethic of the river being floated. Some agencies require broadcasting above high-water mark (particularly those with a flow of less than 500 cfs). Others recommend a cathole. Still others subscribe to "dilution is the solution to pollution" and require wastewater be dumped into the main current. Check with your river authorities to be sure.

Kate's Lunch Clean-up Kit:

Imagine twenty-one hungry boaters around a small roll-up table feasting on make your own tuna-tortilla roll-ups, salami 'n' cheese, dried fruit, carrots, and gorp. Someone brings out last night's leftover rice dish (without a spoon) and someone else spills lemonade powder.

But, not to worry. Kitchenbox Kate packed the lunch clean-up kit: a small collapsible bucket (also useful for handwashing) with a sponge, a squirt bottle of disinfectant, extra food storage baggies, and a cardboard tube stuffed with grocery bags for the trash. Waterless hand cleaner's a nice touch, plus scrim cloth, and graywater strainer. Whatta trip member she is!

Photo: Todd Swanson

The hammock method of air-drying dishes under the camp table.

Protect the Katadyn's ceramic filter with a layer of protective bubblewrap while traveling. Remove it before pumping water.

Photo: Todd Swanson

Good privy location includes a view and seclusion. To tell others the privy was "in use," this trip used a rubber ducky instead of a flag to go with the user from the handwashing area. If the duck was gone, the privy was in use.

CHAPTER TEN
Water, Privy, Loading

Our team's gonna win the prize for the most scenic spot,
Novice declares to Old Timer.

Yep. That's what we call "shitting pretty,"
Old Timer replies.

– THE YEAR THE PRIVY SAT ON THE BLUFF
ABOVE CLIFFSIDE RAPIDS

CAMP TOILET ("PRIVY") DUTY

When you hit the first night's camp, Water-Privy-Loading team's priority is helping unload the rafts so others can set up the kitchen and establish campsites. But perhaps there will no outhouse, in which case, the team will spring to action.

When Team C sets up the toilet facilities on the first night, they also must set up a handwashing station, complete with rinse water, soap, and towel, if desired, but air-drying is best. Position a flag – or the river-booty red cap you scrounged – near the handwashing set-up, so users of the privy can display it, and keep their experience "priv-y." Some groups have the following custom: the person using the privy picks up the flag and carries it with them to the privy. Others will see the flag is gone from the handwashing station, or see it hanging in the distance, and know the privy is occupied. When the person returns to the handwashing station, the privy user hangs the flag back up to show the privy is available again.

Follow the ethic of your river, but generally instruct portable toilet users to put tampons, plastic, or trash into a garbage sack for carryout disposal. Powdered lime can be sprinkled (lightly!) over privy deposits to suppress odor. Some systems (Mr. Peat) require also

The Scoop on Poop:

Did you know that the average adult boater eating balanced meals (yes, that means fiber) contributes 0.12 gallons (about 2 cups) of fecal matter and TP to the privy per day? Our 2002 test validated this Forest Service standard, extrapolated from ammo can privy volumes, to translate into four 5-gallon privy buckets for 21 boaters. Right on target!

that no urine go into the toilet. Other systems may tolerate fluid as well as solid waste, but in the interest of keeping raft weight to a minimum, encourage urination into the river current or "broadcast" a respectable distance from toilet set-up if that is not possible. The SCAT-machine operators at North Fork, Idaho advise boaters to include some urine or water in the buckets to aid in the clean-out process at their facilities. Some trips add water at the take-out, retape the buckets, and let them slosh around all the way to the facilities for easier cleaning. Need I mention gloves?

An expedition-sized water filter can deliver a gallon of drinking water in 1-2 minutes.

WATER DUTY

Either you have carried water into the backcountry (a 6 gal. jug weighs about 50 lbs.) or you need to treat river water. The team needs to provide the river camp with potable water and can demonstrate the correct method to newbies on the trip. This may mean only careful handling of the carried-in water, but it usually means boiling or pumping/filtering some.

a quick summary

... if you don't carry your water in or boil river water:

1. get a reliable filter, and follow the manufacturer's instructions;

2. add iodine or chlorine (halogens) if you want to kill all viruses; and

3. consider using a charcoal filter to remove any remaining chemicals.

Depending on the source and degree of contamination, you may need to boil, filter, and chemically disinfect "Nature's Finest" to avoid illness. The Centers for Disease Control (CDC) find the protozoa *Giardia lamblia* ("beaver fever") to be the most frequently identified cause of diarrhea outbreaks associated with drinking water in the U.S. Most beavers are infected and guess where they defecate. Assume that ALL rivers and streams are a source of contamination by *Giardia* and *Cryptosporidium parvum*, which is ubiquitous in animals, notably livestock. Both of these protozoa pathogens have an oocyst (egg) stage that is highly resistant to iodine or chlorine. To learn more, contact the CDC website at http://www.cdc.gov.

A backcountry trip has two major choices in treating water:

- Option one, you bring river water meant for drinking to a rolling boil for a full minute, effectively killing all protozoa, bacteria, and viruses (according to the CDC).

- Option two has two parts – combine them to reduce your infection risk to negligible:

1. Use of a filtration system guaranteed to meet the "NSF standard 53 for cyst removal" or having a porosity of "absolute 1 micron." Filtering pumps with pore diameter less than 0.2 microns, such as the Katadyn or PUR, will protect your float trip from bacteria (0.2 - 1.5 microns) and protozoa/cysts (2 - 100 microns).

About household chlorine bleach (5%) to disinfect drinking water:

Using Gill's standard of 2-4 drops of bleach per quart of water for a 4-8 ppm concentration, you'll need 32-64 drops (about 1/2 - 1 teaspoon) of bleach for four gallons of river water in your 5-gallon bucket. Remember to allow sufficient contact time: 15 minutes for 86° water and 60 minutes for 41° water to reach the 8 ppm level. This roughly corresponds to the Coconino Health Department's standard for the Grand Canyon – 1/2 teaspoon bleach in a 5-gallon bucket, left to stand for 30 minutes.

2. Use halogens (iodine or chlorine) to kill all viruses (0.004 - 0.1 microns). For five gallons of spring-fed river water, disinfect with one half teaspoon of household bleach (8 drops/gal., 2 drops/qt.). Mix and let stand 30 minutes. For details, consult Halogen Doses and Techniques table, Gill's *Wilderness First Aid*.

Neither boiling nor filtration-plus-chemicals, however, will remove heavy metals or pesticide contaminants. Know your watersheds and act accordingly.

Further tips for the water crew:

- Use two containers on most rivers in addition to your empty potable-water containers. Never get river water in them. Some crews even color-code all potable-water containers.

- Begin by allowing murky water to settle for half an hour. Then pour slowly from one bucket into another through a clean T-shirt, leaving the sediment behind. If it's excessively cloudy, add 1 tsp. of alum per 5-

gallon bucket. Watch the sediment precipitate out in a clump (known as flocculation). On clear rivers we forgo using two buckets and pump from a settling bucket directly into our water jugs.

- Never stick the filter intake tube all the way to the bottom of the river water bucket or you'll be cleaning your filter more often than necessary due to settled-out particles.

- After you've pumped enough potable water for at least dinner, take a jug and two buckets of river water to the kitchen crew (for handwashing and pre-soak for dirty dishes). The clean-up team will need more later. Extra-safe trips use lots of filtered and disinfected water, especially for dishwashing. Some trips with fuel concerns use cold, filtered water for this last rinse, instead of a hot rinse.

RAFT LOADING AND UNLOADING

Most rafters appreciate help with loading and unloading, especially as the trip progresses and backs ache. It goes without saying that everyone usually helps haul gear into camp and then back to the boats, even if they're not on the Water-Privy-Loading team. Some rafters like help securing the load, others want to do it themselves.

Straps and Ropes

Don't be careless and drop the rafters' cam straps (buckled webbing) into sand or lose them in the river during your burst of loading/unloading enthusiasm. Walking on ropes also brings bad karma. Sand weakens the fibers. Care for straps and ropes, and they'll be there when needed.

Photo: Todd Swanson

In bear country, hanging camp garbage "high 'n' wide" in a tree is standard practice for the clean-up crew.

CHAPTER ELEVEN

Day Off!

The advantage of leisure is mainly that we may have the power of choosing our own work, not certainly that it confer any privilege of idleness.

– JOHN LUBBOCK: THE PLEASURES OF LIFE VI

To conclude the Team Approach discussion, according to the duty roster shown in Table 1, Team B has "Day off!" duty beginning with the afternoon of Day 1. This doesn't mean they should scamper off without helping unload the rafts or shirk the group if they are genuinely needed to pitch in with a problem (like setting up tarps to shelter the kitchen from a storm). All it really means is they have no major duties until the evening of Day 2.

Many day-off teams like to use the time to go hiking, read, or sleep in. Others will use the time to sit around in camp chairs, chatting and kibitzing, offering helpful advice to those who have a camp duty.

Photo: Mike Norell

Maria and Barry on "dress-up nite."

You can probably guess that it's fun having your day-off on layover day, especially if there's a dress-up night. You'll have lots of costume- and skit-planning time should you be partial to such antics.

High above the river canyon, day-off and layover day hikes give boaters fresh views and a lower body workout.

Now that you're familiar with the Team Approach. you may wonder how leadership fits in. What are the permit-holder's responsibilities? What can trip members do to help, other than the camp duties we've discussed?

Here's a hint: the permit-holder's first river trip responsibility is to decide which leadership duties to keep and which to delegate. This advances group comfort and river safety.

Part Four: Responsibilities

Honeymooning trip leader Pete (center with new bride Monica) assigned duties using the River Otter team and responsibilities approach. He decreased his stress and increased everyone's participation. Kitchen Notes: Scrim cloth to protect Mother Earth, hanging utensil container on collapsible table, hand sanitizer bottle handy, and math teacher John measuring water into freeze-dried dinner packets.

CHAPTER TWELVE

Leadership Style

by Barry Eschen

Reason and judgment are the qualities of a leader.

—TACITUS: *HISTORIES*, C. 116

LEADER SELECTION

Circumstances often determine who the trip leader is and the extent of the role. If a person organizes a trip, that person is the de facto leader. If a permit is involved, the person signing the permit is responsible and usually the leader. Sometimes the leader chosen by circumstances does not have the personality, inclination or knowledge to lead.

On my first river trip the permit-holder was much more interested in spontaneity than organizing. To his credit he recognized this and designated another person as the organizational leader, which worked very well. On another trip I had the permit but was struggling with a son over control issues and fortunately decided to let another experienced member be the leader. This allowed me the freedom to relate with my family on the trip without involving the leadership issue.

As in workplace organizations, there is often an informal leadership structure that is quite separate from the formal one. The informal structure recognizes a person's skill and power based on personality and experience, rather than the formal organization. If differences between the two structures are not dealt with it can lead to serious consequences.

On one trip the unresolved differences between the formal and informal leadership had serious consequences. At the morning meeting the leader announced that the group would scout a certain rapid. Later, the leader was on the bank scouting the rapid and watched an experienced member look at the situation from the water and lead the group into the rapid. A rafter flipped; his boat pinned in an undercut cliff wall. He dove into the water and went 200 feet through a cave before popping back up in the river, shaken but physically unharmed. It took six hours to recover the raft and most of the gear, and left all of us shaken to the core.

It is very helpful if the formal leaders anticipate such conflict and incorporate the informal leaders in a constructive way. Sometimes the formal leader needs to confront the informal leader for the safety of the group, but the formal leader should be sure it is a major issue before challenging. It is best if every trip member can be sensitive to such conflicts and try to support constructive resolution of them.

On a later trip I remember appointing a member with much experience to be in charge of equipment, so he wouldn't feel left out. On packing day I realized he had done nothing about checking the equipment. I finally "had to" stand next to him and hand him the list and watch him make sure the items were present. The items were present, because other trip members had brought the items they volunteered for.

LEADERSHIP STYLE

There are as many variations in leadership style as there are boaters. Obviously, the group decision-making process is an amalgam of the personalities involved and may vary greatly from one situation to the next, even with exactly the same group of boaters. Styles I have seen include controlling, democratic, manipulating, and spontaneous.

- The "controlling" style is most efficient at getting major decisions made. The leader assesses the situation, makes a decision and all do what they are told. It can save lives in an emergency. It breaks down, however, when the leader decides to control every detail of day-to-day operations. Once I was one of the novices among eight people trying to pack the night before a trip. The leader needed to know what went in every dry box and 5-gallon bucket. At one point he asked everybody to stop, so he could think; held his head in his hands; and then resumed the process. I got tired of waiting around to be told what to do and left before the job was done.

- The "democratic" style requires multiple meetings and consensus seeking or voting. It allows people to feel part of the decision-making process. It takes time. People may get frustrated with those with a differing opinion. In an emergency it is often too slow.

- The "manipulating" style uses others to advocate the leader's ideas. The manipulator will talk with a second person, encouraging the person to speak up; or, if that person agrees but does not speak up, this leader will go to a third person and say, "the second person thinks…what do you think?" The manipulating leader avoids being seen as dictatorial, but the process is time and energy consuming.

- The "spontaneous" style lets things happen. People are gathered for an adventure. The spontaneous leader lets people do what they like and lets the group solve the problems that emerge. I remember a bunch of people arriving to load up for a trip. The leader gave some direction as to what went where, but did not arrange for an inventory of items. The next day at launch time there were no paddles for the paddle raft! Two breakdown kayak paddles were available, so the members fashioned stick handles for the four half-paddles and the merry band launched down the river for a week in the wilderness.

LEADERSHIP TECHNIQUES

The techniques the leader chooses will depend on your group's size, experience and personality. The larger the group, the greater the likelihood that something will be forgotten. The more novices, the more detailed your directions will need to be. Six techniques that may help your organizing are:

- **CENTRALIZING:** Concentrating all aspects of trip organization in one leader works reasonably well with small groups and helps when there are many novices. It does not develop the leadership skills and confidence of other trip members.

- **DELEGATING:** Assigning certain tasks to others works well in most situations. The leader then is responsible for checking that the delegated tasks are accomplished and arranging assistance, if needed. The leader may take on certain tasks, but the more detail work the leader does, the less available the leader is to attend to the big picture.

- **LISTING:** Making lists of items (supplies and responsibilities) and sharing these ahead of time allows people to volunteer items and ideas. But just because you write it, does not mean it gets read and followed! On a May trip on the Owyhee River with three recent college-graduate river novices (yet all with other outdoor experience), the personal gear list said to bring wool or polypro clothing, not cotton. Late on a windy afternoon a couple of wet, cold young men realized they had ignored the recommendation. However, people can be obsessive-compulsive about lists, too. Once I asked an experienced river traveler to measure the volume of the pot he was bringing, so I could put the size on the list. He chuckled and refused. When it came time to cook, his pot was adequate, so the group ate well without the exact size being on the list.

- **DAILY MEETINGS:** Getting together with your party after breakfast every day on the river is helpful. You can discuss the day's rapids, safety issues and any administrative questions. The information shared by experienced boaters may still have to be screened. I remember one morning on the Middle Fork of the Salmon an experienced boater describing The Chutes rapid in low water as "a piece of cake." I chose not to disagree publicly. An hour later I ran this bony stretch, eddied out, and looked up The Chutes to see four paddle rafters and two kayakers swimming. Since the group responded well to the swimmers, the most serious consequence was some wet clothes.

- **SETTING AN EXAMPLE:** This technique can be powerful and avoids putting explicit demands on people. Two examples I commonly use are picking up micro-trash and relieving tired rafters in easier water (I'm a kayaker).

- **DON'T WORRY (CHILLING OUT!):** Combined with spontaneous leadership style, this works well with experienced people, plenty of gear, and good water levels.

No leader perfectly fits the stereotypes I have presented, and skilled leaders change style and technique with the situation. Awareness of the options gives the leadership more possibilities. Generally, the purpose of the trip is to have fun and a few little glitches often add to the challenge and fun, as long as there are not long-term consequences.

We've all worked with leaders, some autocratic, others democratic. Depending on the situation, we've probably been impressed by both types of leaders: the autocratic firefighter at the accident who thankfully told you exactly what to do and the democratic group facilitator who opened up a meeting so folks could say what was really bugging them at work. "All leaders have concern for task and relationships. However, in any one situation, different types of leaders will emphasize these concerns differently." (Fiedler, Chemers, and Mahar, 1977, p. 12)

If folks have a good relationship with the leader, they'll be more motivated to work effectively as a team regardless of the situation. Consider the relative importance of performing a river rescue versus picking a layover campsite. Our respect for and positive relationship with trip leaders lays a solid foundation for a smooth trip.

Additionally, leaders have the potential to be powerful teachers through their experience and application of life skills to the countless specific tasks involved in planning and conducting a multiday river trip. Paul Petzoldt, the grandfather of American wilderness leadership, called this ability to assess priorities "judgment," and ranked its importance as high as perfecting techniques. In his 1974 *Wilderness Handbook* (W. W. Norton & Co., Inc.) he noted that "the teaching of techniques without judgment can be dangerous." Something for river trip leaders to ponder.

CHAPTER THIRTEEN

Trip Treasurer

Neither a borrower nor a lender be:
For loan oft loses both itself and friend...

—SHAKESPEARE: *HAMLET, I, III*

A noncommercial trip by definition requires that all trip members share equally in the expenses for the trip. On some rivers supervised by the U.S. Forest Service, the trip leader must sign a statement to that effect prior to launch. On our trips we delegate the "treasurer" duties:

- collecting deposits

- paying bills

- reimbursing trip members for expenses.

Usually there's a ready trip member who's honest, not number-challenged, or easily intimidated. Many of our treasurers have been novices on multiday trips, but know numbers. Having that virtuous soul use his/her personal checking account for deposits and payments saves the trip from setting up a separate account. Some trips set up a computerized accounting system, but paper accounting has worked for us. There probably won't be more than twenty transactions if individual reimbursements are delayed and combined with end-of-trip reconciliation (final trip refunds or additional trip charges).

The treasurer's first duty is to collect deposits (reservation fees) from potential members. Sometimes that task is better initiated early in the spring to weed out folks who are low potential for actually going on your trip. Because the private party group size is limited according to the river and available campsites, deposits serve as a proxy for how interested someone is in joining your trip. It's wise to make a budget and calculate roughly how much the trip's going to cost per person. Ask early for a third to a half of the per-person cost to hold a spot on the trip. The earlier the trip, the earlier the deposit is needed.

Imagine having a waiting list that includes river runners you really want to be on the trip and, as time trickles away, they make other vacation plans. You call them in June and say you've got a cancellation because lazy Larry Late and His Date didn't come up with the cash after all. It's sad when your friends ask why you didn't call sooner. Worse yet, Larry was a rafter, and now all you kayakers must self-contain!

Be reasonable, however, and give lots of notice as to the date when the reservation deposit is no longer refundable. Ditto for when the final payment is due. A month and a half before the trip still gives you time to make replacements and adjust the projected expense budget to rent gear, pay the air-drop/shuttle, or buy more food. People do have changes in plans, real emergencies, and unexpected financial hardships. You'll probably be surprised who finally goes with you on your multiday float trip. We've never had a trip list stay the same from February to July.

Hints for treasurers:

- Seek agreement from group about deposit-due dates.
- Remind trip members to save their receipts for reimbursement.
- Tally income and expected expenses at the last river trip meeting.
- Tally final expenses a week after you get home from the trip. Make adjustments and mail everyone a draft statement.
- Present final accounting at the post-party and either collect more or give refunds!

One caution for the unsuspecting treasurer: somehow it is very difficult for the average river trip member to save receipts (for group food, gas, and supplies purchased), yet it is amazingly easy for them to ask for rapid reimbursement. Paying trip members back for their group purchases as soon as possible keeps folks happy. The one exception is trying to settle up all accounts the night you return from your trip. Don't risk river friendships quibbling over reimbursements when you're tired and unpacking gear from your successful trip.

The easy way out on the final accounting dilemma is to give everyone a week after getting off the river to get their receipts in. Then compile all trip expenses, dividing by the number on the trip for the overall trip cost per person. Adjust each person's account for any unpaid deposits and unreimbursed expenses and show a draft bottom line for every trip member. Mail this simple cash-in/cash-out table to the gang. In the case of leftover expenses, unpaid deposits, or a shared reimbursement for an agreed-upon off-budget item (i.e., a broken oar), your trip members can see their portion of the entire bill and how much they've already paid. Give them a few days to offer amendments and then create the final accounting for the post-trip party.

If you're lucky, the trip will be flush (deposited income is more than needed to cover expenses). Then the treasurer can split the pot and write everyone a check for overpayment. That's the best of all possible worlds, but it takes good planning to make it happen.

CHAPTER FOURTEEN
Individual Leadership

To capture Dame fortune's golden smile,
Assiduous wait upon her;
And gather gear by ev'ry wile....

—BURNS: *EPISTLE TO A YOUNG FRIEND*

PERSONAL GEAR

Each person decides whether they want to come on a river trip or not and what they need to bring. It's an adult thing. Yet you and your fellow boaters can benefit from a personal gear list. There will be fewer misunderstandings about what to bring (a coffee mug, sunscreen, water bottle, etc.) and your cold friend won't be borrowing your fleece jacket when you want it.

Depending on trip logistics (water flow and raft support), some items on the personal list may be part of the group gear and others may be "personal." For example, if it's a low-water year, kayakers may be requested to carry their own mugs, plates, and utensils to keep the kitchenbox light.

This rafter and passenger demonstrate proper gear (helmets and lifejackets) to run Tappan Falls in Idaho.

Table 14-1 is an individual gear list that has evolved thanks to many requests from trip newbies asking "what do we bring?" It is based on having one 14-foot oar boat (not a paddleraft that lacks storage space) per each four to five people. The list assumes that hardshelled kayakers and canoeists will self-contain as much gear as they ask the rafters to carry. For brevity, "rafter" is synonymous with raft passenger; "IK" means inflatable (or sit-upon) kayakers; and "kayaker" includes both hardshelled kayakers and canoeists.

TABLE 14-1: **PERSONAL GEAR LIST**

RIVER CLOTHING
❏ WET SUIT
❏ BOOTIES/RIVER SANDALS
❏ RIVER GLOVES
❏ POLYPRO SHIRT (NOT COTTON)
❏ SWIM SUIT
❏ LONG UNDERWEAR – e.g. polypro
❏ SPRAY JACKET
❏ CAP
❏ HELMET

WARM WEATHER CLOTHING
❏ SHORTS
❏ LIGHT SHIRT(S)
❏ LIGHT SOCKS
❏ KERCHIEF
❏ LIGHT FOOTWEAR (SANDALS)

COLD WEATHER CLOTHING
❏ RAINJACKET/PANTS
❏ PILE PANTS
❏ PILE SWEATER
❏ HEAVY SOCKS
❏ WARM CAP + GLOVES
❏ LIGHT HIKING BOOTS OR SHOES

BRING YOUR OWN
❏ DRINKING MUG
❏ WATER-BOTTLE(S)
❏ PLATE (FRIZBEE)
❏ EATING UTENSILS
❏ DRY BAG (Rafters + IK get
   4 cu. ft.; Kayakers 2 cu. ft.)

ACCESSORIES
❏ SLEEPING BAG
❏ SLEEPING PAD
❏ TENTS W/GROUND TARP
❏ PERSONAL (DAY-USE) DRY BAG/PACK
❏ MINI-BOTTLE SOAP/SHAMPOO
❏ TOOTHBRUSH, TOOTHPASTE, FLOSS
❏ INSECT REPELLENT
❏ MEDICINE/GLASSES/CONTACTS
❏ SUN SCREEN + LIP PROTECTANT
❏ SUNGLASSES
❏ POCKET KNIFE
❏ FLASHLIGHT
❏ SMALL TOWEL
❏ COMB OR HAIR BRUSH
❏ CLOTHES FOR DRESS-UP NIGHT
❏ WRITING PAD/NOTEBOOK + PEN
❏ WATCH

OPTIONAL
❏ BINOCULARS
❏ CAMERA + EXTRA FILM
❏ FISHING GEAR + FISHING LICENSE
❏ BOOKS
❏ EXTRA CLOTHES FOR CAR TRIP

 Copy if you like. From *River Otter: Handbook for Trip Planning*

These four swam 400 miles to call attention to the plight of their endangered cousins, the sockeye salmon smolts. See Appendix 12 for more info on Idaho Rivers United.

CARING FOR THE RIVER

River health, and the balance of life along and in rivers, is a delicate matter – easily upset by human intrusion and thoughtlessness. All too often, we take our rivers and the life they support for granted. River runners must realize that our rivers are precious resources that require great care.

When you run rivers and camp next to them, keep in mind the top eight things we all must do to preserve, protect, and enhance watershed health. If we don't, we risk losing the precious resource we love and that deserves to be passed onto generations to come.

1. Treat the river and riverside campsites as if you are a guest – an invited guest in the most remarkable of all royal castles – one built by a powerful, but sensitive force:

   • good campsites are found, not made, so camp in existing sites on durable surfaces

   • use trails, don't make your own

   • preserve the past, leave artifacts alone

   • don't spread non-native species of plants; cooperate with river authority programs

   • use maps, plan your day's journey to avoid careless camping in the dark

- avoid hiking and driving on backcountry trails and roads when conditions are wet

2. Respect other living things – this is their home, not yours:

- never feed wildlife, and don't leave scraps of food that wildlife will find
- store your food and cooking gear to avoid attracting critters
- control your pets
- listen to the sounds of wildlife, relish quiet
- watch wildlife from a distance

3. Be kind to other human visitors – set a "golden rule" example of good behavior:

- leave river camps like you'd like to find them
- keep the noise down
- be courteous, take turns at stopping points and viewing natural wonders
- decide on traveling order; keep your trip together, not spread up and down the river

4. Manage your garbage – pack it in, pack it out:

- prepackage food eliminating wrappings and cardboard; use plastic bags
- do "micro-litter" patrols after meals and when leaving a campsite
- remember that such waste as cigarette butts and orange peels may be "organic" in some folks' book, but are human trash; they belong in a garbage bag – not on the ground, in the bushes, or under rocks
- don't burn garbage; keep foul smells and toxic byproducts out of backcountry air
  - take an elegant sufficiency of garbage bags and use them
  - clean up riverside messes you find, even though you didn't make them
  - leave camps cleaner than when you arrived

5. Manage your human and animal waste – abide by the rules of your river authorities:

- use a portable toilet system in areas without outhouses, even on short trips
- pack out (don't burn) feminine hygiene products, diapers, and emergency-use toilet paper

- dig emergency-use poop catholes with discretion and per advice of river managers depending on the soil type and conditions (and don't bury toilet paper)
- urinate into the river or into wet sand where it will be diluted
- wash your hands or liberally apply alcohol-based hand sanitizer after toilet use or cleaning up after your pet

6. Manage your fire – it can be your best friend or worst enemy:

- use a propane or gas cooking stove to limit ash residue from wood and charcoal
- use a firepan with 3" sides and a grill, preferably with legs to protect soils and sand from scorching
- bring your own wood (BYOW) or charcoal; use driftwood and downwood sparingly (it's part of the natural environment)
- make small fires, especially during windy conditions, to avoid ash overflows
- use metal ashcans (good containers include ammo boxes and gallon paint cans)
- spread your firepan with a thin layer of sand or soil upon first use to keep it from warping; when fire is out, add a small amount of water to that ash-sand-soil mix in the ashcan; for the second and subsequent uses, spread the ash mixture into firepan, thereby reducing ash residue with each burning
- use a fireproof blanket under the firepan to catch runaway embers and ashes
- always carry a shovel and bucket in case your fire escapes the firepan
- follow your river authorities' direction regarding use or dismantling existing firepits/rings

7. Manage your soapy washwater ("graywater") – abide by the rules of your river authorities:

- remove grease and particles from dishwater by cooling the water and straining it; put strained material in the garbage sack
- dispose of strained graywater by broadcasting it above the high water mark, preferably 200' from water sources; don't leave unsightly sumps for insects and animals to find
- on big rivers, especially in desert areas, river managers may advise dumping graywater directly into the current where it will be diluted and not harm fragile plant life or attract critters; ditto leftover coffee, soda pop, and beer

- use small amounts of toothpaste, rinse, and spray or spit in garbage or ashcan; never leave white globs on the ground
- bathe above the high water mark with as little soap as possible, never use soap in creeks, rivers, or hot springs
- consider using solar showers and/or bathing *above the high water mark* with the help of a friend and a bucket

8. Educate yourself, your friends, and especially young people about river ecology:

- join river conservation/preservation groups
- be alert for threats to rivers – a tip of my helmet's visor to Verne Huser who grouped them as the eight "D's": dumping, development, dewatering, diking, direct disturbance, dam-building, diversion, draining wetlands in his book *River Running* (see bibliography)
- attend public hearings, fill out surveys, learn more about river issues and make your voice heard
- to influence public policy, write letters and e-mails to public officials, call them
- practice water conservation at home and at work.

This wilderness river trip included Roy Akins, one of the Sockeye Survival Swimmers. The party practiced respectful leave-no-trace techniques along the corridor home of the mighty Salmon.

CHAPTER FIFTEEN

Quartermaster: Group Gear List

Quartermaster...an army officer who provides clothing and subsistence for a body of troops.

—MERRIAM WEBSTER'S COLLEGIATE DICTIONARY,
TENTH EDITION

Remember when I mentioned a co-worker said one of our river trips looked like an army ready to take over a small country? We joke around every time the trip leader appoints a "quartermaster," but we are grateful someone is organizing the group gear. The U.S. Forest Service will send the permit-holder a list of required trip items (the Four Rivers in Idaho call it "The Required Equipment Checklist"). You must present these items for the ranger's inspection prior to launching, or you don't go down the permitted river. All hail the quartermaster who always comes through for us!

The remaining items on your trip's list of equipment and supplies are a function of your camping style. A trip of self-contained kayakers or canoeists,

Thanks to the trip quartermaster and a competent rafter using a cargo net, this fully-loaded cataraft's gear stayed in place through Class IV rapids.

Group gear list for this party of sixteen included two stoves to accommodate a delicious, but elaborate, ethnic cuisine.

for example, will probably carry several small, lightweight water filters, rather than a heavy Katadyn expedition pump with a breakable ceramic filter (refer to the end of this chapter for more hints). But just because your trip has rafters, avoid taxing them with everything, including the kitchen sink (amusingly enough, there is a "camp-sink" contraption on the market complete with legs and counterspace). On one low-water trip, the trip leader woke up to find the heavy Dutch oven roped to his kayak by a tired rafter.

On a leave-no-trace trip, this is one item you can't be without: a porta-potty toilet system. One privy team's equipment looked like this: a toilet, set to go with seat screwed on; a backup privy bucket with traveling screw-top lid; a supply bucket with plenty of TP; and for handwashing – soap-on-a-rope and water container.

Table 15-1 is an example of a customized group gear list for a raft-supported trip for eighteen people and eight days. Note the columns for assignments ("Who 1" and back-up "Who 2") and easy check-off potential on loading-up day. Use the "Qty*" column to jot in your quantities, adjusted for your trip size.

TABLE 15-1: GROUP GEAR LIST: EIGHT-DAY PARTY OF 18 ON A FOREST SERVICE (F.S.) RIVER

Copy if you like. From *River Otter: Handbook for Trip Planning*

** = Required by F. S.

Item	Qty	Qty*	Size	Who 1	Who 2	Notes
Equipment:						
Camping/Cooking Equipment:						
Stove, 2 Burner	2		2 Burner			
Backup Stove	0		—			
Propane Tank	2		2.5 gal. (11 lb. size)			
** **Fire Pan**	2		w/grill			
Lantern	18		Headlamps/ Flashlights			Personal Item
Roll-Up Table	1					
Other Table	1		Kitchen			
Coolers:	1		120 Qt.			
	1		80 Qt.			
	2		60 Qt.			
	1		Soft lunch			
Dry Box	2		Kitc/Food			
** **Ash Bucket**	1					
Folding Saw	1					
** **Folding Shovel**	1					
Rocket Box	0		—			
Ammo Box	2					
Kitchen Equipment:						
Pots:	2		8/14 Qt.			
	1		6 Qt.			
Coffee Pot	1		24 cup (or one smaller & a carafe)			
Lg.Mixing Bowl	1		2 gal. size			
Plastic Gold Pan	1		For salads			
Hot Pads	2					
Leather Fire Gloves	1					
Frying Pan	1					
Dutch Oven	0		12"			
Dutch Oven	1		16"			
Can Opener	1					
Measuring Cup	1					
Flapjack Spatula	1					
Whisk/beater	1					

* * = Required by F. S.

Item	Qty	Qty*	Size	Who 1	Who 2	Notes
Scraper Spatula	1					
Large Knife	1					
Paring Knife	1					
Peeler	1					
Pastry Cutter	1					
Spoons	2		Large			
Towels	2		Cloth			
Dishpan	1					
Pot Scrubber	2					
Brush	1					
Cutting Board	2					
** **Strainer For Dish Water**	1					
Dish Drying Hammock	1					
Silverware Bag	1					
Dinner Plates	18					
Mugs	18					Personal Item
Tablecloth	1		Oilcloth			
Sanitation Equipment:						
Water Purifier	1		Katadyn			
Small Hand Filter (Backup)	2					
Water Bottles	2		5 Gallon			
Collapsible H2O container	2		2.5 Gal. Cubes			
** **River-Water Bucket**	2		5 gal. empty *Extra collapsible ones good for for bathing*			
** **Portapotty System**	3		Screw-lid, gasketed, 5-gal. buckets			
Handwashing set-up	1		Plastic H2O jug + towel + soap-on-a-rope in mesh bag			
Trowel for catholes						
Shelter Equipment:						
Tents:	1		3 Prsn.			
	1		2 Prsn.			
	1		3 Prsn.			
	1		2 Prsn.			
	1		3 Prsn.			
	1		2 Prsn.			
Tarps	1		Large			
	1		Blue			

** = Required by F. S.

Item	Qty	Qty*	Size	Who 1	Who 2	Notes

Supplies:
Cooking Supplies:

Item	Qty	Qty*	Size	Who 1	Who 2	Notes
Matches	1		Box			
Hvy. Alum. Foil	1		1 Roll			
Parchment	10		D.O. sheets			
Zip-Lock Bags	3		1 Gal.			
Zip-Lock Bags	4		1 Qt.			
Zip-Lock Bags	3		1 Pt.			
Zip-Lock Bags	1		Snacksize			
Zip-Lock Bags	2		Sdwch			
Clorox (bleach)	1		2 Qt. jug			
Dish Soap	1		1 Pt.			
Box Trash Bags	1		Compactor			
Charcoal	1		25# sack			
Spices			Mixed			
Frozen H$_2$O jugs	4		1 Gal.			
Disp'bl Propane	1		Canister			
Deet	1		Spray can			
Paper Towels	2		Rolls			
Clothlike Paper Dishcloths	1		Pkg.			

Camping Supplies:

Item	Qty	Qty*	Size	Who 1	Who 2	Notes
Cord	1		100 Ft.			
Duct Tape	3		Rolls			
Marking Pen	1		Thick			
Marking Pen	1		Thin			
Sunscreen-generic/ waterproof	15		SPF			

Sanitation Supplies:

Item	Qty	Qty*	Size	Who 1	Who 2	Notes
Toilet Paper	9		Big Rolls			
Lime	1		Bag—2 lbs.			
Baby Wipes	1		canister			
Wash gel	1		large			
Trash sacks	7		Gal. size			
Supplies for Takeout Trip to SCAT Machine	3 pr		Disposable gloves			
	1		Roll paper towels			

Medical & Safety:
Ouch Pouch:

Item	Qty	Qty*	Size	Who 1	Who 2	Notes
Contents in Chapter 17	3					

First Aid Kit:

Item	Qty	Qty*	Size	Who 1	Who 2	Notes
Contents in Chapter 17	1					

** = Required by F. S.

Item	Qty	Qty*	Size	Who 1	Who 2	Notes
Extraction Kits:						
Throw Bags	4		75'			
Throw Bags	2		25'			
Throw Bags	3		Belt			
Rope (2 ton test)	2		150'			
Parachute Cord	1		150'			
Large Pulley	3					
Small Pulley	3					
Std. Carabiner	9					
Locking Carabiner	2					
Pearabiner	1					
Prussicks	7					
Slings	4					
Face Mask	2					

Transportation:
Craft:

Item	Qty	Qty*	Size	Who 1	Who 2	Notes
Aire Cataraft	1		14'			
Aire Cataraft	1		16'			
Aire Raft	1		14'			
Maravia Raft	1		14'			
Hardshell Kayaks	15					
Inflatable Kayak	1		2-person			
Trailers:						
Utility	1					
Flat Bed	1				·	
Vehicles:						
Jeep	5		Prsn.			
Explorer	6		Prsn.			
Big Van	4		Prsn.			
Suburban	5		Prsn.			

Drop your sunglasses or camera? Bring along a facemask and snorkel to hunt for them or other river booty.

Hints for Self-Contained Kayak and Canoe Trips

• Plan your trip like you would an ultra-light backpacking trip. Analyze bulk and weight, *or else:* 1. it won't fit in your craft; 2. you'll be sorry when you go to negotiate a turn or rapid.

• Use a backpacking stove and kitchen equipment. A collapsible bucket is handy, especially when you use your small filtering device. Remember, if you want to kill viruses, boil water hard for one minute.

• Dehydrate as much of your food as possible (read Kesselheim's *Camp Cook's Companion*).

• Pack food in plastic baggies, which can be turned into trash bags later.

• Plan equipment to be multi-purpose, e.g., your sleeping tarp can double as tablecloth for food prep/eating, even as a water-pumping "settling pond" liner.

On a self-contained desert river kayak trip with cloudy water, using a "settling pond" made from a plastic tablecloth takes the place of a 5-gallon bucket.

- Abide by the river authorities' rules for human solid waste disposal. If they require "pack it in, pack it out," consider making a toilet tube from a length of 4" PVC pipe with a cap glued on one end and a threaded lid (like a sewer cleanout cap) on the other. When using, squat over the tube and aim carefully. (Don't laugh; this is challenging.) Alternatively, make a target of a few TP squares on the ground, squat, then place the deposit in the tube manually and congratulate yourself at going the extra mile for leave-no-trace camping. Pack a shaker of lime to sprinkle inside the tube before closing. Don't forget to grease the inside before you leave home with nonstick cooking spray or solid shortening to facilitate post-trip cleanup (yes, this is not a throw-away item — after dumping the contents at an RV station or sewage treatment plant, use lots of chlorine bleach or other disinfectant before reusing it).

On this four-day, self-contained trip, Lisa and David wished for longer arms to find small items stuffed deep in their kayaks.

- Even if a firepan isn't required on your river, bring one for emergency use. Find one that can protect the environment and prevent wildfires (hubcaps and turkey pans work, but may be either too stiff or too flimsy). We've used 9" by 13" baking pans and folded the sides so it can be molded to fit a kayak. Remember to sprinkle the bottom with sand or dirt to prevent warping. Save this ash mix for re-burning by storing it in your ashbucket – a small paint can with tight-fitting lid.

Backpacking stoves, kitchen equipment, and tents make self-contained trips a fun way to reach gorgeous campsites.

- Always test your load to see if it fits in your boat BEFORE you leave home.
- Refer to Alan Kesselheim's *The Wilderness Paddler's Handbook* for other hints, especially if you are a canoeist.

Back in 1972 we threw our gear (and little Christian) into the canoe and took off. Wet gear and food were common in those days.

CHAPTER SIXTEEN

Transportation Coordinator

Are we there yet?

—ANONYMOUS CHILD

Delegate fact-finding on the price of a shuttle service, bus, friends, etc., to a trip member. Have the person report to the group so that travel plans go smoothly. Trust your "coordinator of all things wheeled" to resolve questions of vehicles, trailers, and possible shuttle bus, airplane, or jet boat service.

Transportation Coordinator's dream: all packed up and ready to roll. This bus and trailer held twenty-one boaters, twenty boats, and eight days worth of food and gear.

Hints for transportation coordinators:

- Use the collective knowledge in your group to come up with the best shuttle plan

- Call around to the professional shuttle services to compare prices and services

- Review shuttle service requirements with drivers of all vehicles (remember to leave keys!)

- In low-water years, evaluate costs of flying in some gear and supplies to drop point

- Don't be afraid to speak up about questionable spare tires and other vehicle necessities

- Develop a contingency plan in case any vehicle breaks down and doesn't make it to the put-in – mobile phones are great for staying in touch.

Even a "simple" multi-day, self-contained kayak trip needs someone to drive and arrange the shuttle.

CHAPTER SEVENTEEN
Medical/First Aid Coordinator

First aid...the knowledge and skills to recognize and
provide basic first aid and care for injuries and sudden
illness until advanced medical care personnel arrive and
take over.

—AMERICAN RED CROSS:
HEALTH AND SAFETY SERVICES FACT SHEET, 2000

Although every trip would like Marcus Welby and Florence Nightingale along to care for emergencies and health care questions, you may have to settle for some other health-conscious team member to be your point person for medical/first aid. Perhaps it's someone with a recent CPR certification, or just a conscientious person who's willing to organize and watch out for the trip medical/first aid supplies.

Kate Krakker has helped our trips capably handle a number of first aid situations and agreed to offer practical advice on preparing for medical emergencies on the river.

Photo: Todd Swanson

Nurse practitioner Kate Krakker conducts sick call in camp. (Massage is optional.)

FIRST AID

by Kate Krakker, RN, MS, FNP

First aid involves careful preparation of a person, or a team of persons, to oversee medical issues on the trip. Wilderness first aid encompasses prevention of medical emergencies, treatment of minor emergencies, stabilization of serious emergencies, and the transportation of serious emergencies out of the backcountry to the closest medical facility. By the end of this chapter I hope you'll understand what is involved in being the first aid provider and how to:

- Provide the supplies needed in a first aid kit
- Understand the medical needs of your group
- Know prevention for common medical problems
- Feel comfortable holding "sick call"
- Have references/resources available to you on medical emergencies.

THE MEDICAL TEAM involves the most experienced medical person/ persons on the trip. It is my hope that you always have a licensed medical person on your trip. If not, don't be shy – encourage someone with skills, or train yourself to be that individual. Most first aid is given by individuals with basic training, intense interest, and/or just plain enthusiasm for the task dealt them. Many times medical care is provided by one person, but consider a team if there is more than one individual interested. The team approach will give you the ability to collaborate on problems, train individuals with less experience, and have medical care available at different locations. And, best of all, you may secure more friends with medical capabilities for future trips. Always a good thing.

Photo: Todd Swanson

Injuries to toes and feet are the most common reason to visit the river trip first aid coordinator.

Whoever does volunteer (or is assigned) to first aid should be trained. Many basic courses are given through local hospitals, ambulance companies, recreation companies training their employees, and day care referral services. Volunteer groups such as Boy/Girl Scouts and the American Red Cross conduct periodic first aid classes for the public. Know cardiopulmonary resuscitation (CPR) and stay updated. If you are a medical professional, stay current in emergency training. Obtain books to the level of care you are comfortable giving, and be familiar with them. Review the text resources listed at the end of this chapter. I have rarely pulled out a book in the wilderness to understand what to do, but many times have been very thankful I took the time to read them before I was faced with that emergency. Treatment action comes to mind clearly in an emergency when you have done the homework.

SUPPLIES FOR A FIRST AID KIT should be planned out ahead of time and be a priority for the group. They may be costly and do expire, so include them in preplanning your trip costs. Most supplies can be obtained at your local pharmacy. For prescription medications, ask your primary care provider. At your annual physical exam, take your first aid kit and show your practitioner what you carry. They are usually agreeable to refill medications that have expired, or come with a great story on how they were used. Only carry medications you feel comfortable with – whether they are prescription (Rx) or over-the-counter (OTC) – and know their use and side effects. Never give medication to others without checking for an allergy to that medicine.

Organize your supplies. I have sewn a bag with many pockets for my kit. Day backpacks provide enough space and compartments to make great first aid kits. I use a red bag with a white cross sewn on so it is readily recognizable. Tying a white bandanna to a red bag is easily done and again highly visible. When all else fails, use duct tape and mark the bag. This is helpful to you when there are large piles of gear going on trips. A well-marked bag is also easy to describe when you need others to fetch it. Organizing supplies within the bag can be done with compartments, mesh bags, and/or plastic zipper baggies. Zip lock baggies are helpful in grouping supplies into packets as they may be used. You can label the tops of the baggies so packets of supplies can be recognized while foraging through the first aid bag with a flashlight between your teeth. Organization before the trip can be great help in future unforeseen circumstances.

I recommend a small ("ouch pouch") kit and a larger first aid kit to be on all trips. With these two kits I have cared for up to twenty-two individuals. You may consider more than one ouch pouch that can be placed with different individuals and at different locations. It should be close to you and easily accessible on a boat, backpack, or hip pack.

The small kit should include commonly used items for minor emergencies:

- ❏ Means of cleansing a wound – soap and water, small alcohol or Betadine wipes, brush
- ❏ Antibiotic ointment – Bacitracin or Polysporin
- ❏ Anti-inflammatory ointment – Hydrocortisone 0.5%
- ❏ Bandage strips (Band-Aids)
- ❏ Gauze dressings
- ❏ Tape
- ❏ Medications:

OTC: ❏ Acetaminophen
　　　 ❏ Aspirin
　　　 ❏ Benadryl tablets, 25 mg.
　　　 ❏ Ibuprofen, the nectar of the weekend warrior

Rx:　 ❏ Anaphylaxis kit
　　　 ❏ Narcotics

- ❏ Tweezers
- ❏ Safety pins
- ❏ Scissors
- ❏ Small pen flashlight

 Copy if you like. From *River Otter: Handbook for Trip Planning*

The large kit carries more of the above supplies, medications, and any special supplies you feel you need to carry. It should be well protected from the elements. I use a river dry bag whether it is going on a river trip, a car-camping trip, or to the beach. The large kit should be double-stocked. Keep in mind the size of your group.

The large kit supplies include:

- ❏ Anaphylaxis kit
- ❏ Antibiotics:
  For skin infections, I recommend Keflex or Duricef (both Rx)
- ❏ For *Giardia* and other diarrhea-causing microbes, I recommend Cipro (Rx)
- ❏ Topical antibiotic ointments: Bacitracin or Polysporin (OTC)
- ❏ Anti-inflammatory medicine:
  - ❏ Ibuprofen
  - ❏ Hydrocortisone ointment
  - ❏ Prednisone taper (Rx)
- ❏ Antacids (Tums, Tagamet, Zantac, Mylanta, Pepto – whichever is your favorite)
- ❏ Antibacterial soap
- ❏ Anti-itch (Benadryl ointment or Rhuli juice for all that itches)
- ❏ Anti-diarrheals (Imodium or Lomotil)
- ❏ Bandages:
  - ❏ Gauze, Telfa, moleskin
  - ❏ Gauze wraps, such as Kerlex, Kling, Conform
  - ❏ Ace bandages
  - ❏ Vet tape
- ❏ Adhesive tapes
- ❏ Triangle bandage
- ❏ Blood pressure cuff
- ❏ Calamine Lotion to dry weepy poison ivy
- ❏ Charcoal Suspension for ingestion of poisons and as a compress on venomous stings (available at health food stores)
- ❏ Colds and Allergies: pseudoephedrine (OTC) and chloropheniramine (OTC)
- ❏ Glasses for reading to magnify, or a magnifying glass, to see splinter, foreign bodies in eye, etc.
- ❏ Eye wash (ophthalmic saline, eye tears solution)
- ❏ Flashlight
- ❏ Pain Medicines:
  - ❏ Ibuprofen
  - ❏ Tylenol
  - ❏ Narcotics
- ❏ Consider sedatives
- ❏ Phenergan Suppositories for vomiting
- ❏ Pliers and Small Wire Cutter for fishhooks

❏ Reference books

❏ Rubbing alcohol for swimmers' ear

❏ Safety pins

❏ Scrub brush to cleanse wounds:
- ❏ Can buy a wound scrub brush
- ❏ Some have been known to use a clean toothbrush

❏ Suture Kit for the experienced

❏ Space blanket

❏ Sun screen

❏ Stethoscope

❏ Scissors

❏ Splinting material may be carried, but is most times readily available in the environment and in trip equipment

❏ Thermometer (to go down to 86 degrees for hypothermia)

❏ Tweezers

❏ Wound irrigation supplies

Physicians and emergency professionals will many times carry additional equipment:

❏ Endotracheal tube

❏ Needle for pneumothorax

❏ IV and IV solutions

❏ Oto-ophthalmascope

Copy if you like. From *River Otter: Handbook for Trip Planning*

UNDERSTANDING THE MEDICAL NEEDS OF YOUR GROUP MEMBERS

is a task completed before you leave. Announce at trip meetings and by e-mail that you would like to hear from each individual on the trip. Ask them to update you on any medications they take or potential medical problems they foresee. If they have none, you would also want that information. This opens a dialogue for concerns they may have and alerts you to potential problems on the trip. It's best to redirect concerns/problems back to them and their medical provider, but form a plan and alert them to your limitations, which are many on a wilderness trip. I ask all individuals who are taking medications to store and take their own medications. Also, it's the individual's responsibility to provide required supplies for a known wound or medical problem that's present before the trip. One trip we had five anaphylaxis kits due to known bee allergies. It is great to have back-up supplies and trip members who plan ahead.

PREVENTION IS THE KEY TO A SUCCESSFUL TRIP once you have pulled out of the driveway. If you are in charge of medical emergencies, it is best to just avoid them all together. I inform my trip members I love to see every little boo boo. It is the smallest of problems that, if undetected, may worsen and affect not only the individual's trip, but may alter the group's plans as well. There are common incidents on trips that cause injury. During these times I stay alert, reminding members that we are on vacation and "let's be careful." They are as follows:

- The loading and unloading of vehicles and gear is a time to slow down, use proper body mechanics, and take breaks if necessary to evaluate the load.

- During the summer months, you cannot use enough sunscreen. Remind trip members in the morning and at lunch to lube up – especially those fair-skinned friends looking for that perfect tan.

- All wounds should be scrubbed clean, antibiotic ointment applied, and an occlusive dressing applied when out in the elements. Check the wound every day.

- Be alert for environmental hazards. Some individuals on your trip may not be familiar with hazards in your region. In the Western United States snakes love warm places. They sun out on rocks, crawl into boats, sleeping bags, and tents. Point out poison ivy. Bear, moose, and other animals are not our friends, and we are in their backyard. Inform others when you see these hazards.

- Day hikes almost always turn into longer hikes than planned. Don't leave camp without proper footwear (socks and well-fitting boots), and water. A power bar in your pocket is a good idea.

- Dehydration occurs quickly when you are active and in the sun. Drink water and say "have some more water" and "can I fill that water bottle for you?" Dehydrated individuals rarely recognize their problem. They believe it is the flu or something they ate. Get them to drink.

- Alcohol is a great thing in camp. Avoiding it through the day's activities 1) improves the safety of the trip; 2) keeps non-drinking trip members as your friends; and 3) gives you a full day of energy and alertness should problems occur.

- Fires are a potential danger for burns. Be careful around them. A burn wound can deplete the gauze dressing supplies very quickly.

- I also spend time around the kitchen. Cleanliness is close to godliness. Washing hands before food preparation and proper dishwashing techniques help avoid stomach upsets.

- In the off season and on cooler rivers, be aware of hypothermia. Again the individual rarely recognizes the problem. Prevention of hypothermia includes stopping the group, even though you may have just pushed out of camp, and getting the individual properly dressed.

MAKE TIME IN THE DAY FOR SICK CALL. This is a time to invite trip members to stop by and chat on any medical concerns they have, show you their boo boos, and tell of great adventures. I choose after the evening meal, when activities are winding down. A good whistle and an announcement signal the group that you have your first aid kit out and are open for business.

Common things happen commonly. This is where your pre-trip planning is tested. Do daily wound care on any open wounds. Follow up on known medical concerns.

KNOW AND HAVE AVAILABLE RESOURCES ON FIRST AID. It is not the intention of this chapter to update you or have the treatment for the many medical emergencies that may occur in the backcountry. The following resources have been helpful to me and to others on first aid duty, doing our best to treat medical emergencies in the wilderness:

- Gill, Paul G., Jr. *Wilderness First Aid: A Pocket Guide.* Camden, ME: Ragged Mountain Press, 2002;

- Auerbach, Paul S. *Field Guide to Wilderness Medicine.* St. Louis, MO: Mosby, 1999;

- Alloway, David. *Wilderness 911.* Seattle, WA: The Mountaineers Books, 2000; and

- Wilkerson, James A. *Medicine for Mountaineering & Other Wilderness Activities.* Seattle, WA: The Mountaineers Books, 1992.

Filling a personal water bottle from a side creek is a risky proposition, best left to experienced back-country boaters with gambler's luck.

CHAPTER EIGHTEEN

Safety Leader and Tips

by Barry Eschen

> Whitewater is a challenging sport and the rewards are great, but the inherent risk of injury or death must be recognized.

—BECHDEL & RAY (APPALACHIAN MOUNTAIN CLUB BOOKS), *RIVER RESCUE*

My river safety attitude comes from being a disciple of Les Bechdel (see bibliography). His perspective of going down the river thinking about what could go wrong and how could I prevent or handle it fits my personality well. I enjoy talking with the group about what could go wrong and how to avoid it. For others, this approach takes the joy, spontaneity and fun out of a trip. Having one of the most experienced trip members be in charge of safety allows the trip leader to focus on other things. It also allows the leader to let someone else be point person in announcing an unpopular decision.

The safety leader does not take on all responsibility for safety. Each person has to decide how much personal risk to take. Each person has to decide if

Safety Leader Barry gives a pre-launch talk to assure all trip members are on the same page (refer to Appendix 1 for details).

Photo: Todd Swanson

Photo: Todd Swanson

Some kayakers won't boat without protective faceguard and sunvisors on their helmets.

they are comfortable going down the river with the available group, considering the group's organization, planning and equipment. Obviously, it is much better to meet the group and make the decision about whether to even go before leaving for the put-in.

Each person also has to decide what personal equipment to bring. My style is pretty careful. I have a football plastic faceguard on my helmet. In Idaho the only people you see with faceguards are the people who have smashed their faces and the ones who care for them. (I tried a metal face guard, but it was too heavy and gave me neck strain.) Even on day trips next to a road I carry in my kayak an extra paddle, hand paddles, a first aid kit, a water bottle, extra dry clothes, gloves, a space blanket, matches, Gatorade powder, a Power Bar, insect repellent, sun screen, a folding saw, a trowel, toilet paper and bags for waste. A buddy or I have needed all of them at least once. My paddle has light-colored blades, so people can see signals better in poor visibility or against a dark background. My life jacket is yellow, so it will be easier for rescuers to find me under water when seconds count. The safety person can help by making sure someone helps novices select their gear.

The group should work out ahead of time how much emergency preparedness is appropriate. Obviously, the length of the trip and the availability of assistance are major factors in deciding the appropriate level.

The safety person needs to use judgment about when to speak up. One year at Big Creek on the Middle Fork of the Salmon the wind was strong. I asked the rafter with the extraction gear on board to go behind our weakest rafter, so the gear would be easy to get, if needed. (Hauling gear up rapids costs time and energy.) The rafter brushed me off and went ahead. He was shocked to see the wind lift most of a sweepboat three feet out of the water. Unlike our rafts the sweepboat had very little gear in it, so it was very light for its size, but it was an impressive sight. As it turned out, our rafters had no problem, so my caution was not needed, but it may have been appropriate.

In addition to monitoring dangers, the safety person may teach water flow mechanics, boating skills and respect for the water. Some people enjoy surprises. Yet I've seen novices never go on a river again after one too many surprises. I prefer to explain to novices where the dangers are and what to do if they find themselves in a bad situation. It allows them to be careful about specific situations rather than worry about the great unknown. It may help people make more informed decisions about running a particular line, getting on a raft, or portaging.

Six particular subjects merit further discussion: practice and graduated risk, an accident plan, alcohol and drugs, staying together, camp accidents and natural dangers.

1. PRACTICE AND GRADUATED RISK are the key elements in turning novices into successful, experienced trip members. The safety-conscious trip member is part "mama-duck" when it comes to helping novices with new experiences on the river. Repetition of skills allows the skills to be there when danger crops up. Graduated risk involves taking on easy situations and then harder ones. I recommend starting novices in water they can handle easily, extensive practice of needed skills and slow introduction to more challenging situations. Over-protecting your trip members does retard their progress and may cause them to chafe under your instruction. Strive for the middle ground and involve them in the decision as to how much they are ready for.

2. AN ACCIDENT PLAN can increase everyone's sense of safety and just might be needed. In a major disaster seconds can count. On most overnight trips I have been on, there has been a designated person to take charge in case of an accident, with one or two back-ups. The person who takes charge directs the effort. Suggestions are welcome, but should go through the leader. A head trapped under water is an emergency. The nearest person(s) should do whatever appears to be best for the victim without jeopardizing another life. In any other situation, there is time to organize. The accident leader should

Practice for accidents can greatly improve the skill of response to the real thing. For example, Les Bechdel recommends throw-rope practice. It can be done as a game at an organizational meeting. I support this, but have never been in a group that did it. I have been in one that practiced after lunch one day on the river.

delegate as many tasks as possible in order to be free to focus on the big picture of the rescue. Most accidents occur in rapids. Usually some people are above the rapid, some in the rapid, and some below. People should group above and below the rapid while a plan develops. If the river is blocked, be sure to send someone upstream to warn other parties to eddy out. Arguing over the best approach is to be avoided. Solo hero actions not cleared with the leader can lead to more problems. The group should understand the plan and the alternative, if the plan fails. The accident leader should be thinking of anything that could go wrong with the plan and how to respond if it does. Obviously, for most people thorough planning and scouting to avoid accidents is preferable to a successful rescue (See Appendix 1 – River Safety Talk).

Tidbits:

The most common injury I've seen on the river is a gouge in the foot from rocks and sticks encountered bare-foot in the sand.

The sand or soil under a firepan is extremely hot. If possible, elevate firepans on rocks to reduce the danger and protect soil and vegetation. I showed how macho I was by continuing for 10 more days on the river with second-degree burns on both feet from stepping where a firepan had been. I'd have had more fun if I were a little more careful.

Between a boat and rock is not where you want to be – stay up-current from a boat, so it is squished between you and the rock, not vice versa.

Spouses get upset if you get close to bears. (You can even bicker over the definition of close.)

3. ALCOHOL AND DRUGS on your river trip is a mixed bag. For some a day without beer is a day without sunshine. In Idaho beer is a major supply item for a river trip. The thank you for favors, like retrieving someone's lost gear, is often a beer. However, alcohol both slows the thinking and dilates the blood vessels in the skin, so a person in the water or wind gets colder faster. After the group is in camp, the risk for hypothermia is usually gone and the consequences of accidents are lessened. On the water my attitude is that at any time I may need the skills of a companion to assist me or even save me. I want both of us to be as clear-headed as possible. Granted, many of my companions are better kayakers after a beer or two than I am without a beer, but I may need them at their best – not just better than I.

4. STAYING TOGETHER increases the safety for all. The river rangers prefer that groups stay together so that the river appears empty ahead, rather than full of strung-out groups merging into each other. A person way out ahead or behind is on his or her own. One mistake can ruin the day for the loner and the trip

Despite the best planning, Ma Nature can have tricks up her sleeve. Always carry a raft repair kit.

members. However, boating alone, with no one visible ahead or behind, only wilderness, can be a special experience.

5. CAMP SAFETY. Once off the water, accidents can happen, too, but the odds of a major disaster are lower. Drowning is not a factor, and assistance and the first-aid bag are readily available.

Like boating alone, hiking alone in the wilderness is a special experience. The trail lures one on with new vistas around each bend. It can be very helpful if the group agrees ahead of time on what the guidelines for hiking will be. We expect hikers to let the group know where they are going and to be back before dark. I remember building a large fire to serve as a beacon for a hiker who returned well after dark. He did not tell us where he was going. I had picked up his tracks early in the day, off the trail, and had seen where he got back on the trail, so I had an idea where he was headed. However, he was one the strongest in our party, so we would have been hard pressed to travel the next day as far as he did, much less find him. We ask solo hikers to carry a whistle.

6. NATURAL DANGERS are part of the excitement of wilderness travel. Besides you do not have the benefit of solid shelter, news service, weather reports, and emergency services. That's part of the fun of it, but it also is cause for caution.

WEATHER

Predicting the weather can be fun and useful. In the Northern Hemisphere storms usually come on a south wind. This also means it gets warmer. If you are in a canyon, the local wind direction may be very different from the wind up above. Watch cloud movement to determine the wind direction. Classically, thin cirrus clouds are followed by stratus and/or cumulus clouds. As the storm passes, the wind switches to the north and it gets colder. Thunderstorms form when a column of warm moister air rises into the colder upper atmosphere. This is most common in the afternoon in humid conditions. Watch for the rapid development of large dark clouds. There are violent up and down currents in a thunderhead. Ice particles going up and down get coated with more and more water producing larger and larger hail. The up and down motion also produces an electric charge and consequent lighting. If the updraft becomes strong and organized, a tornado forms. If a tornado goes over water it takes up the water producing a waterspout. Then it won't rain cats and dogs, but can rain fishes and frogs.

If you see a storm developing, it may be a good idea to make camp early. Prepare for wind and rain. Look for a sheltered spot. Line tents up to present the least resistance to the expected wind. Check for any lone or weakened trees or branches in choosing your tent site. Stake tents. Add rocks on top of the stakes. If the wind comes up, get in the tent to hold it down. You may want to get a quick meal going. Put some clothing and firewood where it will remain dry. The temperature is going to drop.

Cumulus clouds may mean lightning soon. If you see a flash, count the seconds till you hear the thunder. Divide the seconds by 5 and that gives you the number of miles it is away. Anything under one mile is cause for immediate caution. Lightning can hit anywhere and far from the previous strike. The following ideas make some sense in reducing your risk. Get off the water. Avoid isolated trees, high spots and slight depressions. Do not handle long metal objects like tent poles. If you feel tingling and your hair standing on end, tuck into a ball and get on your toes. An alternative is to run like hell, but it's probably too late.

Microbursts occur with thunderstorms where the rain enters very dry air. As the rain falls it evaporates, chilling the air around it. This creates a column of heavy cold air that rushes to the ground and spreads out. The wind can topple isolated trees or even every tree on a hillside. The best protection is getting next to a large rock that will catch the falling trees. The "eddy lines" of microbursts are the windshears that trouble landing planes.

Tornadoes come with huge dark thunderheads. There is often large hail. From a distance a potential tornado cloud often has an anvil shape extending to one side at the top of the cloud. The anvil is formed by rapidly rising warm moist air that cannot penetrate the colder air above. You cannot outrun or outpaddle a tornado, but you can move to the side. If it appears to be getting larger and larger, it is approaching. Turn ninety degrees and run for shelter.

FIRE

Fire is a natural part of the ecology. On half of my trips down the Middle Fork of the Salmon there has been a fire somewhere along the eight-day trip. The mountainside forests are a patchwork of young and old and dead trees, depending on the fire patterns. I have seen fire scampering across what appeared to be a barren hillside, jumping from blade of grass to blade of grass to dead leaf. Most of the time fire just means use your head. Stay away from burning trees that may shower burning debris on you or fall because the base is weakened. If the fire gets to the tops of the trees (crowns) it is much more intense and dangerous. Usually the authorities will alert you of such danger and won't permit parties to launch on the river if a fire is expected to crown. If the fire gets more intense, it becomes a firestorm and generates its own weather including fierce winds. If there is a fire and you hear a sound like a freight train, seek immediate shelter in rocks, in the water if possible and away from any trees. Expect fierce winds with flying embers.

EARTHQUAKES

Earthquakes happen. The immediate danger is falling trees and falling rocks from the cliffs and mountainsides above you. After a quake make sure everyone is accounted for and avoid spots where trees or rocks may fall in aftershocks.

NEW RAPIDS

Rainstorms, snowmelt, fires, and earthquakes all can put debris in the water, creating a new or changed rapid. If there is debris in the water, be alert for strainers and for trees caught against rocks, which make a drop much more technical. Scout. If you come upon quiet water that covers vegetation on the bank that once grew in the air, you are approaching an obstruction. Watch for a horizon line, a place ahead where the water disappears without going around a bend. Eddy out and scout.

When a side-creek backs up during a storm with logs and debris, it can let go with powerful forces. The result is a "blow-out" that may create new holes like this one at Orelano Creek in Idaho.

Bears:

Forest Service River Ranger Sara Whittier of the Middle Fork of the Salmon District knows her bears. After two black bears had to be shot for menacing camps in 2002, she lectured all float parties on methods to keep them from returning to river camps. "It'll save their lives and maybe your own," she said.

- Keep a clean camp.
- Keep all food in dry boxes, not in tents or jacket pockets.
- Strap coolers closed at night, even form a giant cube with dryboxes and coolers.
- When confronting a black bear, stay aggressive and don't run.
- Use long-range (30-foot) bear pepper-spray.
- Use an air-horn to frighten them.

LARGE ANIMALS

Humans have hunted large animals for generations. They will protect themselves. They will protect their young. If they know you are around, they will usually skedaddle out of there. If you are sneaking up on them to take a picture, they do not understand that you do not have a weapon. Carnivores only hunt people when desperate – it's too dangerous for them. Carnivores will protect their kills from you.

Of the large animals, bears are probably the most troublesome. North American bears are divided into black bears (which may be black, brown or cinnamon in color), brown bears or grizzlies (have a hump over the shoulders and lighter hair over the shoulders), and polar bears. My experience is limited to black bears. Do not surprise bears: they can be cranky. Make noise in bear country. If you do confront a black bear, be aggressive. Do not turn and run unless the bear is running at you and there is a climbable tree available. If a black bear grabs you, conventional wisdom says play dead. If it starts to drag you off, it is going to eat you. Fight. With brown bears, just fight.

Bears need food, especially during drought and in the fall when they must store fat for hibernation. If they learn to get food from camps, they become a major problem. Do not camp near populated areas where bears have been getting into the garbage. Put your food in coolers and dry boxes. Strap coolers shut. Gary Payne watched a bear lie on its back and spin a cooler in its paws, trying to pop it open. Don't take food into your tent or clothing with food on it. Don't forget the energy bar in your pocket. Scented soaps and lotions can interest bears. Hang your garbage in a tree or put it in a cooler in a raft. If bears are in the area it's a good idea to have an air horn and bear pepper spray available. Regular pepper spray is too weak. Air horns are very effective in scaring bears.

Moose are big! A female will protect her calf, even if you think you are not threatening. Stay well clear.

Wolves and mountain lions will generally leave you alone. Reciprocate.

MEDIUM ANIMALS

Skunks, raccoons, porcupines, foxes, and other medium animals generally leave people alone. If you or your pet get sprayed by a skunk use acid, such as vinegar, vitamin C, or tomato juice to denature the odorant.

Snakes like to leave you alone too. Rattlesnakes will warn you if you give them a chance. River people encounter rattlesnakes most often while hiking, scouting or portaging. Snakes like to sun themselves when the temperature starts to warm after a cool time. Look before you step or place your hand on a rock or ledge.

SMALL ANIMALS

Golden mantled ground squirrels (large "chipmunks") love to enjoy your food. We nicknamed one Hep Yurself. One chewed through a drybag of supplies of ours directly into the wrapped fruitcake within. One rode down the

This mama moose and her calf swam across the river into our camp at daybreak. When she saw Gary move, she feigned an attack charge that sent us all running for cover. Then she sniffed our boats and proceeded with her breakfast grazing.

river in one of our coolers. One tore the pocket out my life jacket to get the Power Bar wrapper I had left there.

Ground squirrels can carry plague. Stay clear of a sick squirrel.

Deer mice carry hanta virus, but are not dangerous out of doors. If you want to sweep up mouse feces in closed locations such as cabins, wear a mask. At lower elevation sandy beaches, mice forage at night. I have two good river shirts that I put out to dry overnight, only in the morning to find them chewed wherever a food particle had been. Look for tracks in the sand before you make camp to know whom to expect that night. At the same beach where my shirts were chewed we were entertained by a screech owl the next year. No mice!

"Live and let live," Eric said to the snake. "Just don't crawl in my kayak tonight." (Hint: always shake your kayak in the morning to roust out any snoozing critters.)

Minnesota's not the only place where the mosquito is known as the State bird. Sue likes the protection her "no-see-'em" tent provides.

INSECTS

Bees and wasps are generally not your friends, but they too like your food. Wasps, including yellow jackets, like meat. They can be very persistent in getting at your food, so watch every bite when they are around. You can put a bit of meat off to the side for them while you eat, but be sure to clean it up when you finish. Otherwise they will be there for the next meal eaten at this spot. Wasps can sting multiple times.

Bees like sugar. Look for them on the rim of your soft drink can or Gatorade cup. One trip Maria had a pouty lip like a lingerie model thanks to a farmer bee. Bees sting only once. Farmer bees are colored like yellow jackets but are chunkier and like sugar, not meat. They are less aggressive.

Mosquitoes are aggravating and carry disease, most recently West Nile virus. Use netting and repellant. Mosquitoes breed in standing water and feed on grasses until the females need blood to produce their eggs. If you are going to be in a warm, damp location, expect mosquitoes. Small black flies are tricky. Their bite is hardly noticeable, but then itches like crazy the next day. Use insect repellent. If they are very small, put baby oil on your skin and it will trap them, so that they are much too busy to bite you.

SPIDERS, SCORPIONS, AND TICKS (ARACHNIDS)

In the United States tarantulas and scorpions look fierce but do not kill people. Their bites do hurt and may form an open sore. Black widow and brown recluse bites can be more serious. Be careful if rummaging around in rotting logs, woodpiles or cabins.

Ticks carry rickettsial diseases, such as Rocky Mountain spotted fever and Lyme disease. Like mosquitoes, the females need blood to produce eggs. They generally feed on bushes and drop off onto you when they sense a good meal passing by. If you are in tick country examine each other carefully before going to bed. Don't forget children and pets.

CHAPTER NINETEEN

Spontaneity Catalyst:
Beer 'n' Bears, Photos and Games

There was a jolly miller once lived on the river Dee;
He work'd, and sung, from morn till night, no lark more
blythe than he.

—ISAAC BICKERSTAFFE: *LOVE IN A VILLAGE*

You may wish to appoint some jolly trip member to lead spontaneous camp activities, like dress-up night festivities, riverbank games, beer/beverage service, and photography rules for bear (bare?) shots. Spontaneous fun needs only a tug-of-war rope and some skipping stones, or remembering to pack the Frisbee® or *peteca*/Volleybird®. This campground-fun catalyst can also do a group purchase order for maps or publications, or special games and prizes for an "awards" ceremony. Perhaps your leader of things spontaneous will bring a musical instrument or lead off songs or group story-telling or joke sessions, with humor like this:

The Forest Service has issued a BEAR WARNING in the national forests:

They're urging people to protect themselves by wearing bells and carrying pepper spray.

Campers should be alert for signs of fresh bear activity, and they should be able to tell the difference between Black Bear dung and Grizzly Bear dung.

Black Bear dung is rather unformed in quality and copious in quantity. Sometimes you can see fruit seeds, insect parts, and/or squirrel fur in it.

Grizzly Bear dung is also rather unformed and copious, but it has bells in it and smells like pepper spray.

Perhaps one or more members of your party will be spontaneous from time to time and surprise others, practicing random, elf-like acts of kindness. Here are a few "Kind Baby Otter Tips," a term coined by our son Christian.

Kind Baby River Otter Tips:

- If you find someone's wet clothes in a heap, spread them out to dry.

- If you're the first up in the morning, surprise the cooks by getting hot water/coffee started.

- If the wind's coming up in camp and the trip leader's already shouted for everyone to secure their belongings, take a minute and put the loose helmet and paddle jacket inside the owner's boat before they blow away. Also works for staking someone's tent if they're off on a hike.

- If you suspect that a cooler needs to be drained from melting ice, open the drain plug for a second to check, even if you're not on kitchen duty.

- If you come across a pile of empty cans, smash them with a rock and put in a recycling sack.

- If you find a wet map, stretch it out to dry, or put sticks between the pages if it's the plastic page booklet style.

- If you have some skills, share! This means songs, poems, jokes, neck and shoulder massages, story-telling!

- If you're an expert boater, consider letting a newbie or a kid sit in your craft in a calm eddy. When there's time, offer an introductory lesson in your sport to interested folks. Includes helping someone practice kayak rolls, sharpen their rowing strokes, or read water better.

- If someone's had a particularly rough day, offer a bit of help with their camp chores.

- Keep your sense of humor like rafter Daryl when he broke an oar (below).

A tied score: River: 1 (broken oar); Rafter: 1 (sense of humor)

CHAPTER TWENTY

Meal Planning Guru

> Food is essential to the success of a trip, but it's a
> mistake to bring too much. Get a jump on waste
> management by planning....
>
> —LEAVE NO TRACE CENTER FOR OUTDOOR ETHICS:
> *WESTERN RIVER CORRIDORS*

Nothing makes river trip camping successful like well-planned meals.

And no one is more important to a well-organized trip than the meal planner (guru). Need I mention that some appreciative paddlers have crowned meal gurus with wildflower wreaths and given them the first massages?

You and your group have expended huge numbers of calories paddling, hiking, and swimming. Meals need to be high in variety, calories, nutrients, and enough fat for satiety (feeling full). The ingredients must be preserved

*Meal Planning Guru and cooking team make two Dutches of lasagne. Note recipes
are protected by plastic zip bag.*

without a refrigerator and cooked without a microwave oven. Cooking items and ingredients cannot be too heavy or your rafters will complain. Glass is best left at home, with one exception: if you must have Tia Rosa's bottled hot sauce on the trip, duct-tape it like a little mummy.

So, what does your meal guru do to get started?

Remember the pre-trip meeting agenda? People love to discuss their favorite camp foods. A smart guru listens and gets others involved by asking for recipes and help in advance-prep cooking. On our trips the meal guru assembles volunteers to assist with the trip preparation duties. They draw up a judicious list of menus using the recipe-adjusting table in Appendix 5 – far from the frenetic activity of the group meeting. Considerations must include space and weight limitations, food allergies, and ease of preparation (see Appendix 7 for hints).

Because natural fuel is limited, especially in many western river corridors, the guru in charge of meals should be familiar with propane-stove and Dutch-oven cooking methods. Consult Sheila Mill's *Kettle Cuisine* (Paragon Press, 1996). Her discussion of "The Cooking Environment" is packed with pearls about low impact stoves, sanitation, and coolers.

For hints about dehydrating foods for wilderness camping, consult Alan Kesselheim's *Camp Cook's Companion.*

Part Five is an example of how to turn a one-page 8-day/7-night trip *master menu* into easy-to-follow *daily menu sheets.* Quantities are for a trip size of twelve hungry men and women, aged 15-73, but space is provided for you to adjust volumes for gender and age of trip members using the hints for conversions in the appendices. Then you're set to use the rest of Part Five:

- the *advance prep food assignment* list to assure advance cooking help

- the handy *shopping lists* to divide up among volunteer shoppers

- the practical *packing lists* to guarantee all items are available.

Spontaneous music serenades cooking team and day-off boaters.

Photo: Todd Swanson

Part Five:
Mastering River Meals

First night riverside review of the master menu and cooking protocol.

CHAPTER TWENTY-ONE
Master Menu

The achievement of, the mastery of the thing!

—GERARD MANLEY HOPKINS: *THE WINDHOVER*

Reducing a multiday trip menu to its bare bones is like writing an outline for a dreaded term paper. First, you procrastinate, then you hear Yoda's voice: "without first step, no journey can begin." Start with the basic fact: food is only paddler fuel. Amounts, varieties, and methods of preparation involve more art than science. So ponder the type of trip you have ahead.

Once you have answered these questions, the Meal Planning Guru has several options – all of which can work well in cooperative groups.

OPTION 1: The same people cook everyday, but are relieved of other duties.

OPTION 2: Different people cook in rotation, using their own menus and supplies.

OPTION 3: Different people cook in rotation, using group menu plans and supplies.

Menu Planning Variables and Considerations:

- Who's in your group? Teenaged kayakers, playing in holes all day can easily eat three times the food any sane raft passenger would want.
- What's the weather like? We all eat more when air and water temperatures are cold.
- Any time and distance considerations? A trip with easy ten-mile days has more in-camp time than a one where on-river time takes most of the daylight hours. Match menus to itinerary.
- Any weight and space limitations? A cruise-ship smorgasbord can't be carried on a self-contained kayak trip. Plan menus that fit type and number of support craft.
- Any economic limitations? Of course. Food expenses rank first in most trips as the big ticket item, unless you have expensive vehicle and airplane shuttles. It's your call: lobster au gratin or canned tuna, mates?
- Any personal preferences limitations? This includes food allergies and keeping the carnivores and vegans happy. Analyze your party's camping and cooking styles. What compromises need to be made?

I offer the following pages as a fun way to get started on meal planning using Option 3. Pick some meal themes after getting group input, then jot down the basics for three meals per day. For example, Mexicali Monday might include a spicy omelet for breakfast, tortilla wraps for lunch, and a taco bar for dinner. The goal is to fuel your river crew with adequate nutrition and keep them happy campers without killing off the meal planners, shoppers, and packers.

It all begins with the Master Menu sheet, a summary listing of meals by river day number. The Master Menu doubles as the trip calendar, guiding the packing and use of the contents of all food containers:

- Ice chests (coolers)

- Freezers (a cooler packed with dry ice)

- 5-gallon buckets with lids we fondly call "PBs" – a nickname derived from the old pickle buckets once so easily obtained from restaurants

- Aluminum dryboxes

- Waterproof gear bags of unquestionable sturdiness and reliability

Whether you use the sample Master Menu in Table 22-1, a variation, or your own creation, safeguard the original of your trip's meal plan for easy reference. It tends to serve as the trip calendar because paddlers remember river days by the menus consumed, as well as by the rapids run. Encase it in a plastic zippered bag and tape it inside the lid of the kitchen drybox or other accessible spot. You might want to keep a copy for back up also. Keep in mind that river camp cooking is usually fun for everybody. Simple language and easy recipes encourage participation. Some trips can do fine on instant soups or stir-fry every night, but our boaters enjoy the variety of "theme" dinners featuring ethnic foods and quirky instruction sheets – what I call the Daily Menu Sheets described in Chapter 22 and detailed in Appendix 2B.

The Master Menu example is for twelve boaters on a raft-supported, fairly luxurious (but low-water year) trip. Based on our August trips on the Middle Fork of the Salmon River, it favors going as light as possible to keep rafters cheerful while navigating the tricky rock gardens of the upper sections (picture Fred Flintstone in a loaded cataraft in a creek). The schedule demonstrates building in variables:

- how to plan a launch camp feast before leaving the comforts of a Forest Service campground

- how to keep meals on Days 1 and 2 ultra-lightweight and easily prepared without a full kitchen or a large ice chest

- how to plan for a Day 3 airplane drop of heavy kitchen equipment, food, and coolers at Indian Creek (mile 25 when the water levels pick up)

- how to use and re-use food containers to optimize space requirements

A final note: unless you choose Option 1 (a trip where only designated folks cook), different hands will be searching for meal ingredients every day. Good labeling and orderly packing make cooking easy for everyone. Food containers on the Master Menu are listed to correspond to the first river day they are used. They are clearly labeled with

attention veggie boaters and metric cooks:

The Master Menu choices are easily adapted. Consult Appendices 3-10 for ideas on meat substitutes and a metric conversion table.

duct tape and waterproof marker (e.g., "PB #1" means Day 1 and "PB #5" means don't open it until Day 5). The location of all ingredients is listed on the Master Menu with an arrow (→) denoting where they are packed (e.g., in "The Cooler"). This helps track menu ingredients for shopping and packing lists (Chapters 24 and 25).

To see a one-page, copy-ready, generic version of the Master Menu, go to Appendix 2A.

TABLE 21-1: **MASTER MENU**

RIVER DAY: WRITE IN DAY OF THE WEEK/DATE	TENTATIVE DINNER CAMP NAME and RIVER MILE

"Launch Camp"_____/_____/ Boundary Creek Campgrounds – mi. 0

- **B:** Coffee and Donuts at Eschen's before leaving Boise between 10-11 a.m.
- **L:** Sack Lunch (BYO) or stop to buy on the road (Stop again for downwood for BBQ pits as no wood available in camp)
- **D:** "All-American BBQ": Steaks, Potatoes, Garden Salad, Pies

→ BOUNDARY CK. COOLER #1 MORPHS INTO A TRASH CONTAINER THAT STAYS IN A SHUTTLE VEHICLE.

→ RE-LABEL BOUNDARY CK. COOLER #2 THE "LUNCH COOLER" FOR THE REST OF THE TRIP.

"River Day #1"_____/_____/ Trail Camp – mi. 7

- **B:** Kielbasa sausages heated on Camp BBQ pits (firepan is loaded for launch), Muffins, Oatmeal, Melon Slices
- **L:** Pack Lunch Cooler with Tortillas to make wraps, Cheese, Turkey Breast, Carrots, Oreos
- **D:** "Moroccan Delight": Lemon Chicken, Rice, Tabouli, Cucs, Onion & Tomatoes, Pita Bread, Halvah 'n' Sesames

→ INGREDIENTS ARE IN THE LUNCH COOLER AND PB #1 (RE-LABEL THIS "LUNCH PB #1." USE FOR SNACKS + DRY LEFTOVERS FOR REMAINDER OF TRIP.)

"River Day #2"_____/_____/   Pistol Ck. Camp – mi. 21

- **B::** Bagels and Cream Cheese, Oatmeal, Dried Fruit, Summer Sausage
- **L:** Leftover Tabouli in Pitas, Bagels, Carrots, Ham + Cheese 2-3# ea.
- **D:** **"Goin' Light"**: MRE's or Freeze-dried meals, Carrots, Pemmican, Candy Bars, Pan Cookies

→ INGREDIENTS ARE IN LUNCH COOLER, PB #1, AND PB #2.

"River Day #3"_____/_____/   Jackass 1 or 2 – mi. 38

- **B:** Oatmeal and Dried fruit, Amaia Chorizo Sausage (or other dry type)
- **L:** Pitas with leftover Tabouli and Hummus (Stop at Indian Ck. mi. 25. Pick up "The Cooler," "The Freezer" and PBs.)
- **D:** **"Hail Britannia"**: Salisbury Steaks, Spuds, Chutney Salad, Fruitcake (make Breakfast D.O. Appley Coffeecake)

→ INGREDIENTS ARE IN LUNCH COOLER, THE COOLER, AND PB #3.

"River Day #4"_____/_____/   Camas Creek – mi. 60

- **B:** English Muffins, Kielbasa Sausage, Appley Coffee Cake
- **L:** Bagels, Cream Cheese, Peanut Butter, Salami, and Pan Cookies
- **D:** **"Pax Romani"**: Lasagne, Radicchio/Cabbagio Salad, Dolci di Limone

→ INGREDIENTS ARE IN LUNCH COOLER, LUNCH PB #2, THE COOLER, AND PB #4.

"River Day #5"_____/_____/   Layover Day + Dress-up Nite,
Camas Creek – mi. 60

- **B:** Bring out the eggs and bacon from The Cooler! Make E. Indian Monkey Bread
- **L:** Pitas, Cheese, Summer Sausages, Turkey Ham, 3rd sack of Baby Carrots
- **D:** **"Spanish Conquest"**: Bean Burritos, Arroz Vasco, Mexican Fudge (make Breakfast D.O. Blueberry Cobbler)

→ INGREDIENTS ARE IN LUNCH COOLER, LUNCH PB #2, THE FREEZER, THE COOLER, AND PB #5.

"River Day #6"_____/_____/   Survey/Woolard – mi. 74

- **B:** Blueberry Dutch Cobbler, Oatmeal, Frozen Sausages
- **L:** Use up any leftover Burritos, Tortillas, Carrots, Cheese 'n' Salami.
- **D:** **"Tuscan Village"**: Antipasti, Pasta Marinara, Dutch Oven Panne, Tiramisu

→ INGREDIENTS ARE IN LUNCH COOLER, LUNCH PB #2, THE COOLER, THE FREEZER, AND PB #6.

"River Day #7"_____/_____/   Last Night on the River, Cliffside – mi. 89

- **B:** Kielbasa Sausages, Oatmeal, Leftover Tiramisu
- **L:** Tuna, Red Onion, Mayo, Thawed Tortilla Wraps
- **D:** **"Irish Eyes"**: Pilot Biscuits/Smoked Fish, Heavenly Ham, Mashers, 3-Bean Salad, Cherry Fudge D.O. Cake

→ INGREDIENTS ARE IN LUNCH COOLER, THE FREEZER, AND PB#7.

"River Day #8"_____/_____/   Going Home Day, Take out at Cache Bar – mi. 99.7

- **B:** Fried Ham and Leftovers
- **L:** Lunch Leftovers in Lunch Cooler, The Freezer (which by now is only luke...but it'll keep out the chipmunks)...optional: Dinner on the Road Home.

CHAPTER TWENTY-TWO
Daily Menu Sheets

No receipt [*recipe*] openeth the heart but a true friend,
to whom you may impart griefs, joys, fears, hopes,
suspicions, counsels, and whatsoever lieth upon the
heart to oppress it.

—SIR FRANCIS BACON: *OF FRIENDSHIP*

This section describes Daily Menu Sheets: detailed recipes, advance preparation instructions, and packing checklists. Table 22-1 is an sample of one of the eight actual sheets our Middle Fork of the Salmon boaters used in riverside camps (copy-ready daily menus are in Appendix 2B).

We've found that getting the food ready for a dozen drooling paddlers is all the Meals Team cares about, not about how to whip up the best curry powder from scratch. Separate sheets for each evening meal – on heavy paper, darkened and enlarged with a copier – are helpful when light grows dim on late nights in camp. We pack a reference copy of all Daily Menu

Creative presentation of Nite 2's appetizers on a plastic gold pan.

Notes on Daily Menu Sheets:

- Each Daily Menu sheet shows date, location, food theme, menu-at-a-glance, and containers.

- Instructions for Cooks comes first, then Advance Prep Details (♣), and lastly Checklists. The symbol ♣ denotes a meal item, often a whole recipe that requires (or is amenable to) advance preparation. The ♣ is a cooking term.

- The symbol ♦ denotes a dedicated meal ingredient, one easily used for another purpose. These items needs to be labeled and packed to go with a recipe. The ♦ is a packing term.

- The symbol → shows where to locate the ingredients for each Daily Menu.

- River Days begin with Day 1 on the river (and launch camp is Day 0).

Sheets in the zipper bag with the Master Menu in the kitchen drybox. The working copy (with color highlighting for Meal Team use) is protected in its own zipper bag and stowed in the appropriate 5-gallon bucket ("PB") or drybox along with the evening meal's ingredients. Several of the menu items can be pre-mixed or pre-cooked to save in-camp prep time and fuel.

While this level of detail may seem too much for some, rest assured, these sheets will save you trouble in camp. You'll see at a glance what food containers you need to get into for your ingredients. You'll easily assemble the necessary ingredients and advance prep items. You'll use the right sized cooking containers and conserve fuel. And best of all, you'll have foolproof instructions that will give you more time to sing otter songs.

I used to tell novice cooks to "just be creative," but their panicked looks made me change my approach. You'd think they'd prefer to take on a gnarly rapid. This could be because we tend to have more teens and twenty-somethings than Julia Childs-types on our trips. Anyway, I've had success with more detailed menus. Young folks seem to enjoy clear directions and learning by doing, whether in kayaks or in kitchens!

To see the copy-ready versions of Table 22-1 and others for a eight-day trip (and a blank form you can adjust to fit your group size) go to Appendix 2B.

TABLE 22-1: **SAMPLE DAILY MENU SHEET: MOROCCAN DELIGHT**

"River Day #1"_____/_____/   Trail Camp – mi. 7

B: Kielbasa sausages heated on Camp BBQ pits (firepan is loaded for launch), Muffins, Oatmeal, Melon Slices

L: Pack Lunch Cooler with Tortillas to make wraps, Cheese, Turkey Breast, Carrots, Oreos

D: **"Moroccan Delight":** Lemon Chicken, Rice, Tabouli, Cucs, Onion & Tomatoes, Pita Bread, Halvah 'n' Sesames

→ INGREDIENTS ARE IN THE LUNCH COOLER AND PB #1 (RE-LABEL THIS "LUNCH PB #1." USE FOR SNACKS + DRY LEFTOVERS FOR REMAINDER OF TRIP.)

"Welcome to zee cahzbah…"

INGREDIENTS – NITE 1

(♣ = Advance Prep.)	Amounts for 12:	Amount for (___):	DIRECTIONS IN CAMP:
Boiling Water	1 gallon-2 cups (14 cups). Remove 6 c. for tabouli, leaving 8 cups for rice.		Bring to boiling in large pot. Remove amount needed for tabouli. Use remainder for rice.
Rice	4 cups		Stir into boiling water, cover, simmer 20".
Rice Seasoning Pkt: ♣			Add all with rice to boiling rice water.
Yellow Raisins	2 cups		
Curry Powder	2 Tbsp.		
Oil	2 Tbsp.		
Salt	1 Tbsp.		
Moroccan Chicken ♣	12 boneless, skinless breasts, lusciously marinated, pre-cooked at home.		In camp thaw sacks (warm 'em in the boiling water), wrap in towel until rice is done, then mix well w/rice in large serving bowl or pot.
Pita Pocket Bread	4 packages of 5 ea.		Fill w/chicken & rice or tabouli; or use as pushers.
Tabouli Mix	4 cups (includes dried herbs, onion, parsley, lemon, mint, salt)		Place sack of tabouli in a small pot or bowl to hold up sides. Add boiling water, stir, soak for 30", then add veggies, oil, lemon juice.
(Boiling water above)	6 cups		
Cucumbers	2 large		Dice into sm. pieces; add to tabouli.
Green Onions	2 bunches		"
Cherry Tomatoes	1 pint box		"
Oil	3/4 cup		Add to tabouli.
Lemon Juice	1 plastic lemon		For those who like to pucker!
Halvah Dessert	2 8-oz bricks		Cut into cubes.
Sesame Candies	About 36		*"Shalom!"*

♣♣♣ ADVANCE PREP. nITE 1 DETAILS ♣♣♣

(♣ = Advance Prep.)	Amounts for 12:	Amount for (____):	DIRECTIONS:
Moroccan Chicken			
Chicken Breasts	12 boneless, skinless		Cut chicken into 1" cubes.
Marinade: Cornstarch White wine Lemon juice Olive oil Garlic powder Salad herbs Salt	 2 Tbsp. 2 cups 1 cup ¹/4 cup 1 Tbsp. 2 tsp. your choice 2 tsp.		Sprinkle chicken w/corn-starch; stir to cover all pieces. Mix marinade; pour over chicken in baking dish. Fully cook in home oven – 40" at 350°; stir twice while cooking. Cool; put chicken and gravy into two freezer zip bags; label "Nite 1, Moroccan Chicken." Freeze flat.
Rice Seasoning Pkt.			
Yellow Raisins Curry Powder Oil Salt	2 cups 2 Tbsp. 2 Tbsp. 1 Tbsp.		Mix these and seal in a zip bag. Label "Nite 1 Rice Seasonings."
Tabouli Oil			
Olive Oil	³/4 cup		Double bag in a plastic container and tape. Label "Nite 1 Tabouli."

CHECKLISTS – nITE 1

PB #1:			Label all packages
❑ Rice	4 cups		Nite 1 and write the
❑ Packet w/Raisins, Oil	2 cups, 2 Tbsp.		name of all non-
Curry Pwdr. + Salt	2 Tbsp. + 1 Tbsp.		obvious ingredients on
❑ Tabouli	4 cups		outside of their sacks.
❑ Oil	³/4 cup in bagged jar		
❑ Plastic Lemon	1		
❑ Halvah Bricks	2 8-oz bricks		
❑ Sesame Candies	About 36 in a zip bag		
Cooler nite 1:			Keep frozen chicken
❑ Chicken Breasts	12, frozen, cut-up		away from veggies, so
❑ Pita Breads	4 pkgs. of 5 each		veggies don't get ice
❑ Cucumbers	2 large		burn (insert lunch
❑ Green Onions	2 bunches		items in between or
❑ Cherry Tomatoes	1 pint box		wrap frozen chicken in
			newspaper).

Daily menus guide the food-sorting process.

Daily Menu Sheets provide a helpful way to keep track of all the food items. First, there's the built-in shopping list feature (more in Chapter 24). Second, once the food is purchased, the sheets aid food sorting by river day. The week before the trip, we attach a copy of each day's menu to our food sorting boxes at the staging/packing area. Then, using the sections of the sheets called "Advance Prep Details" and "Item Checklists," our Meal Planning Guru has a big jump on packing the items. Keeping all info relating to a meal in the same place is important in crosschecking. I encourage volunteer shoppers, sorters, and packers to use highlighters, colored inks, and other methods of consistent crosschecking. The creative ways the lists get marked up change every year. The key thing is that the right items go into the right food container on packing day, whether yellow highlights mean a missing item or one that is accounted for and safely packed away.

Curious about those little advance prep (♣) icons? Instructions for advance prep items look easy, you say, but who does it? And how?

Ramey and Jamie in the thick of advance food prep (with carrots 'n' onions) for a week-long trip on a wilderness river.

CHAPTER TWENTY-THREE
Advance Food Preparation

April prepares her green traffic light and the world
thinks Go.

—CHRISTOPHER MORLEY: *JOHN MISTLETOE*

As a part of the agenda for one of your river trip planning potluck
meetings, I suggested you pass out a sign-up list of advance food preparation
assignments. Nobody flinched, right? That's because it's fairly logical to ask
for help – early and often. It maximizes participation according to the
teamwork ethic, spreads the work around, and gives your buddies ownership.

Here's how it works. First, the Meal Planning Guru drafts out the Master
Menu and rough Daily Menu Sheets. Certain menu recipes will fall into the
advance prep category because they are too messy to make on the river, or
have products (i.e., frying up ground beef or soy burger) that everyone wants
to eat, but no one wants to clean up. Other recipes make good advance prep
material due to their consumption of fuel on nights when you don't have the
Dutch oven along (Moroccan Chicken on Night 1 in the Upper Middle
Fork). Still others (Cherry Fudge Cake) allow personal creativity, but save
hungry boaters waiting around during measuring, sifting, and maybe baking
(Chocolate Chip Pancookies ready to eat).

Steps in Advance Prep:

1. Cut apart a copy of the Daily Menu Sheet to make a pile of ♣Advance Prep
   Detail♣ sections. Using the Moroccan Delight dinner, for example, cut off the ♣
   sections for cooking the chicken, making the rice seasoning packet, and tabouli
   oil. Take these instructions to the planning meeting and distribute to willing prep
   chefs. Bring actual recipes for the curious to look over.

2. Set a delivery date for completed items a week prior to shopping day.

3. Remind your advance prep cooks to turn in their ingredient receipts
   for reimbursement.

Table 23-1 lists the assignments we made from the meals in Appendix 2B. The blank items at the end of the list are available for additional jobs that the Guru and food packers might have to do themselves, if they don't request help. (Find a copy-ready version of this in Appendix 2.)

TABLE 23-1: **SAMPLE ADVANCE FOOD PREP ASSIGNMENT SHEET**

Please sign up for items to prepare in advance for the trip meals...we'll provide you with instructions.

PERSON(S):	ITEMS:	Guru check-off & location* column:
	Pre-bake Potatoes & Marinate Steaks for Day 0 (Launch Camp)	
	Bottle up 3 salad dressings for Days 0, 4, and 7	
	Moroccan Chicken, Rice Seasoning Packet, Tabouli Oil for Day 1	
	Chocolate Chip Pan Cookies for Days 2, 4	
	Pemmican for Day 2	
	MRE's for Day 2	
	Salisbury Steaks for Day 3; **Potatoes, Milk, Gravy Mix** Days 3 and 7	
	Chutney Salad for Day 3	
	Appley Coffee Cake Mix Bags for Nite 3	
	Lasagne Meat Filling for Day 4	
	Cheesecake Packet Assembly for Day 4	
	Monkey Bread Caramel Mix for Day 4	
	Chorizo Meat Mix for Arroz Vasco for Day 5	
	Chocolate Fudge for Day 5	
	Antipasto for Day 6	
	Panne Bread Mix for Day 6	
	Pasta Marinara Meat Sauce for Day 6	
	Tiramisu for Day 6	
	Chocolate Yogurt Cake Mix for Day 7	
	Cut **ten sheets of parchment** for the Dutch	
	Make 12 **team assignment work cards**	

Copy if you like. From *River Otter: Handbook for Trip Planning*

*****Location** indicates where the items are stored prior to packing day.

CHAPTER TWENTY-FOUR

Shopping Lists

It is better to buy a quart of milk by the penny than to keep a cow.

—JAMES HOWELL: *LETTERS II*

Would you like to avoid scraps of handwritten notes for your river trip shopping lists?

Developing shopping lists is a logical outgrowth of menu planning and recipe compilation. We've learned that for volunteer shoppers facing today's hangar-sized grocery stores it pays to divide the shopping lists into five categories:

- Can 'n' Bottles
- Dry Good + Bulk Bin Stuff
- Bread + Sweet Stuff
- Veggies + Fruits
- Dairy + Meat Case

The sample shopping lists that follow are designed to show all necessary recipe ingredients. Groups that use advance prep chef and group "cook-a-thon" methods can use them. In the case of a trip where advance prep chefs signed up and purchased their prep ingredients, those items are marked by the advance prep icon (♣) so group-buying shoppers can eliminate the item from their shopping lists. Granted, some trips may wish to buy all the items

Advance Prep Saves Money as well as Time:

A trip treasurer once discovered a money-saving feature of advance prep. Let's say you ask Monica and Pete for receipts for reimbursement for making the Mexican Chocolate Fudge. When they donate a teaspoon of cinnamon instead of having trip shoppers buy a whole bottle, it improves the trip budget. Small items like exotic spices and baking powder don't need to come on the trip in bulk or be charged to the trip. But, *it's only fair if everyone does some advance prep or otherwise contributes* to the shopping or supply lists.

and distribute those needing advanced prep to the cooks. It's a matter of preference.

All shopping lists should correspond to ingredients in whatever daily menus you choose. Table 24-1 is a sample shopping list for fresh veggies and fruits. Mine reflect the Daily Menu Sheets in Appendix 2A-B and are copy-ready in Appendix 2C. The sample shows when the items will be needed and if it's in someone's advance prep recipe. Prior to shopping day, the Meal Planning Guru should cross these off as the advance prep items are delivered. Otherwise, they'll need to be purchased and made up in the final pre-trip days (or hours).

Because the shopping lists catalogue all the items by "river day," they have an additional use.

Photo: Todd Swanson

Thanks to advance prep work on this cheesecake, the hard part is waiting for it to set up in the cool evening river.

The results of a well-planned shopping trip are easily divided into meal boxes.

On packing day they serve as a helpful tool to quickly identify an item by its day of use as the volunteer packers find mystery items and wonders where they should go. (Yes, just grab the Cans and Bottles list when you find the plastic lemon juice container that rolled away from its assigned box...ah – it goes in the Day 1 box. You get the idea.)

If an odd item *must* be there for camp cooks to assemble a recipe, and if the item could get lost or used up, mark it with the ♦ symbol (e.g. below, the apple for Day 3 coffeecake.) See Appendix 2C copy-ready version of this table.

TABLE 24-1: SAMPLE SHOPPING LIST: VEGGIES AND FRUIT

♣ = ADVANCE PREP. ITEM (If the item is prepared in advance by someone, DON'T buy it.)

♦ = DEDICATED ITEM (This item or portion of an item is necessary for a recipe. Since it's apt to be used at another time – innocent mistakes happen – label and pack with care.)

X = VARIABLE USE ITEM (some mustard, mayo, cocoa mix, etc., used daily)

1. If your trip number is different than twelve (12), calculate amounts in the last column.

2. Check on all Advance Prep. items. If some are missing, highlight the ♣ ingredients needed to make them yourself.

3. Make a back-up photocopy of this list and use as reference in packing.

4. Highlight all remaining items to be purchased and give the list to the shopper so they can make purchases.

ITEMS:	River Day								Total Amt. for 12	Your Amt. ___#
	0	1	2	3	4	5	6	7		
Veggies + Fruits:										
Apple, Green (Coffeecake)				♦1					1	
Cabbage, Green					1				1	
Carrots, Baby, 2 lb. sacks			1	1		1			3	
Carrots, Large for ♣ Salad										
Cucumbers (♦ tabouli, and lunches)		♦2	2						4	
Garlic Cloves, fresh ♣					♣4	♣8	♣4		♣16	
Lettuce, equiv. 2 heads	2 hd								2 hd	
Melons:										
Cantaloupe		2							2	
Seedless Watermelon, sm.	1								1	
Onions, Green bunches for ♦ tabouli		♦2							2	

ITEMS:	River Day								Total Amt. for 12	Your Amt. __#
	0	1	2	3	4	5	6	7		
Onions, Red for salad and lunches	1	1			1			1	4	
Onions, White or Yellow ♣ (♦1 is dedicated for burritos condiments – buy)				♣1	♣2	♣2 ♦1	♣3		♣8 BUY 1	
Peas, frozen 2 lb. sack				2#					2#	
Peppers, Anaheim ♣						♣4			♣4	
Peppers, Green for lunches		2	2						4	
Peppers, Red for lunches		1	2	1					4	
Potatoes, Bakers	12								12	
Radicchio					1				1	
Spinach, frozen, box					2				2	
Spinach, fresh lg. sack for lunches		1							1	
Tomatoes, Cherry, Pt. Bskt.	2	1							3	
Tomatoes, Slicing ones for lunches		3							3	

Bring the Shopping Lists to Final Group Meeting:

It's helpful to have the shopping list ready at the big planning meeting held one week prior to launch (see Chapter 6: Sample River Meeting Agenda). At the time when the trip leader divides the group into work groups, the shoppers can receive their lists and discuss the best stores to use. This will contribute to both economic decisions and cut down on waste. For example, bulk food like rice, oatmeal, and dried fruit are much cheaper when purchased by the pound from bulk bins in discount grocery stores. Also, delivering items to the food packing area in plastic bags will cut cardboard box waste way down, e.g., gravy mix, lemonade powder, tea.

CHAPTER TWENTY-FIVE

Coolers, Dryboxes, and Five-Gallon "Pickle Buckets"

Come help me lift this cooler. I think they packed it
with concrete.

—A RAFTER ON LOADING DAY

This chapter puts it all together, right into the correct river-bound container.

If you have followed the logic of the Daily Menu Sheets and their appended Packing Checklists, you can skip this discussion because it's not nuclear physics. All the Meal Guru has to do is fit the items into as few containers as possible, protect perishable items, and measure twice and cut once so to speak (an old carpenter's rule, but you get my drift: check and recheck!).

The easiest items to deal with are the durable (non-perishable) foodstuffs because they don't need to be kept cold. While your options are as varied as

Some Hints (heretofore unmentioned) about "Dry" Item Packing:

- Pack the heaviest items (like cans) on the bottom of the container or bucket.

- Double-bag (freezer-weight plastic zipper bags) and tape closed any item with oil or butter in it, such as the caramel mix for monkey bread.

- Tortillas, pita breads, and bagels pack better than the sturdiest bread.

- Duct tape any glass bottles. Better yet, don't bring glass on the river.

- 5-gallon buckets need their lids taped closed – even if you think they are watertight.

- Secure them under a cargo net – don't trust their wire handles to carabiners or cam straps.

- If you put food into dry bags, always double-bag each item also. A small hole in a dry bag can allow large amounts of water to enter the bag (a holey bag exposed to water and pressures in a raft load gets pumped like a CPR manikin: air is squeezed out and water is sucked in).

the multi-colored ads in the supply catalogs, our trips rely on old standbys for packing food: aluminum dryboxes, 5-gallon lidded pickle buckets, and an occasional ammo can and soft-sided dry bag. It's been years since we've hauled the heavy army surplus "rocket" boxes with their sharp corners. And it may be years before we adapt to expensive new resin containers with ads cautioning gaskets aren't warranted.

First, the aluminum drybox. The continuous-steel lid hinge, the tension-adjustable latches, and reliable gaskets make these large containers our choice for "pantry" items: coffee, tea, cocoa, granola, oatmeal, sugar, dry milk, and the spice box. We all get a workout hefting the thing into camp by its collapsible handles, but we've yet to seen one ravaged by a bear. It's a luxury to travel with more than one of these "kitchenboxes." The second is great for breakable gear like the ceramic filtered water pump and the camp lantern and can be left attached to the raft where it usually doubles as a passenger seat.

The pickle buckets are our favorites for separating out each day's dry foods. We generally label one or two for lunches (early and late in the trip) and keep another for snacks/hors d'oeuvres. Easily labeled and stowed, these containers must have their seals and lids tested before you leave home…or

Some Hints (heretofore also unmentioned!) about "Perishable" Item Packing:

- Pre-freeze as many items as possible before they go into the ice chests.
- Use water frozen in plastic jugs instead of loose ice (less messy; yields fresh water later).
- Cover dry ice with newspaper and fill in dead space around it with crushed ice.
- Place frozen water jugs, block ice, or dry ice in a well space in the center of other foods.
- If possible, drop the sealed freezer into a chest freezer for a day or two before departure.
- All coolers and freezers must be sealed shut with duct tape.
- Cover them with wet towels or burlap bags on scorching summer days.
- Open ice chests no more than once a day for the "freezers" and not more than three times a day for "coolers."
- Don't trust cam straps (buckle webbing) and duct tape alone to keep coolers watertight – old bike tubes or bungee cords work well in addition, especially in a flip.
- Empty coolers make great garbage bins, but contain all rubbish in heavy plastic garbage sacks.

Can Cans of Carbonated Beverages Sub as Ice?

On the eighth day of a hot summer trip we had icy Guinness Stout (in the cans containing CO_2 cartridges) that we'd frozen in a chest freezer before we left. The Irish beer did double duty as ice until then. My research with other brands was inconclusive, but favored beers frozen in the chest freezer rather than the freezer compartment of my self-defrosting fridge.

Adrienne Ward, a Wyoming friend of my kayak mentor Gary Payne, e-mailed me that she posted the frozen beer idea back in the mid-90's on a boater website, then listed her idea in *Canoe and Kayak* a few years later in "Tips from the Field." She agrees research is incomplete. She advises folks to conduct their own tests by freezing their favorite beers for 24 hours. Use plastic zipper bags to contain any explosions. Miller, Bud, Olympia worked well for her, but Coors and carbonated sodas like Coke and Pepsi burst in both chest freezer and fridge freezer.

your favorite crackers will end up soggy, not to mention what river water does to Gummy Bears and gorp. Yes, just dunk 'em in the bathtub and look for leakage.

For our perishable foodstuffs we rely on heavy ice chests with sturdy latches and handles, such as the 60-quart Gotts and the 128-quart Igloos. For our eight-day trips with 10-18 people we pack all our perishables in two 60-quart coolers (a "lunch" and a "freezer") plus one 128-quart cooler (the "cooler"). If you have fewer or more people, or fewer or more days, adjust accordingly. Some rafters actually carry a beer cooler and a chest of clean ice for their battery-operated blender drinks, but we opt for lighter rafts and getting our highs from river corridor adventures. "It's a matter of taste," like our Irish auntie said about the cousin's blue hair....

Table 25-1 is an example of the packing check-off list we use for our coolers (others are in copy-ready format in Appendix 2D).

TABLE 25-1: **SAMPLE PACKING LIST: LAUNCH CAMP COOLERS (#1 AND #2 [LUNCH COOLER])**

Boundary Ck. Cooler #1
(when empty, fill w/trash, open vent, leave in shuttle vehicle)

Check-off	Item	Amount for 12	Amount for ___#
	Chips 'n' dip (guacamole)	2 sacks 'n' 1 pint	
	Spanish Olives	1 can	
	Steaks London Broil ♣	6 lbs.	
	Potatoes – Bakers ♣	12	
	Butter for Spuds	2 cubes (1/2 lb.)	

Check-off	Item	Amount for 12	Amount for ___#
	Sour Cream for Spuds	1 pint	
	Bacon Bits for Spuds	1/2 jar	
	Garden Salad ♣	2 heads lettuce equiv.	
	Tomatoes, Cherry	2 baskets	
	Other salad veggies	Broccoli, red onion	
	Salad Dressing ♣	Homemade, 1 cup	
	Pies	2 large bakery pies	
	Kielbasa Sausages for Breakfast	5	

Don't forget the Watermelon, Beverages, Canned Fish 'n' Crackers, Breakfast Muffins/Melons!

Boundary Ck. Cooler #2
(use for overflow from Cooler #1 and label "Lunch Cooler" from now on)

Check-off	Item	Amount for 12	Amount for ___#
	Breakfasts: Butter	2 sticks	
	Breakfast Cream Cheese	2 – 8 oz. containers	
	Bagels	18, frozen	
	Summer Sausage (Day 2)	2	
	Chorizo"Amaia"Sausage (Day 3)	1	
	Lunch Day 1: Tortillas	20	
	Monterey Jack Cheese	2 lbs.	
	Turkey Breast	1 – 4 lb.	
	Mayo + Mustard	1 bottle each	
	Carrot babies, Spinach + Peppers	2 lbs. / Lg. sack / 4 peps.	
	Tomatoes, slicing	3	
	Dinner Nite 1: Chicken Breasts	12, frozen, cut-up	
	Pita Breads	4 pkgs. of 5 each	
	Cucumbers	4 large (extra for lunch)	
	Green Onions	2 bunches	
	Cherry Tomatoes	1 pint box	
	Peppers	2 red, 2 green (snacking)	
	Lunch Day 2 and 3: Bagels	12	
	Cheddar Cheese	2 lbs.	
	BlackForest Ham + Gallo Salami	4 lb. ham/1 lb. salami	
	Pita Breads	8 pkgs. of 5 each	
	Dinner Nite 2: Carrots, baby	2 lbs.	

Part Six:
Packing Puzzles

When going light in low water, prepackage pantry items in smaller quantities for the first leg of the trip.

CHAPTER TWENTY-SIX

Staging

If this were played upon a stage now, I could condemn it as an improbable fiction.

—SHAKESPEARE: *TWELFTH NIGHT*

Launch day approaches.

Non-perishable food items have accumulated over time according to sales and the whims of your food purchasers. Your boxes, labeled *Day/Night 1, Day/Night 2, Days/Nights 3-4,* etc. and a copy of the menu for that day(s) taped on the box, help you keep track. The boxes for *Breakfasts, Lunches, Snacks, Kitchen Misc.* (including such kitchen pantry and drybox items as spices, oil, sugar) are brimming. All the frozen items came to your central packing site. They've been labeled with tape or marker according to when they'll be needed, and kept frozen in a separate sixty-quart cooler plunked right down inside your mostly empty chest freezer. No chance your frozen turkey will get mixed in with the river trip food.

Food boxes for pre-sorting items are numbered by river day.

Examples of water-tight storage containers: gasketed wooden drybox, two sizes of aluminum dryboxes, 5-gallon pickle buckets.

After non-perishables have been safely stored in their appropriate watertight river container and labeled, you catch your breath with thoughts of what comes next. As other gear and supplies come flowing in, you wonder: how will four rafts ever carry the pile of personal gear bags, ice chests and food containers, emergency first aid and rescue supplies, and miles of rope?

Remember the joke about being so prepared we could take over a small country?

Somehow river-runners we know have adopted the military term "staging." Just like moving troops, military supplies and equipment, we establish a base in preparation for our planned operation – the multiday river trip. Figure 26-1 shows the three stages we use.

Previously, I've suggested that an area of someone's living room might be set aside for organizing the food by river day, using labeled boxes before the items go into the pickle buckets or dryboxes. That's **STAGE ONE**. Like any supply-based maneuver, it helps to have space to lay items out for inspection and labeling. It's no different than what you do when you lay out your personal gear on the bed in your room. You put it on stage, so to speak. So, staging begins long before the big packing day.

Let's now assume Stage One is empty because all the buckets (packed, labeled, and duct-taped) are now out in the garage. You've moved out the car(s) and swept up a bit to accommodate **STAGE TWO**. The doorbell rings

FIGURE 26-1: **PACKING AND STAGING MAP**

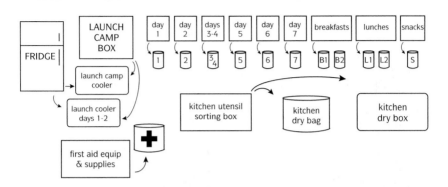

STAGE ONE (inside) :: on packing day transfer items from fridge & boxes to river trip containers

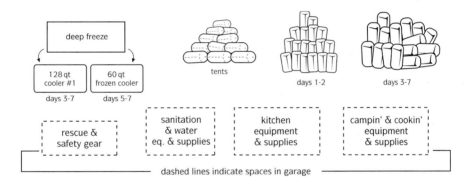

STAGE TWO (garage) :: on loading day pack up using checklists (group gear, coolers, personal gearbags)

dashed lines indicate spaces in garage

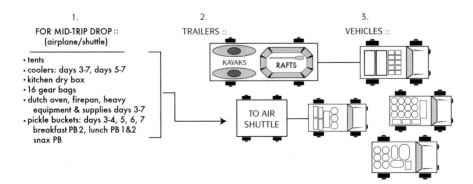

STAGE THREE (outside) :: on departure day load vehicles; use checklist for mid-trip drop pile

1.
FOR MID-TRIP DROP ::
(airplane/shuttle)

• tents
• coolers: days 3-7, days 5-7
• kitchen dry box
• 16 gear bags
• dutch oven, firepan, heavy
  equipment & supplies days 3-7
• pickle buckets: days 3-4, 5, 6, 7
  breakfast PB 2, lunch PB 1&2
  snax PB

2.
TRAILERS ::

KAYAKS   RAFTS

TO AIR
SHUTTLE

3.
VEHICLES ::

and it's someone dropping off a propane tank they topped off. You put it in the garage and the trip teenager pulls in with a camp shovel and his gear bag to drop off early because he's riding his bike over on packing day. You put them next to the propane tank and the buckets even though you know if this continues you'll never find a thing.

You call the trip member who agreed to be "Quartermaster." This person hustles over with the group gear list from Chapter 15. Fresh from the copy shop, he has it enlarged, printed on heavy paper, and cut into pieces. Like most humans of the river persuasion, you stand back in awe as he tacks and tapes parts of the list to your garage walls and one big one that says "Airplane." The middle of Figure 26-1 shows how this brilliant boater laid out Stage Two.

Highlighted on the posted lists are the items that the river ranger will check before your party is allowed on the river. As you help take items to their respective piles and more people drop items off, the grizzled quartermaster tells you stories. Once upon a trip, he drove two-plus hours before he realized the firepan was missing. Another tale followed – the time when the paddle-raft paddles lay in a pile by the vegetable garden for the duration of the trip. Long hours from the staging area, paddle-rafters carved stick handles at launch camp to fit into halves of kayak breakdown paddles. Lastly – the thing that made him volunteer to be quartermaster – the sad time his drive-day steak-sandwich lunch got lost in the hot staging garage until they returned nine days later.

The names of "Piles" for Stage Two:

1. Personal Gear (gear bags, lunches, water bottles)
2. Camping/Cooking (firepan, shovel, stoves, roll-up tables, coolers, ash buckets, etc.)
3. Sanitation (water filters, buckets, toilet and supplies)
4. Shelter (tents and tarps)
5. Kitchen (aluminum kitchenbox[es], pots, Dutch ovens, pans, utensils, strainer, etc.)
6. Supplies:
   a. Cooking/Clean-up (matches, bleach, soap, trash bags, etc.)
   b. Camping (cord, duct tape, group sunscreen, etc.)
7. First Aid Kits (small one for each raft, trip medical bag)
8. Extraction Kits (rescue throw bags, ropes, pulleys, carabiners, slings, face mask for diving)

Garage gear piles of Stage Two morph into Stage Three vehicle loading.

You thank him, head inside to double-check your personal gear list, and then make a lunch with your name on the sack. Meanwhile, you hear the rafters drive in with their trailers, the kayakers leaving off their boats and paddles, helmets, jackets, and spray skirts. **STAGE THREE** is developing in your driveway and on your front lawn – the craft and their accoutrements. You wonder how all this is going to get to launch camp and make it down the river.

Kitchenbox Secrets:

- An aluminum drybox is a most ideal kitchenbox – watertight and commodious. Packing it with cooking equipment and supplies from the Quartermaster's list is a nesting puzzle. Experiment with using easy-nesting items (like the plastic gold panning pan for a salad bowl). Save receipts to return any pieces of the kitchenbox puzzle that don't fit and try again.

- Bringing the kitchenbox into camp each night may be a hassle, but it and the serving table and stove are the focal points for an easily organized camp kitchen.

- A cloth utensil holder with compartments not only keeps order in the kitchenbox, but doubles as a cooking organizer when you hang it from a serving table in camp.

- If pantry items (oil, sugar, spices, etc.) are included, pack them well to prevent all utensils from becoming covered with whatever spills.

- The most awkward item in the kitchenbox is the collection of coffee mugs and lids each person brings. These always seem to end up in the kitchenbox, so encourage your crew to be respectful of size…twenty people can't bring 32 oz. insulated mugs and have them all fit in an aluminum drybox with other items.

- Depending on space available, the morning coffee/tea/sugar/creamer/cocoa may become part of your kitchenbox. Try restocking daily-use containers from the breakfast pantry drybox.

Enlarge each day's packing list on heavy paper. Tape them to the pre-sorting boxes for final check-off as items are packed in their water-tight containers.

Label coolers with destination and plastic-encased packing lists showing contents and dates of use. Note the "deep freezer" cooler for days 5-8 nestled in a chest freezer (arrow) to freeze solid before dry ice is added on departure day. Remember to seal all lids with duct tape.

CHAPTER TWENTY-SEVEN

Loading

I's born in the night when the moon shone through.
I picked up my paddle and walked to Stage Two.
Then loaded 13 tons of gear and grub,
Told Quartermaster, "Hey! I need a backrub!"

—A SONG FOR LOADING DAY

The quartermaster and senior raft captain pull up chairs at the kitchen table and pencil out possibilities for loading the trip's four rafts. The combinations seem practically endless as they search for the fairest way to distribute the heavy group gear. Because they've talked to their rafters, however, they build their plan on two pieces of information: 1) the rowing abilities/experience of the rafters and 2) the optimal rigging for each kind

Raft frames and oars are loaded on the trailer above fully packed coolers, aluminum dryboxes, and pickle buckets.

of raft based on its design. Table 27-1 is what they came up with for the eight-day trip for 18 people:

TABLE 27-1: **RAFT LOADS**

First Leg (3 days, low water, before the airdrop):		Second Leg (after air-drop):
The Jag (16' cataraft):	gear bags	The Freezer
	lunch cooler (80 quart)	
	main river rescue bag + 2 ropes	
The Ocelot (14' cataraft):	**Porta Potty Toilet**	Dutch oven
	medical bag	cataraft floor
	pickle buckets (3: Breakfast 1, Lunch 1, PB Days 1-2)	pickle buckets (5: PBs Days 3-7)
The Aire (14' raft):	Kitchen Dry Box (& **mesh strainer**)	The Cooler (120 qt.)
	collapsible water bucket	
	river rescue bag #2 + rope	
The Maravia (14' raft):	dry box #2 (water filter, **shovel, ashcan, aluminum firepan**)	pickle buckets (3: Br. 2, Lu. 2, & extra bread PB)
		more gear bags
		heavy duty firepan

When the rafts are moored at the launch site put-in, each rafter knows what "mandatory" items they have loaded (**in bold**) and can quickly show the river ranger where they are. These rafters get the ranger's commendations for their organization. Those of us who wave goodbye to her as we launch know planning skills come from years of learning through experience, capable friends, and a few good books.

For the graphically-oriented, sketching out the craft can help more than a list. This is very useful when large items such as coolers and dryboxes are split up into two or more legs of the trip. Whenever there is an airdrop of provisions, weight and volume are big issues, not only for the rafts, but also for the airplane making the delivery. It'll save you money if you pack efficiently because air taxi services usually charge by weight.

So another trip drew a sketch like Figure 27-1 to illustrate the food/beverage/gear distribution in a way that helped everyone in camp. When color-coded and posted inside the kitchenbox's lid (next to the Main Menu), volunteer cooks didn't have to wander from raft to raft looking for the cooler they needed for the evening meal.

FIGURE 27-1: **RAFT LOADS**

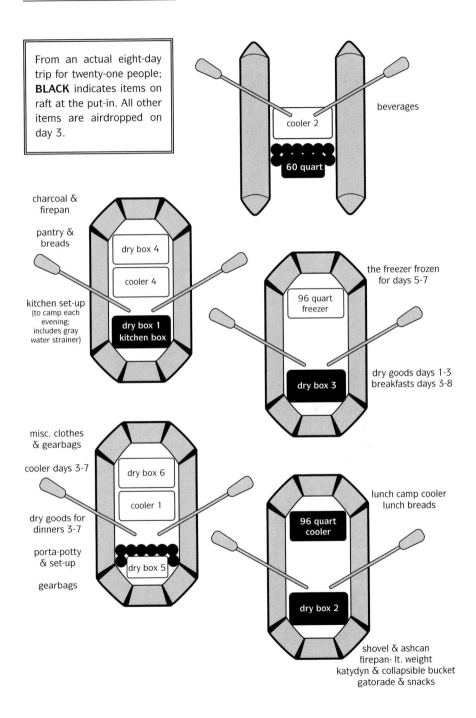

From an actual eight-day trip for twenty-one people; **BLACK** indicates items on raft at the put-in. All other items are airdropped on day 3.

beverages

cooler 2

60 quart

charcoal & firepan

pantry & breads

dry box 4

cooler 4

kitchen set-up
(to camp each evening; includes gray water strainer)

dry box 1 kitchen box

the freezer frozen for days 5-7

96 quart freezer

dry goods days 1-3 breakfasts days 3-8

dry box 3

misc. clothes & gearbags

cooler days 3-7

dry box 6

cooler 1

lunch camp cooler lunch breads

96 quart cooler

dry goods for dinners 3-7

porta-potty & set-up

dry box 5

gearbags

dry box 2

shovel & ashcan
firepan- lt. weight
katydyn & collapsible bucket
gatorade & snacks

Photo: Todd Swanson

Unloading at the launch site requires strong backs and cool heads. Well-labeled gear is less likely to find its way into another party's load.

Water's edge question: "How's all this gonna fit?" Answer: "Ask the raft captain."

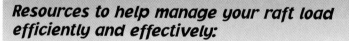

Resources to help manage your raft load efficiently and effectively:

The Complete Whitewater Rafter, Jeff Bennett, Camden, ME: Ragged Mountain Press, 1996.

River Running, Verne Huser, Seattle, WA: The Mountaineers, 2001.

The White-water River Book, Ron Watters, Seattle, WA: Pacific Search Press, 1982.

Part Seven:
Post Trip

*Clean-up duties begin with a washtub full of soapy disinfectant and plenty of water.
End with fresh air drying. Who wants to open coolers and dryboxes for next summer
and have them anything but fresh and ready to go?*

CHAPTER TWENTY-EIGHT

Clean-up Duties, Photo Party, and Future Planning

By the waterside I will lay my head
Listen to the river sing sweet songs
To rock my soul.

—ROBERT HUNTER: *BROKEDOWN PALACE*

The river tugs at your heartstrings on the way home. You might even wish you could find a way to spend your life "by the waterside."

Photo: Keith Taylor

It's normal to have recurring flashbacks of your incredible river trip. Photos like this preserve your fond memories.

After the adventure is over and you're on the drive home, remember to get commitments for next day clean-up and return of rented and borrowed items. Also, be sure your party has agreed to a date for the post-river trip potluck party. Allow enough time for everyone to develop their photographs and sort their gear. Party planning and photo-sharing ends the trip on an upbeat note.

On clean-up day the quartermaster's list will help sort gear, but leaders shouldn't keep the fun of washing out coolers and disinfecting privy buckets to themselves. Get help! Require everyone to show up unless they want to risk never being invited on another trip…too strong? Well, *invite* everyone to come to the clean-up site unless they have a very good excuse. Have gloves and cleaning materials like a washtub of soapy disinfectant, bleach, brushes, scrubbers, and trash bags ready for everyone to take a turn with a cooler or drybox. Tell young helpers to watch science in action as household bleach performs its job on the privy buckets. Set aside miscellaneous socks, sunglasses, and other personal items in a lost-and-found pile, with unclaimed items brought to the picture party about a week later. Likewise, create a stash of all extra dried food and supplies for a game at that get-together.

Here's how some trips handle extra food and supplies. First, line the stuff up on kitchen counters or the floor (yes, even partially used rolls of aluminum foil and the last of the sesame candies). During the potluck meal your party can cruise by the items, making a mental note of the choicest stuff. After your awards ceremony (if you have one), play some kind of a brief game to determine the order folks will follow as they circle through the goodies, taking one item each pass. An easy, quick method is to have the order determined by picking a Scrabble letter (A goes first, etc.) or by birthday: January 8 is first, March 15 is next, then May 3, etc. You will be amazed at what people want from the leftovers!

Unless you have a friend with a photo developing shop, most trips can't afford to make copies of everyone's film (unless you put them on a compact disk). So, some trips ask everyone to make up double prints and bring one initialed, numbered set (i.e., Phyllis Photog labels the backs of the pictures in her envelope with *PP-1, PP-2*, etc.). Then, when Staircase Steve and Carly see her shot showing them crashing through Devil's Tooth, they'll put their initials on the back, and Phyllis will kindly make copies for them, mailing them later using the trip list info. Of course, Carly will give her extra copy of the one Steve wants out of her pack or will make him a copy, etc. Other trips go high-tech, have a slide show from the CD photos, and give everyone a disk copy. The important thing is that everyone has a good time and no one quibbles about making it come out exactly fair to the penny.

Running your pantry containers and water bottles through a sanitizing wash in a dishwasher is good preparation for your next trip.

Hopefully, the trip treasurer has been able to pull together everyone's receipts in time for the party. Presenting a spread sheet of income and expenses along with the refund checks (or the invoices for additional payment) helps trip members understand the true costs of the non-commercial river trip. It never hurts to divide up the total expense figure by the number on the trip, then ask if anyone could take a commercial trip for that amount!

Money aside, as your post-trip party winds down, share some final hugs and congratulations on successfully completing your self-outfitted river adventure.

The Future Beckons:

So, your trip members go home from the Post-Trip Party with full stomachs, some extra supplies, and an urge to watch the mailbox for those prized photographs. Some paddlers might even begin thinking of organizing next year's trip since you showed them how...if they could only figure out how to be as lucky as you were this year. Have them check out Appendix 11 for a source list of contacts for obtaining river trip permits. And drop a hint that you might be available...

Happy Boatin' !

Photo: Todd Swanson

Remember Amanda up to her chin in whitewater?

Photo: Todd Swanson

Remember the put-in?

Seeing photos like this one at the post-trip party brings back great memories ... and a few opinions about how many bighorn sheep were really spotted.

Remember Dave running the falls?

Photo: Phylis King

Raft captain Joe gives the trip a "thumbs up" at post-trip party.

Photo: Todd Swanson

And arm-wrestling in layover camp?

Photo: Swanson family files

Above: Some trips designate a trip photographer like Todd. Here he's caught relaxing from his ubiquitous lens.

Photo: Todd Swanson

Appendices

Matt is side-surfing a hole formed by water pouring over a rock and backwashing back in. He is about to be flipped on his upstream side. In big sticky holes "window shading" (or "washing machining") can roll a kayak over and over.

APPENDIX ONE
Barry's Safety Talk

Run and get Barry. We can't leave until he gives his safety talk.
—LISA JOHNSTONE BEFORE WE LAUNCHED

A safety discussion is essential on trips where there are novices and any overnight trip where there are people who have not boated together before. Talking about signals, how to avoid dangers, and what to do if someone gets in trouble gives the group a common knowledge base and a rudimentary approach to organizing in the case of an emergency. Safety talks elicit responses from "very helpful" to "waste of time when you could be boating."

When I give a safety talk, I usually use an outline (one follows) and ask questions so volunteers can explain each subject. It keeps me from doing all the talking and allows others to contribute and me to pick up some new ideas. I tailor the content to the current trip, the river knowledge of the newest boater, and the level of group interest. Sometimes I take the newbies aside for the basics rather than ask the whole group to listen. One time I gave the talk in each car as we traveled to the put-in. I like to illustrate points with examples from my experience with group members and people known to the group.

As I mentioned, I like to discuss safety topics with people rather than give a lecture. The text that follows fleshes out the outline for reading or for preparing a talk. It eliminates the questions and responses I ordinarily include.

HAVING FUN

We are going on the river to have fun. Part of the fun is knowing that there is a certain amount of risk. For most people knowing what the risks are and where they are allows them to relax when there is minimal risk and to get prepared when risk approaches. The river is more powerful than we are. Even the best boaters cannot go against the current for long. However, we can learn to play together with the river and dance upon the waves.

We each decide whether to get in the water, how much risk to take, and how prepared we want to be. The information that follows provides some basics. The bibliography lists books with much more information. Remember, accidents happens, but if you know where they commonly occur, you can get out of the way or get prepared.

RIVER BASICS

You can't fight the river, but you can get in the water that is going where you want to go. Whether in your boat or out of your boat and swimming, you

FIGURE APPENDIX 1-1: **RIVER FEATURES**

EDDY

can learn to spot where you want to be and where you do not want to be. Eddies form where an object, such as a rock or bank protrusion, blocks the flow of water. Water flowing downstream pulls along water from behind the object, so other water flows upstream to fill the space. This creates a place where the water flows upstream. The place where the water going down rubs on the water going up is called the eddy line. An eddy is a good place to be if you want to rest, get out of the river, or go back upstream. As my first kayak teacher Jay Rosentretter said, "Eddies are your friends."

By convention the left and right sides of the river are defined as left and right as a person faces downstream. River left will be on the right side of a person facing upstream. To avoid confusion people use the terms "river right" and "river left," rather than just "right" and "left."

When water flows over a rock the downward momentum creates a dip in the surface of the water, called a hole. An eddy often forms behind a hole. If the water coming upstream forms a wave pouring into the hole, a keeper hole is formed. Something floating in the hole has water crashing down from both upstream and downstream. If you are swimming this is not a good place to be. If the edges of the hole slope down river (smiling hole), you can move to an edge and will be swept out by the current. If there are any irregularities in the wave, they may provide an exit. If the edges of the hole slope upriver (frowning hole), you have to fight the current. If you are stuck in a frowning

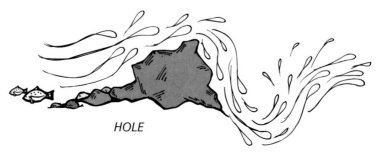

HOLE

KEEPER

hole, how do you get out? If water is crashing in on you from all sides, where is it going? That is the way out. Dive down and there will be a rush of water to carry you downstream from the hole to where you can swim up and breathe. Of course, the hydraulics of holes make a fun place to play for those with the craft and skills to handle them. The most dangerous keeper holes form behind low-head dams. They look innocent. There are usually no irregularities and the hole extends all the way across the river with no way around and no way out, except down.

Rooster tails are pulses of water shooting up in the air. They indicate very turbulent water, usually with a keeper hole and often with exposed or shallow rocks. Sometimes skilled rafters want to play near rooster tails, but for swimmers and kayakers rooster tails indicate where you do not want to be.

Pillows are elevations in the surface of the water that form upstream from a rock as the water crashes into it. They can help turn a swimmer or your boat

No pillow! Where is the water going? This undercut at Whistling Bird on the Owyhee in Oregon is a bad place for a boat to be.

Downstream view of the Whistling Bird Rapid. Rafter works hard, avoids the hazardous undercut, and negotiates the rock garden with skill.

toward the current running beside the rock. If water crashes into a rock and does not form a pillow it is going down into an undercut or even a cave. This is a very dangerous place to be. If the current pushes you into the undercut, it may be impossible to get out. If caught in such a situation, try to make small moves along the rock parallel to the current rather than just push against the current.

Strainers are formed by objects, usually trees that have fallen in the water, that allow water to pass but not you. You do not want to be in a strainer. If you are swimming and cannot avoid a strainer, turn and go headfirst. You do not want to get caught with one leg on one side of a branch and the other leg on the other side with the current plastering you to the branch. If there is clear space above a tree trunk, as you approach, place your hands on top of the trunk like you were doing a pushup and vault over it. It you cannot vault over the top, go under the trunk and use you hands to work your way through the branches. Strainers are clearly to be avoided.

Boulder sieves are rocks scattered in the river that allow the water to pass but not your boat. If your boat is pushed sideways against a rock, it is broached. In a kayak you need to lean into the rock and try to move either forward or backward till the current catches more of one end of your boat, turns the boat and frees you.

Safety kayaker positioned on a rock, guiding oarboats with throw rope ready.

A pin occurs when the end of something, usually the tip of a kayak, catches on the bottom in moving water. This is a very serious situation. The current can push the kayak over, folding the front of the kayak and trapping the kayaker's legs. Similarly, a person can catch a foot on the bottom and be bent over by the current. This is called an entrapment. The current may then fold the person forward and hold the head under water. A pinned or entrapped person should push down with the arms locked at the elbows, letting the water crash against their back. This will create an eddy with an air pocket in front of the face. Buddies of a pinned or entrapped person should immediately get a rope across the current and pull it up against the person's chest. Hopefully they can get this done before the person's arms collapse. Once the chest support is in place the buddies can slow down and plan an extraction. To avoid foot entrapments never walk in moving water that is higher than your knees.

To ferry is to head up or down stream at an angle to the current. The force of the water causes you to scoot to the side. An upstream ferry is a very useful way to avoid a hazard. It is amazing how quickly it will move you to another part of the river, when you can't make it swimming directly upstream and wouldn't get clear in time if you swam sideways to the current. Try it so you have it down when you need it.

EQUIPMENT BASICS

Just like understanding how the river works helps you be safer, understanding how your equipment acts in the river can help you.

Ropes can be very handy, even lifesaving, but a coil of rope can be very dangerous. Although the commonest use for a knife on a life jacket is to help prepare lunch, the most important is to cut a rope that is holding someone under water. When pulling a person or a boat out of moving water never wrap the rope around your arm or hand. If the object goes down river and the rope is wrapped around your arm, you are going to go down the river too, and maybe with a dislocated shoulder to boot.

If you tie objects to your boat, tie or strap them tight to the boat. Do not leave something on the end of a length of rope (tether). In an accident the rope may wrap around an arm or leg or the object may fly through the air in an arc like a medieval mace.

Under a raft or dory (drift boat) is not a place you want to be. Use your head and get out. If you are under an upside-down raft and need air, there will be a bubble under the raft.

If you, a boat and a rock are rubbing on each other, who do you want in the middle? A swimmer hanging on the side of the raft in moving water with protruding rocks is an emergency. Someone in the raft should face the swimmer, grab the shoulders of the life jacket and fall backwards into the raft. At the same time the swimmer should kick their feet to help. The swimmer will slide right into the raft. Two people, one on each shoulder, are even stronger. Maria was on a commercial raft trip where they did not cover this in the safety talk and she was the only passenger who knew how to help when a passenger went overboard in a rapid.

SELF RESCUE

If you are out of your boat (swimming), you should immediately assess the situation and take action. It is helpful if you can hold onto gear, such as your paddle, but you are much more important than your gear or boat. If you need to take action to avoid danger, let go of the gear and take care of number one. The usual defensive way to swim is to get on your back with your feet downstream. You can use your feet to fend yourself off rocks. Your face will be up and your back will be protected by your life jacket. There are exceptions to this approach. If you are in deep water and think you can make an eddy, get on your stomach and crawl stroke for it. If serious danger is downstream, crawl stroke, using an upstream ferry to get to a better position in the current, so you will go around the danger. As discussed above, if you must enter a strainer, do it head first and face down.

In certain situations self rescue may be the only option. If you go about helping yourself, your companions may not need to endanger themselves to help you.

ASSISTED RESCUE

Part of the fun of river travel is working together to help each other out. I joke that I cut a notch in my kayak paddle for every swimmer I pull out. I, too, have been pulled out plenty of times, but I don't cut notches for those. Assisted rescue requires teamwork. Even for a simple situation of a kayaker swimming in a pool of slow water, there should be organization. One person helps the swimmer, another goes for the kayak, another for the paddle. Let people know who is doing what. One time my son was swimming with a cut on his eyebrow in the Middle Fork of the Salmon. I assumed another kayaker would rescue him, so I went for his boat and Maria for his paddle. Suddenly, I realized nobody was helping Christian! It was a deep slow pool, so I got to him quickly, and there was no long-term consequence of our poor organization.

Trip members should know where first aid and extraction gear are located and which trip members are knowledgeable of its use. It is very helpful to designate a safety team and who will take charge in case of an accident. Very often, if there are ten boaters, there are at least eleven opinions as to what to do and six people start executing four different plans. This is not satisfactory in serious situations.

One safety person should go down the river last, lagging back for anybody who needs to go more slowly. It is appropriate for the last safety boater to encourage others not to lag too far behind.

When there is a free swimmer, several options are available – tell the swimmer what to do, approach the swimmer with a craft, and use a throw rope. If the swimmer is broached, entrapped or pinned, the situation may be much more serious and require carefully planned, skillful extraction. This is best organized and executed by people trained in river safety by a hands-on training course. The forces generated by the water, Z-drags and groups of people pulling with all their strength are tremendous and dangerous.

The first priority for the rescuer is self-preservation. Size up the situation quickly for dangers to you and to the swimmer. No one appreciates heroics that end with two victims in serious trouble instead of one. Sometimes the swimmer is in good condition and in a safe place and can care for themselves. However, a few clear instructions and words of encouragement may be very helpful. You may see the nearby eddy that the swimmer does not see. Even though breathing and moving, the swimmer may be dazed. As a kayaker, I often pull people and boats to a friendly eddy. Kayakers need to approach victims with caution, especially if it is someone you do not know. Speak to them and gauge the response. Tell them what to do. If they ignore your instructions and lunge at the side of your boat, move away. The victim is about to tip you over and climb on top of your upside down boat. Since rafts are more stable, they can approach thrashing victims more safely. Look downstream to check for any rock that will scrape the victim off the raft. Have the victim approach from the rear, or, if there is no dangerous rock, the side. Be prepared to immediately pull the victim into the raft.

Swimmers can greatly assist their rescue by a craft. If a kayak is picking you up, move immediately to the stern. You can crawl up onto the stern of the kayak and, if the kayaker agrees, put your arms around the kayaker's waist. Do not press on the side of the kayak. If the kayak tips over, let go so the kayaker can roll; then approach from the stern again. Kick to help the kayaker get you to shore. If you are getting onto a raft, face the raft and grab onto a line if it is available. As you are pulled up, give a good frog or flutter kick to assist. The best way to approach a cataraft with only one person on it is between the tubes on the up-current end. Remember that the cataraft may hit a rock, shallow spot, or boil and stop suddenly.

Rescuing with a throw rope works well from a raft or the shore. Before you throw look down current and plan where you are going to land your catch. Next look right at the swimmer and yell "Rope" as you throw. Hold on to your end of the rope! Aim for just up current of the swimmer's head. Throwing up-current from the swimmer is better than throwing down current. If the swimmer must slow down to await the floating rope they can remain on their back, feet first and kick. If the rope is down current from the swimmer, then the swimmer must get on their stomach and go down current headfirst. As the swimmer grabs the rope brace yourself for the shock. If you are familiar with belaying techniques, this is an excellent time to use them. If you miss your first throw, coil up the rope with a few coils in each hand and toss again. If you need more distance, you can fill the rope's stuff sack with water to weight it.

As a swimmer, you should grab the rope, get on your back and bring the rope over one shoulder. The water will be rushing against your shoulders and head, but there will be a pocket of air in front of your face. You will tend to plane on the surface of the water, making it easier for both you and the rescuer to hold on. Adjust as needed. The rescuer will pendulum you into an eddy. Do not let go until you a very sure you can get yourself out of the water. If your hands are too cold to grasp the rope, get it across your chest and press it against your sides with bent arms, "chicken-wings" style. Never wrap the rope around any body part. If you do and the rope goes tight, the current will pull you under water and hold you there. In order for you to get up to breathe, the rescuer will have to give you slack or even let you go. If the rescuer lets go of the rope, you should let go as well and stay clear of it. You do not need to be tangled in a rope while trying to save yourself.

  If you are in your boat and broached or pinned, your buddies may be able nudge you free. If you are entrapped (part of your body caught in your boat), signal for help and then go about trying to get free. If one thing does not work, try another. Try to conserve strength through purposeful movement.

  If your buddy is broached, pinned, or entrapped in a dangerous situation, use your head. A head under water requires immediate action. Otherwise try to stabilize the victim, while the group gathers. One person should take charge. All suggestions should go through the leader. Remember that the person or boat may break free at any time, so there should be a belay rope attached to a trapped boat and there should be a safety boater below the accident site.

Cataraft broached. No amount of high-siding or rocking would dislodge it.

Unloading the broached cataraft so it can be dislodged.

Photos: Todd Swanson

FIGURE APPENDIX 1-2: **HAND SIGNALS**

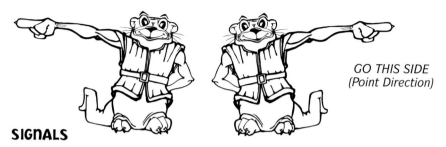

GO THIS SIDE
(Point Direction)

SIGNALS

The roar of water can make voice communication impossible. The group should review what signals it will use before launching. Custom is to always indicate the place to go, never to the danger. Our group of kayakers often reach out an arm and point a finger down at a good surfing spot, but use paddle signals to direct the rafts and less experienced boaters around the hole.

A whistle is extremely useful and should be standard equipment on everyone's lifejacket. One can use a whistle while still paddling. One blast asks for attention. It can call attention to a paddle signal, or an animal on the bank, or alert a dozing boater to a hazard. Three blasts means a problem, such as a swimmer, a trapped boater, a trapped boat, or unexpected danger.

Hand signals should be simple. Point to the way to go. One hand tapping on the head asks if a person is okay. The same signal back means "I'm okay." No response, shaking the head or thumbs down means "I'm not okay." In poor visibility both hands on top of the head is easier to see than one. One finger up and making a circle means eddy out.

STOP

EDDY OUT   *OKAY? I'M OKAY.*   *SURF HERE*

FIGURE APPENDIX 1-3: **PADDLE SIGNALS**

GO THIS SIDE
(Point Direction)

GO WAY OVER

Paddle signals are similar. Straight up means go straight ahead. To indicate a needed turn, hold the paddle up and tilt it 45 degrees to the side in the desirable direction of travel. The signal is given in reference to the position of the person receiving the signal – go left, right, or straight ahead. I remember going down the Owyhee in Oregon in the dusk and signaling to a rafter. There was a low rock in the center of the river so I signaled river right. The rafter immediately scooted over to his far right and got caught in other rocks. Since then we have used tilted left and right to mean left and right of center and tilted to one side with a pumping action in the desired direction to mean get way over to that side. Remember to hold your paddle so that the blade faces the person you are signaling: it makes it easier for them to see it. To signal stop, hold the paddle horizontally and move it up and down.

GO STRAIGHT

STOP

PERSONAL APPROACH AND SELF CARE

As I have emphasized, it's up to you how careful, safe, and compulsive you want to be on the river. I probably score high on all three, but I also like to take on challenges. My helmet has multiple deep scratches from rocks and I have had several ugly bruises and one trip to the emergency room for cut and broken fingers.

You decide whether you should boat that day and whom you go with. You decide what boat you will go in. You are responsible for maintaining your boat and equipment and choosing your clothing.

As you go down the river, listen to your body. Specifically monitor rest, hydration, nutrition, physical condition and mental state. If my shoulder is sore, I tend to roll more sloppily. Maybe I shouldn't hop in that gnarly hole for a possible pop-up. Everybody has off days. Maybe it would not be a good idea to do today what I did last week. If you have a trip member who pushes you to attempt a run you do not want to do, don't boat with them. I have seen boaters walk a drop I knew they could handle easily, but they knew what was in their head that day, and they had fun by not pushing themselves.

Listen to your buddies. Pay attention if they are concerned. I remember one Mother's Day when after a cold swim in Slalom on the South Fork of the Payette I stood in the water and emptied my boat myself. Fighting shivering,

Scout logjams whenever possible. Decide where do I want to be? How do I get there?

Rescuring a swimmer after he tested his limits.

Photo: Todd Swanson

I began to get back in my boat. Gary and Maria asked how I was doing and I growled "I'm okay." At their insistence, I had some food and sat in the sun. Then I started getting nauseated. It was two to one: I was hypothermic. I got out of the river.

As you go down the river think about where you want to be and where you do not want to be. *If you have any doubt, scout,* or let someone more experienced (or stupider) try it first. A couple of guidelines apply to looking at rapids, adapted from William Nealy. The longer you need to look at a drop or hole, the greater your chances of swimming. If you cannot spit, you are either dehydrated or you should portage. While bank-scouting a rapid, take your throw rope with you. You may need it to help someone.

If you do get broached, pinned, or entrapped, keep your eyes open, check possibilities, try a plan. If it does not work, try another one. Try to move parallel to the current rather than against it. Save your air and strength. Your buddies will soon be there to help.

I like to anticipate possible problems and have a plan of action in mind if they materialize. Usually, everything goes fine; but, if it does not, I already know what I will do.

I began with the thought that we get in the river to have fun. Hopefully, this information will give you more comfort in the water and therefore more fun. Go for it!

OUTLINE

HAVING FUN

Object is to have fun

River more powerful than you

Playing together with the river, dancing on the waves

You decide

  Whether to get in

  How much risk to take

  How much caution and preparation you are comfortable with

Stuff happens, but if you know where it comes from you can get out of the way.

RIVER BASICS

Get into the stream of water that is going where you want to go

Where is the water going?

  Eddies

  Holes

  Keeper holes

  Rooster tails

  Pillows

Rocks, undercuts, strainers and sieves

Broaches and pins

Ferrying

EQUIPMENT BASICS

Ropes

Objects on the end of a rope

Under a boat, bubble under a raft

Between a boat and a rock

SELF RESCUE

Usually more efficient, immediate, and preferable

May be the only option

Does not put companions at risk

How to swim

ASSISTED RESCUE

Throw rope
  Planing
  Hands too cold
Pins and entrapments
  Head under water
Grabbing a raft or kayak
Organizing

SIGNALS

Always point to the place to go, never to the danger
Whistle
Hand
Paddle

PERSONAL APPROACH AND SELF CARE

You choose what risks to take
  Decide to go on the trip
  Choose your leader and craft
  Choose your equipment and clothing
  Walk a rapid
  Do not boat with someone who pushes you to risks you do not wish to take
Listen to your body
  Rest, hydration, nutrition, mental state
  Can you spit?
  Listen to your buddies
Where do I want to be in the river?
What could go wrong?
What could I do if the problem occurred?
Self preservation
  Anticipate hazards
  Keep your eyes open
  Analyze quickly
  Act
  If one approach does not work, try another with a different angle of force.
  Use the force of the water, rather than fight it.
Remember the joy, freedom and exhilaration of boating.

The International Scale of River Difficulty

According to a 1998 American Whitewater listing (see Appendix 12), rivers have six classes of difficulty.

Class I: easy. Fast moving water with riffles and small waves. Few obstructions, all obvious and easily missed with little training. Risk to swimmers is slight; self-rescue is easy.

Class II: novice. Straightforward rapids with wide, clear channels which are evident without scouting. Occasional maneuvering may be required, but rocks and medium sized waves are easily missed by trained paddlers. Swimmers are seldom injured and group assistance, while helpful, is seldom needed. Rapids that are at the upper end of this difficulty range are designated "class II + ."

Class III: intermediate. Rapids with moderate, irregular waves which may be difficult to avoid and which can swamp an open canoe. Complex maneuvers in fast current and good boat control in tight passages or around ledges are often required; large waves or strainers may be present but are easily avoided. Strong eddies and powerful current effects can be found, particularly on large-volume rivers. Scouting is advisable for inexperienced parties. Injuries while swimming are rare; self-rescue is usually easy but group assistance may be required to avoid long swims. Rapids that are at the lower or upper end of this difficulty range are designated "class III –" or "class III + " respectively.

Class IV: advanced. Intense, powerful but predictable rapids requiring precise boat handling in turbulent water. Depending on the character of the river, it may feature large, unavoidable waves and holes or constricted passages demanding fast maneuvers under pressure. A fast, reliable eddy turn may be needed to initiate maneuvers, scout rapids, or rest. Rapids may require "must" moves above dangerous hazards. Scouting may be necessary the first time down. Risk of injury to swimmers is moderate to high, and water conditions may make self-rescue difficult. Group assistance for rescue is often essential but requires practiced skills. A strong Eskimo roll is highly recommended. Rapids that are at the lower or upper end of this difficulty range are designated "class IV –" or "class IV + " respectively.

Class V: expert. Extremely long, obstructed, or very violent rapids which expose a paddler to added risk. Drops may contain large, unavoidable waves and holes or steep, congested chutes with complex, demanding routes. Rapids may continue for long distances between pools, demanding a high level of fitness. What eddies exist may be small, turbulent, or difficult to reach. At the high end of the scale, several of these factors may be combined. Scouting is recommended but may be difficult. Swims are dangerous, and rescue is often difficult even for experts. A very reliable Eskimo roll, proper equipment, extensive experience, and practiced rescue skills are essential. Because of the large range of difficulty that exists beyond class IV, class 5 is an open ended, multiple level scale designated by class 5.0, 5.1, 5.2, etc... each of these levels is an order of magnitude more difficult than the last. Example: increasing difficulty from class 5.0 to class 5.1 is a similar order of magnitude as increasing from class IV to class 5.0.

Class VI: extreme and exploratory. These runs have almost never been attempted and often exemplify the extremes of difficulty, unpredictability and danger. The consequences of errors are very severe and rescue may be impossible. For teams of experts only, at favorable water levels, after close personal inspection and taking all precautions. After a class VI rapids has been run many times, its rating may be changed to an appropriate class 5.x rating.

Copy-ready Versions of Part Five Tables

TABLE APP. 2A-1
MASTER MENU

TABLES APP. 2B-1 TO 2B-9
DAILY MENUS
(And Advanced Food Prep, Table 23-1)

TABLES APP. 2C-1 TO 2C-6
SHOPPING LISTS

TABLES APP. 2D-1 TO 2D-4
COOLER PACKING LISTS

Copy? Yes, You Have Permission!

To customize these copy-ready tables for your river trip, copy pages you need at 130% enlargement to fit on an 8½ x 11-inch page. Remember that cardstock, or some heavier paper, works well inside a gallon-sized plastic zip bag.

On your enlargements, fill in appropriate dates, camp names, and river miles from launch camp. Use the blanks for your own daily menus, advance prep, and checklist instructions if you have recipes of your own. Ditto the shopping and packing lists. Customize to your heart's desire!

The following are copy-ready versions of tables mentioned in Part Five for an eight-day, seven-night, twelve-person wilderness river trip with one re-supply point on Day 3. They are based on the Master Menu in Table Appendix 2A-1. There is a layover camp on Days 4 and 5, with an easy meal for dress-up night. You may want to switch meals around, but don't forget, that will have a ripple effect in your shopping, labeling, and packing checklists.

Here's one camp and mileage scenario for the Middle Fork of the Salmon River in Idaho's Frank Church – River of No Return Wilderness:

Launch Camp	Boundary Ceek Campgrounds	Mile 0
River Day #1	Trial Camp	Mile 7
River Day #2	Pistol Creek Camp	Mile 21
River Day #3	Jackass Camp	Mile 38
River Day #4	Camas Creek (layover night 1)	Mile 60
River Day #5	Camas Creek	Mile 60
River Day #6	Camas Creek (dress-up and layover night 2)	Mile 60
River Day #7	Cliffside (last night)	Mile 89
Take out #8	Cache Bar	Mile 99.7

Table App. 2A-1: Master Menu

TABLE APPENDIX 2A-1: **MASTER MENU**

RIVER DAY: WRITE IN DAY OF THE WEEK/DATE	TENTATIVE DINNER CAMP NAME and RIVER MILE

"Launch Camp"_____/_____/ Camp _____ – mi.___

   B: Coffee and Donuts at _____ before leaving between _____ a.m.

   L: Sack Lunch (BYO) or stop to buy on the road (Stop again for downwood for BBQ pits if no wood available in camp)

   D: "All-American BBQ": Steaks, Potatoes, Garden Salad, Pies

   → LAUNCH CAMP COOLER #1 MORPHS INTO A TRASH CONTAINER THAT STAYS IN A SHUTTLE VEHICLE.

   → RE-LABEL LAUNCH CAMP COOLER #2 THE "LUNCH COOLER" FOR THE REST OF THE TRIP.

"River Day #1"_____/_____/ Camp _____ – mi.___

   B: Kielbasa sausages heated on Camp BBQ pits (firepan is loaded for launch), Muffins, Oatmeal, Melon Slices

   L: Pack Lunch Cooler with Tortillas to make wraps, Cheese, Turkey Breast, Carrots, Oreos

   D: "Moroccan Delight": Lemon Chicken, Rice, Tabouli, Cucs, Onion & Tomatoes, Pita Bread, Halvah 'n' Sesames

   → INGREDIENTS ARE IN THE LUNCH COOLER AND PB #1 (RE-LABEL THIS "LUNCH PB #1." USE FOR SNACKS + DRY LEFTOVERS FOR REMAINDER OF TRIP.)

"River Day #2"_____/_____/ Camp _____ – mi.___

   B:: Bagels and Cream Cheese, Oatmeal, Dried Fruit, Summer Sausage

   L: Leftover Tabouli in Pitas, Bagels, Carrots, Ham + Cheese 2-3# ea.

   D: "Goin' Light": MRE's or Freeze-dried meals, Carrots, Pemmican, Candy Bars, Pan Cookies

   → INGREDIENTS ARE IN LUNCH COOLER, PB #1, AND PB #2.

"River Day #3"_____/_____/ Camp _____ – mi.___

   B: Oatmeal and Dried fruit, Amaia Chorizo Sausage (or other dry type)

   L: Pitas with leftover Tabouli and Hummus (Stop at _____ (supply drop) – mi.____. Pick up "The Cooler," "The Freezer" and PBs.)

   D: "Hail Britannia": Salisbury Steaks, Spuds, Chutney Salad, Fruitcake (make Breakfast D.O. Appley Coffeecake)

   ➡ INGREDIENTS ARE IN LUNCH COOLER, THE COOLER, AND PB #3.

"River Day #4"_____/_____/ Camp _____ – mi.___

   B: English Muffins, Kielbasa Sausage, Appley Coffee Cake

   L: Bagels, Cream Cheese, Peanut Butter, Salami, and Pan Cookies

   D: "Pax Romani": Lasagne, Radicchio/Cabbagio Salad, Dolci di Limone

   → INGREDIENTS ARE IN LUNCH COOLER, LUNCH PB #2, THE COOLER, AND PB #4.

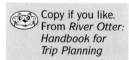 Copy if you like.
From *River Otter: Handbook for Trip Planning*

"River Day #5"_____/_____/   Camp (layover/dress-up?)
                                              _____ – mi.___

- **B:** Bring out the eggs and bacon from The Cooler! Make E. Indian Monkey Bread
- **L:** Pitas, Cheese, Summer Sausages, Turkey Ham, 3rd sack of Baby Carrots
- **D:** **"Spanish Conquest"**: Bean Burritos, Arroz Vasco, Mexican Fudge (make Breakfast D.O. Blueberry Cobbler)
- → INGREDIENTS ARE IN LUNCH COOLER, LUNCH PB #2, THE FREEZER, THE COOLER, AND PB #5.

"River Day #6"_____/_____/   Camp _____– mi.___

- **B:** Blueberry Dutch Cobbler, Oatmeal, Frozen Sausages
- **L:** Use up any leftover Burritos, Tortillas, Carrots, Cheese 'n' Salami.
- **D:** **"Tuscan Village"**: Antipasti, Pasta Marinara, Dutch Oven Panne, Tiramisu
- → INGREDIENTS ARE IN LUNCH COOLER, LUNCH PB #2, THE COOLER, THE FREEZER, AND PB #6.

"River Day #7"_____/_____/   Last Night Camp _____– mi.___

- **B:** Kielbasa Sausages, Oatmeal, Leftover Tiramisu
- **L:** Tuna, Red Onion, Mayo, Thawed Tortilla Wraps
- **D:** **"Irish Eyes"**: Pilot Biscuits/Smoked Fish, Heavenly Ham, Mashers, 3-Bean Salad, Cherry Fudge D.O. Cake
- → INGREDIENTS ARE IN LUNCH COOLER, THE FREEZER, AND PB #7.

"River Day #8"_____/_____/   Going Home Day, Take out mi.___

- **B:** Fried Ham and Leftovers
- **L:** Lunch Leftovers in Lunch Cooler, The Freezer (which by now is only luke…but it'll keep out the chipmunks)…optionaL: Dinner on the Road Home.

Notes to Tables App. 2B-1 to 2B-9: Daily Menu Sheets

Each Daily Menu sheet is titled with date, location, food theme, menu-at-a-glance, and containers.

Instructions for Cooks comes first, then Advance Prep Details, and lastly "Checklists" for packing.

The symbol ♣ denotes a meal item, often a whole recipe that requires (or is amenable to) advance preparation. The ♣ is a cooking term.

The symbol ♦ denotes a dedicated meal ingredient, one easily used for another purpose. The ♦ item needs to be labeled and packed to go with a recipe. The ♦ is a packing term.

"Checklists" tell where to locate the ingredients for each Daily Menu.

River Days begin with Day 1 on the river (and launch camp is Day 0).

Table App. 2B-1 to 2B-9: Daily Menus

TABLE APPENDIX 2B-1: **LAUNCH CAMP NIGHT**

(This meal is optional – a flexible menu for trips camping overnight at the put-in site)

RIVER DAY: WRITE IN DAY OF THE WEEK/DATE	TENTATIVE DINNER CAMP NAME and RIVER MILE

"Launch Camp"_____/_____/   Camp _____ – mi.___

B: Coffee and Donuts at _____ before leaving Boise between _____ a.m.

L: Sack Lunch (BYO) or stop to buy on the road (Stop again for downwood for BBQ pits if no wood available in camp)

D: "All-American BBQ": Steaks, Potatoes, Garden Salad, Pies

→ LAUNCH CAMP COOLER #1 MORPHS INTO A TRASH CONTAINER THAT STAYS IN A SHUTTLE VEHICLE.

→ RE-LABEL LAUNCH CAMP COOLER #2 THE "LUNCH COOLER" FOR THE REST OF THE TRIP.

INGREDIENTS – NITE 0

(♠ = Advance Prep.)	Amounts for 12:	Amount for (____):	DIRECTIONS IN CAMP:
Chips 'n' dip	2 sacks 'n' 1 pint Guac		Set out 'n' munch.
Spanish Olives	1 can		"
Briquets	40 BBQ or firewood		Gather firewood on road into camp.
Steaks London Broil♠	6 lbs.		Cut into 1/2-sized portions (waste-not-want-not and save leftovers).
Potatoes – Bakers ♣	12		Place at edge of BBQ coals while steaks cook; good spuds turn often.
Butter for Spuds	2 cubes (1/2 lb.)		Use leftover butter for breakfast.
Sour Cream for Spuds	1 pint		
Bacon Bits for Spuds	1/2 jar		
Garden Corn or Salad	12 ears; two heads		BBQ corn; tear lettuce in bowl.
Tomatoes, Cherry	2 baskets		Add to salad.
Other salad veggies	Broccoli, red onion		Your choice.
Salad Dressing ♣	Homemade, 1 cup		Drench the salad veggies!
Pies	2 large bakery pies		"Chow down, cowpokes!"

♣♣♣ ADVANCE PREP. NITE 0 DETAILS ♣♣♣

INGREDIENTS:	Amounts for 12:	Amount for (_____):	DIRECTIONS:
London Broil Steaks	6 lbs.		Marinate the day before you leave.
Marinade: Soy Sauce Garlic Powder	1/3 c. 2 tsp.		Cover all sides of steaks; seal in zipper bags in cooler.
Potatoes, baked	12		Grease, wrap in foil, prebake 30" at home – 350°; reheat in BBQ pit.

CHECKLISTS – NITE 0

Use ingredient list above – easy!	Two 60-qt. Gott Coolers. Other personal coolers can be left in vehicles.		Pack dinner items in Launch Camp Cooler #1. Pack any overflow items on top of breakfast and lunch items in Launch Camp Cooler #2.

 Copy if you like.
From *River Otter: Handbook for Trip Planning*

TABLE APPENDIX 2B-2: **RIVER DAY #1 – FIRST CAMP NIGHT**

"River Day #1"_____/_____/   Camp _____– mi.___

B: Kielbasa sausages heated on Camp BBQ pits (firepan is loaded for launch), Muffins, Oatmeal, Melon Slices

L: Pack Lunch Cooler with Tortillas to make wraps, Cheese, Turkey Breast, Carrots, Oreos

D: **"Moroccan Delight"**: Lemon Chicken, Rice, Tabouli, Cucs, Onion & Tomatoes, Pita Bread, Halvah 'n' Sesames

→ INGREDIENTS ARE IN THE LUNCH COOLER AND PB #1 (RE-LABEL THIS "LUNCH PB #1." USE FOR SNACKS + DRY LEFTOVERS FOR REMAINDER OF TRIP.)

"Welcome to zee cahzbah…"

INGREDIENTS – NITE 1

(♣ = Advance Prep.)	Amounts for 12:	Amount for (_____):	DIRECTIONS IN CAMP:
Boiling Water	1 gallon-2 cups (14 cups). Remove 6 c. for tabouli, leaving 8 cups for rice.		Bring to boiling in large pot. Remove amount needed for tabouli. Use remainder for rice.
Rice	4 cups		Stir into boiling water, cover, simmer 20".
Rice Seasoning Pkt: ♣			Add all with rice to boiling rice water.
Yellow Raisins	2 cups		
Curry Powder	2 Tbsp.		
Oil	2 Tbsp.		
Salt	1 Tbsp.		
Moroccan Chicken ♣	12 boneless, skinless breasts, lusciously marinated, pre-cooked at home.		In camp thaw sacks (warm 'em in the boiling water), wrap in towel until rice is done, then mix well w/rice in large serving bowl or pot.
Pita Pocket Bread	4 packages of 5 ea.		Fill w/chicken & rice or tabouli; or use as pushers.
Tabouli Mix	4 cups (includes dried herbs, onion, parsley, lemon, mint, salt)		Place sack of tabouli in a small pot or bowl to hold up sides. Add boiling water, stir, soak for 30", then add veggies, oil, lemon juice.
(Boiling water above)	6 cups		
Cucumbers	2 large		Dice into sm. pieces; add to tabouli.
Green Onions	2 bunches		"
Cherry Tomatoes	1 pint box		"
Oil	3/4 cup		Add to tabouli.
Lemon Juice	1 plastic lemon		For those who like to pucker!
Halvah Dessert	2 8-oz bricks		Cut into cubes.
Sesame Candies	About 36		*"Shalom!"*

♣♣♣ ADVANCE PREP. NITE 1 DETAILS ♣♣♣

Ingredients:	Amounts for 12:	Amount for (____):	DIRECTIONS:
Moroccan Chicken			
Chicken Breasts	12 boneless, skinless		Cut chicken into 1" cubes.
Marinade:			Sprinkle chicken w/cornstarch; stir to cover all pieces. Mix marinade; pour over chicken in baking dish. Fully cook in home oven – 40" at 350°; stir twice while cooking. Cool; put chicken and gravy into two freezer zip bags; label "Nite 1, Moroccan Chicken." Freeze flat.
Cornstarch	2 Tbsp.		
White wine	2 cups		
Lemon juice	1 cup		
Olive oil	1/4 cup		
Garlic powder	1 Tbsp.		
Salad herbs	2 tsp. your choice		
Salt	2 tsp.		
Rice Seasoning Pkt.			
Yellow Raisins	2 cups		Mix these and seal in a zip bag. Label "Nite 1 Rice Seasonings."
Curry Powder	2 Tbsp.		
Oil	2 Tbsp.		
Salt	1 Tbsp.		
Tabouli Oil			
Olive Oil	3/4 cup		Double bag in a plastic container and tape. Label "Nite 1 Tabouli."

CHECKLISTS – NITE 1

PB #1:			Label all packages Nite 1 and write the name of all non-obvious ingredients on outside of their sacks.
❏ Rice	4 cups		
❏ Packet w/Raisins, Oil	2 cups, 2 Tbsp.		
Curry Pwdr. + Salt	2 Tbsp. + 1 Tbsp.		
❏ Tabouli	4 cups		
❏ Oil	3/4 cup in bagged jar		
❏ Plastic Lemon	1		
❏ Halvah Bricks	2 8-oz bricks		
❏ Sesame Candies	About 36 in a zip bag		

Cooler Nite 1:			Keep frozen chicken away from veggies, so veggies don't get ice burn (insert lunch items in between or wrap frozen chicken in newspaper).
❏ Chicken Breasts	12, frozen, cut-up		
❏ Pita Breads	4 pkgs. of 5 each		
❏ Cucumbers	2 large		
❏ Green Onions	2 bunches		
❏ Cherry Tomatoes	1 pint box		

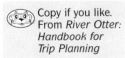

Copy if you like.
From *River Otter:
Handbook for
Trip Planning*

TABLE APPENDIX 2B-3: **RIVER DAY #2 – SECOND CAMP NIGHT**

"River Day #2"_____/_____/   Camp _____ – mi.___

B: Bagels and Cream Cheese, Oatmeal, Dried Fruit, Summer Sausage

L: Leftover Tabouli in Pitas, Bagels, Carrots, Ham + Cheese 2-3# ea.

D: "Goin' Light": MRE's or Freeze-dried meals, Carrots, Pemmican, Candy Bars, Pan Cookies

→ INGREDIENTS ARE IN LUNCH COOLER, PB #1, AND PB #2.

"Boil some water, *mes chèries – et bon appétit!*"

INGREDIENTS – NITE 2

(♣ = Advance Prep.)	Amounts for 12:	Amount for (____):	DIRECTIONS IN CAMP:
Freeze Dried Dinner Or MREs ("Meals-Ready-to-Eat")	12 Army MRE's are sufficient for 12 boaters, but double the packets (24) if you use backpacker dinners		Boil enough water to prepare per directions. When water boils, call troops and let them measure correct amount of water for their pouches (keep outside foil bags to insulate meals).
Carrots – baby ones	2 lbs.		Open sack; display gourmet style.
Dessert: Candy Bars Sacks Pemmican ♣ Chocolate Chip Pan Cookies ♣	12 12 1 tray cut for 12, remaind. for Day 4		Once more, with French chef flourish, lay out the dessert offerings – "Bon Apétit!"

♣♣♣ ADVANCE PREP. NITE 2 DETAILS ♣♣♣

Ingredients:	Amounts for 12:	Amount for (____):	DIRECTIONS:
Pemmican by Mike Cooper ♣	24 servings of 3 oz. each (4.5 lbs.) plus an extra 2 3/4 lb. sack. Total = 7 lbs. 4 oz.		(reprinted with Mike's and *On the Eddy Line*'s permission)
Mixture "A":			
Peanut Butter	2 c. ready-made (or homemade)		(Homemade: use a blender or food processor. ♣ Add 5 c. peanuts (1.5 lbs.), 1/3 c. canola oil, 1 tsp. salt.)
Canola Oil or margarine	1/3 c.		Mix with peanut butter.
Dark Honey	1 c.		"
Mixture "B":			
Any Dried Fruit (e.g., apricots, apples, figs, raisins) Prunes Roasted Peanuts Roasted Cashews	12 c. 1 c. 1 c. 2 c.		Run these items twice through a food grinder (not a food processor).

♣♣♣ ADVANCE PREP. NITE 2 DETAILS (CONTINUED) ♣♣♣

Ingredients:	Amounts for 12:	Amount for (____):	DIRECTIONS:
Mixture "C":			Mix "A" with "B" in a big bowl (used gloved hands) to make "C." Run chunky mixture "C" through grinder again to smooth. Pat mixture out onto two cookie sheets or jellyroll pans and cut into 24 pieces.
Powdered Sugar Dip	1/2 lb. (2 c.)		Roll each piece with a rolling pin, then dip in powdered sugar (or cocoa powder). Cut into 1" x 2" strips.
Want it drier?			Dehydrate for a harder pemmican or freeze directly if you like it softer.
Zipper Bags	24 1/2-pt. snack sacks + 1 quart zipper sack		Can be frozen indefinitely, but no need to refrigerate on the trip. Seal in snack-sized zip bags. Store in 1-gal. bag; label "Nite 2 Pemmican."

Chocolate Chip Pan Cookies – DOUBLE this recipe! And save a batch for Day 4 Lunch!

Flour	2 1/4 c.		Sift flour with soda + salt.
Baking Soda + Salt	1 tsp. each		"
Butter	1 c.		In a bowl, cream butter with sugars.
Brown Sugar	1 c. packed .		"
White Sugar	1/2 c.		"
Vanilla	1 tsp.		Add to creamed mix.
Eggs	2		"
Chocolate Chips Walnuts (optional)	12-oz. package 1 c. chopped		Mix flour mixture with creamed mix, then add chips and nuts (opt.).
			Put into two greased 9 x 13 pans or jellyroll pans; bake 350° for 25." Cool and cut; store in 1-gal. bags; label one "Nite 2," other "Day 4."

CHECKLISTS – NITE 2

PB #2: ❑ MREs ❑ Chocolate Bars ❑ Pemmican Sacks ❑ Pan Cookie	 12 12 24, plus extra sack 12 servings	Label all items PB #2.
Cooler Nite 2: ❑ Carrots	2 lbs.	Label carrot sack Nite 2.

Copy if you like.
From *River Otter: Handbook for Trip Planning*

TABLE APPENDIX 2B-4: **RIVER DAY #3 – THIRD CAMP NIGHT**

"**River Day #3**"_____/_____/   Camp _____– mi.____

B: Oatmeal and Dried fruit, Amaia Chorizo Sausage (or other dry type)

L: Pitas with leftover Tabouli and Hummus (Stop at _____(supply drop) – mi. ___. Pick up "The Cooler," "The Freezer" and PBs.)

D: "**Hail Britannia**": Salisbury Steaks, Spuds, Chutney Salad, Fruitcake (make Breakfast D.O. Appley Coffeecake)

→ INGREDIENTS ARE IN LUNCH COOLER, THE COOLER, AND PB #3.

"I say chaps, this is a lovely meal!"

INGREDIENTS – NITE 3

(♣ = Advance Prep.)	Amounts for 12:	Amount for (_____):	DIRECTIONS IN CAMP:
Briquets	60 (26 to heat steaks, 34 to bake cake)		Set up Firepan and Grill. Light the coals, Oliver and 'Liza Doolittle!
Salisbury Steaks ♣	6 lbs. Ground Beef makes 24 1/4-lb. patties w/mush-room + onion – 2 per person.		Thaw the patties and heat them up on grill to coincide with completion of potatoes and gravy (heating water takes forever!).
Boiling Water	2 gallons		Boil a large pot for potatoes, gravy, peas; pour boiling water into zipper bags to save on pots, esp. the gravy.
Potatoes, mashed, instant ♣	2 lbs. Potato flakes (about 20 cups dry = 12 svgs. 1 2/3 c. ea.)		Add 1 gallon + 1 qt. (20 c.) boiling water to freezer bags of flakes; stir in milk + butter (save papers to grease D.O.).
Milk, instant ♣	2/3 c. in 1 1/2 c. water		Mix up and add to mashed spuds.
Butter	2 sticks (1 cup)		Add to mashed spuds.
Gravy ♣	5 packets, instant, in a gallon freezer bag.		Slowly add 5 c. boiling water. Mix w/whisk. "Good Gravy, Grace! No mess!"
Peas, frozen	2 lbs. (12 1/2-cup svgs.)		Add 2 cups boiling water to pea sack supported in a pot.
Chutney salad ♣			Serve in its sack(s).
Ol' Engl. Fruitcake ♣	1 loaf, bite-sized bites		Slice lengthwise x 3, then x 12.
Appley Dutch Oven Coffee Cake (for morning) ♣			Use 34 hot briquets: 12 for bottom, 22 for top; grease 14 or 16" D.O. w/butter papers from potato project. Place parchment sheets on bottom and magic can* (see note) in center.
Eggs	4, frozen		Thaw and mix in 4-cup measure; add 2 c. water; beat with fork.

(♣ = Advance Prep.)	Amounts for 12:	Amount for (_____):	DIRECTIONS IN CAMP:
Milk, instant, baggie labeled Appley Cake Milk Pkg. #1	2 cups		Beat milk into egg/water, then fill to 4 c. line w/water; mix again.
Premixed Ingredients, labeled Appley Cake Mix Pkg. #2 (the white, dry stuff)			Pour this dry cake mix in mixing bowl or tall plastic bag (s); stir in liquid mixture (lumps are okay). Hold center can firmly in D.O. and spread batter around it.
Premixed Ingredients, labeled Appley Topping Pkg. #3 (the raisin, nut, cinnamon mixture)	Topping ingredients		Layer on top of dough, with apples on top. If your coals are super hot, you can lay a sheet or two of parchment on top to keep raisins from burning.
Green apple or slices of dried apple	Sliced thin for topping		*"Aunt Nell said it was the best coffee cake she ever tasted."* – Grandma
*"Magic can" is simply a 2" diameter empty can with lids removed. Use it to eliminate doughy centers – it works like an angelfood tubepan.			Cover; 22 coals top, 12 underneath; bake 50" rotating every 10". At 30" put bottom coals on top of D.O. When done, remove coals, cool w/lid off, then covered w/lid and a big rock on top to keep critters out until breakfast.

♣♣♣ ADVANCE PREP. NITE 3 DETAILS ♣♣♣

Ingredients:	Amounts for 12:	Amount for (_____):	DIRECTIONS:
Appley Coffee Cake			
"Appley Cake Milk Pkg. #1":			Put in pint zipper bag and label "Appley Cake Milk Pkg. #1."
Milk, instant	2 c.		
"Appley Cake Mix Pkg. #2":			Mix all items; put half into one 1-gal. zipper bag – label" Appley Cake Mix Pkg. #2". Put other half into another bag – label it "Appley Cake Topping Pkg. #3"; add next items.
Sugar	4 c.		
Flour	8 c.		
Butter	2 c.		
Baking Powder	2 Tbsp. + 2 tsp.		
"Appley Cake Topping Pkg. #3":			Add these items to Pkg. #3; seal.
Cinnamon	2 tsp.		
Raisins	2 c.		
Pecans, chopped	2 c.		
Eggs, in freezer bag	4 beaten		Beat; put in pint freezer bag; label "Nite 3 – Appley Cake Eggs."

CONTINUED

♣♣♣ ADVANCE PREP. NITE 3 DETAILS (CONTINUED) ♣♣♣

Ingredients:	Amounts for 12:	Amount for (____):	DIRECTIONS:
Salisbury Steak & Potatoes			
Ground Beef, bulk, not patties	6 lbs. to make about 24 quarter-plus-pounders after mixing		Put on gloves; place meat in a large mixing bowl. Mix meat by hand with all the ingredients below:
Mushrooms, chopped	2 cans, drained		"
Salt Pepper	2 Tbsp. 1 Tbsp.		"
Garlic Powder	1 Tbsp.		"
Onion	1 finely chopped		"
Soy Sauce	1/4 c.		"
Eggs	4 beaten		"
			After mixing, make up 24 patties; layer them in two 1-gallon zipper bags w/plastic wrap between; label "Nite 3 Salisbury Steaks"; freeze flat.
Potatoes, instant	2 lb. sack divided into two 1-gal. bags		Label "Nite 3 Potatoes; save sacks for mixing" on the bags.
Gravy, instant	5 packets sealed in a 1-gal. freezer zip bag		Label "Nite 3 Gravy; save sack for mixing" on the bag.
Milk, instant	2/3 cup		Pack in 1/2 pint zipper bag; label "Nite 3 Potato Milk (add 1 and 1/2 cups cold water to mix up)."
Chutney Salad			
Raisins Carrots Walnuts Pineapple, crushed Mayonnaise Plain Yogurt	1 1/2 c. 12 peeled, grated 3/4 c. toasted chopped 2 20 oz.cans (2 c. ea.) 3/4 c. 3/4 c.		Mix these ingredients in a 1-gallon freezer zipper bag. Seal; label "Nite 3 Chutney Salad"; freeze flat.

CHECKLISTS – nITE 3

PB #3:			Label all items Nite 3 (the non-obvious ones, natch!)
❏ Potatoes, instant	2 lb. sack divided into two 1-gal. bags		
❏ Milk, instant for spuds	2/3 c. in baggie		
❏ Gravy packets + bag	5 packets in big bag		
❏ Fruitcake	1 loaf		
❏ "Appley Cake Milk Pkg. #1"	Instant Milk, 2 cups		
❏ "Appley Cake Mix Pkg. #2"	Coffee Cake Mix		
❏ "Appley Cake Topping Pkg. #3"	Topping		
❏ Green Apple	1		
❏ Parchment Sheets	4 for Appley Cof-cake		
The Cooler nite 3:			Label all Nite 3.
❏ Salisbury Steaks	24 patties, frozen		
❏ Butter for Potatoes	2 sticks		
❏ Peas	2 lbs., frozen, in 1-gal. sack		
❏ Chutney Salad	1 sack, frozen sack		
❏ Eggs for Coffee Cake	4 beaten, frozen bag		

Copy if you like. From *River Otter: Handbook for Trip Planning*

TABLE APPENDIX 2B-5: **RIVER DAY #4 – FOURTH CAMP NIGHT**

"**River Day #4**"_____/_____/ Camp (layover?)_____ – mi.___

B: English Muffins, Kielbasa Sausage, Appley Coffee Cake

L: Bagels, Cream Cheese, Peanut Butter, Salami, and Pan Cookies

D: "**Pax Romani**": Lasagne, Radicchio/Cabbagio Salad, Dolci di Limone

→ INGREDIENTS ARE IN LUNCH COOLER, LUNCH PB #2, THE COOLER, AND PB #4.

"Benvenuto! It's a Layover Campa! – Buon apetito!"

INGREDIENTS – NITE 4

(♣ = Advance Prep.)	Amounts for 12:	Amount for (____):	DIRECTIONS IN CAMP:
Briquets	34		You lights zem in Firepan; oil bottom 14" or 16" Dutchio.
Lasagne Sauce: Ground Beef ♣ Tomatoes, crushed Pesto, optional Dried Tomatoes, opt	Thaw all frozen ingredients: 2 lbs., pre-fried, frozen 2 lg. cans (3¹/2 c. ea.) 1 pt. Homemade, frozen 1 cup		Mix tomatoes and pesto into meat sacks to make sauce and conserve on dishwashing effort! The pesto and dried tomatoes are optional, but tasta *saporito*-good!
Lasagne Noodles	20-24 Noodles (1.5 lbs.)		Pour a layer of sauce into D.O.; squish noodles in. Use broken ones to fill gaps.
Spinach, chopped	2 boxes, frozen (thaw)		Layer onto noodles, then more sauce and noodles.
Ricotta Cheese	1 quart, thinned w/1 cupa water in D.O.		Spread onto noodles, add water, mix a bit, then layer more noodles; si, si, si – squish zem down!
Mozzarella Cheese Water	2 lbs. (brick) 3 cups before slicing		Cut into ¹/8" slices; layer on noodles, more sauce, then rinse sacks with water; add it over cheese; one more layer noodles.
Parmesan Cheese pkt. ("Parmigiano")	1¹/2 c. grated		Add remaining Mozzarella; squish down again; top w/Parmigiano.
D.O. (Note: if windy or cold, add a few extra goals during cooking)			Bake 40" w/21 coals on top and 13 on bottom. Rotate lid and base at least twice to avoid hot spots. After 40" put bottom coals on top; bake 30" more. Cool slightly to set up before serving.
Radicchio/Cabbagio: Cabbage, green Radicchio Oil/Vinegar Dsg. ♣	 1 head, chopped 1 head, chopped Homemade		Chop up the radicchio and head of cabbage; toss with dressing.

(♣ = Advance Prep.)	Amounts for 12:	Amount for (_____):	DIRECTIONS IN CAMP:
Dessert ♣: "Dolce di Lemone"	2 boxes Jello "No-Bake" Cheesecake, for hearty servings		Follow directions on package cut-out. (You see-a da carda, ok?)
Crust package♣: Includes: Butter ♣ and Sugar ♣ Just add Water	1 cupa (2 sticks) 1/3 cupa (labeled) 3 Tbsp.		Find package labeled "Nite 4 Dessert Crust" and add water to crust mix. Mix with fork and press down into pan or serving bowl.
Filling package: Milk, instant ♣ Water	1 2/3 cups, dry 4 1/2 cups		Mix up milk up with water; add contents of filling package; beat well; pour into crust.
Topping: Sour Cream Sugar ♣ Lemon Zest ♣	1 pint 1/3 cupa 1 Tbsp.		Mix sour cream and "Nite 4 Dessert Topping" (sugar/lemon zest); spread on top of filling; let whole thing set up during dinner.
East Indian D.O. Monkey Bread (make in the morning if you can wait that long!) ♣			
Briquets	34		Light 'em!
Monkey Bread Caramel Mix ♣	1 gallon sack, premixed		Put all but 1 cup of "Layover Day Breakfast Monkey Bread Caramel Sauce" into DO (around The Can!)
Croissant Dough Or Crescent Roll Dough	2 sacks, thawed Or 4 tubes of 8, or 3 tubes of 12		If they aren't yet thawed, leave them out to warm up and begin to rise. Watch out that they don't rise too fast and burst out. (Yes, it happened one year on top of a dry box, when left overnight!) Layer out over Caramel Sauce; cover w/remaining 1 c. Sauce.
Milk, instant ♣	1/3 c. dry – add 1 c. water		Mix up in its small packet, then pour over Monkey Bread in D.O.
D.O.			Bake with 21 coals on top and 13 under; in 20", rotate Dutch and lid twice. Then put bottom coals on the lid top and bake for 10 more minutes. Rotate lid once after 5 minutes to avoid hot spots.

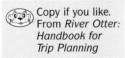
Copy if you like.
From *River Otter: Handbook for Trip Planning*

DAY #4: INGREDIENTS (CONTINUED)

(♣ = Advance Prep.)	Amounts for 12:	Amount for (____):	DIRECTIONS IN CAMP:
"The Tray": Heavy Aluminum Foil Duct Tape	Four 2-foot sheets		**1.** Duct tape bottom of one length of foil to the top of another. Repeat with other two sheets. Place one square on the other; crimp edges to make classy double-thick Tray. Turn tape-side down. **2.** Make a depression in the sand or shallow place. Remove Dutch lid and put Tray with edges bent up on the Dutch; replace lid. Prepare for the Big Inversion when you (AND hot glove and pads and friends) turn the Dutch over, catching caramel in the Tray and lid. **3.** Serve al fresco in the depression as a cure for depression!

♣♣♣ ADVANCE PREP. nITE 4 DETAILS ♣♣♣

Ingredients:	Amounts for 12:	Amount for (____):	DIRECTIONS:
Lasagne Meat			
Ground Beef Onions Oil Garlic Salt Pepper Oregano	2 lbs. 2 chopped 1/8 c. 5 cloves, minced 2 tsp. 1 tsp. 2 tsp.		Fry onions and garlic until transparent, remove from pan. Fry beef until slightly browned. Add spices, then fold in onion/garlic mix. Cool and put into two 1-gallon zipper sacks; label "Nite 4 Lasagne Meat"; freeze flat.
Salad Dressing			
Vinegar, balsamic Oil, olive Garlic Powder Salt Pepper	1/4 c. 3/4 c. 1 tsp. 1 tsp. 1/2 tsp.		Bottle together in a tight-lidded plastic bottle/jar; put in zip bag; label "Nite 4 Salad Dressing."
Dessert Packets:			
Jello No-Bake Cheesecake Mix	2 sacks filling mix plus directions		Empty filling packages into zip bag and cut out directions from box; label "Nite 4 Dessert Filling."
Milk, instant for Dolci di Lemone	1 2/3 cups		Put in 1 pt. zip bag; label "Nite 4 Dessert Milk."
Crust Mix plus Sugar + Butter Mixed	1/3 cup 2 sticks (1 cup)		Mix and Label "Nite 4 Dessert Crust plus Sugar & Butter."
Sugar/Lemon Zest for Topping	1/3 cup sugar 1 Tbsp. lemon zest		Label "Nite 4 for Dessert Topping."

♣♣♣ ADVANCE PREP. NITE 4 DETAILS (CONTINUED) ♣♣♣

Ingredients:	Amounts for 12:	Amount for (_____):	DIRECTIONS:
Monkey Bread			
Caramel Sauce:			Mix these ingredients in 1-gallon, freezer-weight zipper bag. Knead briefly. Double bag; seal and label, "Layover Day Breakfast: Monkey Bread Caramel Sauce"
Butter	1 cup		
Corn Syrup (Karo)	1/2 c.		
Brown Sugar	3 c.		
Cinnamon	1 tsp.		
Cardamom	1 tsp. (ground)		
Raisins and Pecans	2 cups of each		
Milk, instant	1/3 cup		Pack in snack zip bag. Label "Milk for Layover Day Monkey Bread."

CHECKLISTS – NITE 4

PB #4:			Label all Nite 4.
❏ Tomatoes, crushed	2 lg. cans		
❏ Dried Tomatoes, opt.	1 cup, optional		
❏ Lasagne Noodles	1.5 lbs.		
❏ Oil/Vinegar dressing	1 container		
❏ Dessert Filling and Box directions	2 sacks from 2 boxes		
❏ Dessert Milk, instant	1 1/3 cups		
❏ Dessert Crust, Butter, & Sugar	1 cup (2 sticks) 1/3 c. mixed w/crust		
❏ Dessert Topping Mix			
Sugar/Lemon Zest	1/3 c. + 1 Tbsp.		
❏ Monkey Bread Caramel Mix: (includes Pecans and Raisins and Instant Milk)	1 gallon sack (put in PB #4 if room, otherwise in pantry) 2 cups each 1/3 cup		
The Cooler Nite 4:			Label all Nite 4.
❏ Ground Beef	2 gallon sacks		
❏ Pesto, optional	1 pint, optional		
❏ Spinach	2 boxes, frozen		
❏ Ricotta Cheese	1 quart		
❏ Mozzarella Cheese	2 lbs.		
❏ Parmesan Cheese	1 1/2 cups		
❏ Cabbage	1 head		
❏ Radicchio	1 head		
❏ Sour Cream	1 pint		
❏ Croissant Dough OR Crescent Roll Dough	2 pkgs., frozen OR 4 tubes of 8 rolls (or 3 tubes of 12)		

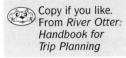 Copy if you like. From *River Otter: Handbook for Trip Planning*

TABLE APPENDIX 2B-6: **RIVER DAY #5 – FIFTH CAMP NIGHT**

"River Day #5"_____/_____/ Camp (layover/dress-up?)_____mi.__

B: Bring out the eggs and bacon from The Cooler! Make E. Indian Monkey Bread

L: Pitas, Cheese, Summer Sausages, Turkey Ham, 3rd sack of Baby Carrots

D: "**Spanish Conquest**": Bean Burritos, Arroz Vasco, Mexican Fudge (make D.O. Breakfast Cobbler)

→ INGREDIENTS ARE IN LUNCH COOLER, LUNCH PB #2, THE FREEZER, THE COOLER, AND PB #5.

"Hola todos! Comed con gusto!"

INGREDIENTS – NITE 5

(♣ = Advance Prep.)	Amounts for 12:	Amount for (____):	DIRECTIONS IN CAMP:
Burritos Elegantos:			
Flour Tortillas Salsa Sour Cream Guacamole Dip Cheddar Cheese Onion Refried Beans, instant w/spices included	30 tortillas, 12" 1 quart 1 quart 2 pint containers 2 lbs., grated 1 onion, chopped 6 c., dry		Lay out the burrito ingredients: Tortillas and Salsa; put a spoon in the Sour Cream; ditto for the Guacamole Dip. Grate Cheese and chop onion; put each on a plate w/ a serving spoon. Stand sack in a pot; pour 8 c. boiling water in; stir and serve!
Arroz Vasco Mas Facil: (This is Basque Meat & Rice – *"kaixo!"* – very easy!)			
Chorizo Sausage Meat Mix ♣	3 packages pre-cooked Cacique (12 oz. ea.) + 6 cut up Chorizo sausages (pre-cooked)		Thaw "Chorizo Meat Nite 5." You can warm up the packets in the heating rice water by putting them on a layer of crumpled foil to keep sack from melting (tightly sealed, *por favor*). As the water approaches boiling, remove the sacks and cover with a towel.
Rice	4 cups		Boil rice w/8 cups water; stir; cover; simmer on low flame 20." After rice is cooked, if you want to avoid a greasy pot, combine cooked rice to meat IN the meat sacks or clean E-Z-fill baggies. Keep the mixture warm in covered pot w/1" hot water at bottom.
Dessert: ♣ Mexican Fudge			Find in The Freezer; take out to thaw.
Horno Dutchia Postre por La Manaña: (D.O. morning dessert)			Bake tonight for morning, *amigos* – or the crumbs of it – if you can't beat off the guerrilla invasion!
Briquets	34		Light 'em! Prepare D.O. by oiling it and placing magic can in center.

(♣ = Advance Prep.)	Amounts for 12:	Amount for (____):	DIRECTIONS IN CAMP:
Blueberry Pie Filling	2 cans large (a #2½ size can = 3½ cups)		Pour into D.O. around the can, naturalmente!
Yellow Cake Mix	2 boxes Duncan Hines		Sprinkle mix on top.
Butter ♦	1 stick (½ cup)		Cut up onto top.
7-Up (or other lemon-lime soda like Sprite)	2 cans, warm (*Ay, caramba!*)		Pour over the top. Bake w/22 briquets on top and 12 under for 35" — rotating at least twice, then put bottom coals on lid; bake 10" more; serve *con amor*!

♣♣♣ ADVANCE PREP. NITE 5 DETAILS ♣♣♣

Ingredients:	Amounts for 12:	Amount for (____):	DIRECTIONS:
Chorizo Meat Pkts.			
Cacique Chorizo Chorizo Sausages, uncooked	3 pkgs. (12 oz. ea.) 6 diced		Fry meats separately, then mix and remove from pan.
Onions Garlic Salt Anaheim Peppers w/o seeds, diced Manzanilla Olives	2 chopped 8 cloves, minced 2 tsp. 4 (or med. can Green Chilis) 1 sm. can, chop		Fry onions, garlic, salt and peppers. Chop olives, add. Seal in two 1-gallon zipper sacks, label each "Chorizo Meat Nite 5"; freeze flat.
Mexican Fudge			
Chocolate Chips Milk, sweetened, condensed Cinnamon	3 sacks (12 oz. ea.) or 2 lbs., 4 oz. bulk 2 cans (Eagle Brand) 1 tsp.		Melt and mix; layer 1" thick on parchment in flat pan; cool, cut into squares, put flat into zip bags; label "Nite 5 Fudge"; and freeze.

CHECKLISTS – NITE 5

PB #5:
- ❏ Salsa — 1 qt.
- ❏ Onion — 1
- ❏ Dried Refried Beans — 1 sack, 6 cups
- ❏ Rice — 4 cups
- ❏ Blueberry Pie Filling — 2 cans
- ❏ Yellow Cake Mix — 2 boxes
- ❏ 7-Up or Sprite Cans — 2 cans

Label all Nite 5 after discarding all unnecessary cardboard packaging.

Copy if you like. From *River Otter: Handbook for Trip Planning*

Cooler Nite 5:
- ❏ Guacamole, Sour Cream — 1 quart each
- ❏ Cheddar Cheese — 2 lbs.

Label all Nite 5.

Freezer Nite 5:
- ❏ Chorizo Meat Pkgs. — 2 packages, frozen
- ❏ Mexican Fudge — 2 qt. sacks
- ❏ Tortillas — 40
- ❏ Butter for DO cobbler — 1 stick (½ c.)

Label all Nite 5.

TABLE APPENDIX 2B-7: **RIVER DAY #6 – SIXTH CAMP NIGHT**

"**River Day #6**"_____/_____/   Camp _____– mi.____

B: Blueberry Dutch Cobbler, Oatmeal, Frozen Sausages

L: Use up any leftover Burritos, Tortillas, Carrots, Cheese 'n' Salami.

D: "**Tuscan Village**": Antipasti, Pasta Marinara, Dutch Oven Panne, Tiramisu

→ INGREDIENTS ARE IN LUNCH COOLER, LUNCH PB #2, THE COOLER, THE FREEZER, AND PB #6.

"When the moon-ah hits the sky…That's Amore!"

INGREDIENTS – NITE 6

(♣ = Advance Prep.)	Amounts for 12:	Amount for (____):	DIRECTIONS IN CAMP:
Antipasto ♣	Plastic jug, full of zesty Italian delights		Set out jug and slotted spoon.
Briquets	34		Light them.
Panne di Bierre:	4-lb. 6 oz. Loaf of Beer Bread – makes 32 slices of 2.5 oz. each		Grease Dutch Oven; put parchment circle in bottom.
Pre-mixed Flour ♣ Light-colored Beer	3 sacks Advance Prep. 3 cans, warm (*O Mama mia!*)		Pour a can of warm beer in each sack. Mix bread dough sacks just until moistened – lumps OK. Empty into Dutch, shaping dough into big donut around a magic greased can.
Butter ♦	1 cup (2 sticks)		Soften butter; spread half on top now; save half for during baking.
Il Dutchi O.	"You now gotta da big *panne di bierre!*"		Put 22 coals on lid top and 12 under; bake 1 hour. Rotate the lid 1/4 turn clockwise and bottom counter-clockwise 1/4 turn every ten minutes to prevent hot spots. At the fourth turning (40-minute mark) move all bottom coals on top of the lid (two-thirds rule). At the fifth turning (50-minute mark), open the lid and spread soft butter over the bread. Bake for ten more minutes (1 hour total).
Butter ♦ Kosher Salt, opt. ♦ Honey, opt. ♦	1 cube for those who must gilda da lily… 1/4 cup, optional 1 8-oz honey-bear type, optional		Let bread cool slightly by removing from Dutch (just pick up the corners of the parchment paper). Then cut into 32 slices and serve warm with more butter (and salt or honey). *"Molto-bene, molto-bene!"*

(♣ = Advance Prep.)	Amounts for 12:	Amount for (____):	DIRECTIONS IN CAMP:
Pasta Marinara Meat Sauce Sacks ♣	3		Remove from freezer, thaw, and add 1 cup water to each sack (use boiling if the sauce sacks are still frozen).
Spaghetti Pasta Water Oil	2 lbs. 2 gallons, boiling 1 Tbsp. pantry oil		Boil water in largest pot; add noodles and 1 Tbsp. oil; stir noodles so they don't stick together; lower heat and cook about 10 min. to "*al dente*, chewy-to-the-tooth" doneness. Pour hot water into pre-soak bucket. Dat-sa smarta!
Parmesan Cheese pkt. Pesto Sauce (opt.) ♣ (for those who want added zest)	2 cup, grated 1 pint, homemade		Use pasta tool to ladle pasta onto plates, then adda da meat sauca and da Parmigiano on top – *Delizioso!* Put out pesto for garlic lovers.
Dessert: Frozen ♣ Tiramisu di Maria			Remove from freezer. Slice and serve *con amore!*

♣♣♣ ADVANCE PREP. nITE 6 DETAILS ♣♣♣

Ingredients:	Amounts for 12:	Amount for (____):	DIRECTIONS:
Antipasto Jug			
Artichoke Hearts Pepperonici Black Olives	2 jars, 8-oz. each 1 pint jar 1 can, medium pitted, drained		Pour veggies into a gallon jug or bottle. Use all the pickling liquid except the black olive juice.
Green Olives Pickled Onions Jardinera (pickled cauli, carrots, etc.) Any other veggies	2 can, stuffed 1 jar, 8-oz. 1 jar, 12-oz. Use your Italian imagination.		Add sliced garlic cloves. Top off with enough vinegar and oil dressing to cover the veggies.
Vinegar + Oil Dsg. (ratio of 1 part vinegar to 2 parts oil) Garlic Cloves	4 sliced		Label "Nite 6 Antipasto"; put in PB #6 or pantry drybox. (Check to see if the jug leaks. If so, double bag.)
Bread (Panne) Mix			
Flour Baking Powder Sugar, opt. (omit for a more Italian taste)	9 cups 1/4 cup 1/4 – 1/2 cup		Sift these three ingredients together. Divide equally into three "E-Z fill" tall sacks (each 1-gal. size). Zip shut and label "Nite 6 Bread."

♣♣♣ ADVANCE PREP. NITE 6 DETAILS (CONTINUED) ♣♣♣

Ingredients:	Amounts for 12:	Amount for (_____):	DIRECTIONS:
Pasta Marinara Meat Sauce			
Oil	2 Tbsp.		Fry chopped onion in oil until
Onions	3, chopped		transparent, add minced
Garlic	6 cloves, minced		garlic. Fry until garlic browns,
Ground Beef	3 lbs.		dump into big bowl. Fry meat
Oregano	2 Tbsp. dried		until it browns slightly, add it
Basil	2 Tbsp. dried		to big bowl. Add the spices
Salt	1 Tbsp.		and then the tomatoes and
Pepper	1 tsp.		tomato paste. Mix well. Put
Tomatoes, crushed	2 lg. can		into three 1-gal. freezer
	(ea. 3 1/2 c.)		zipper sacks, label "Nite 6
Tomato Paste	1 12-oz. can		Pasta Meat;" freeze flat.
Tiramisu			
Pound Cake	2 boxed pound cake mixes, e.g., Betty Crocker's		1. Bake the pound cakes as directed on the box, only use two long flat pans (like jelly rolls or 9" x 13" baking pans)
Eggs per Pound Cake Recipe	4		and parchment liners. Cool; slice cakes horizontally, making four layers total.
Mascarpone Cheese	1 carton, 8 oz.		2. Mix cheese in a bowl w/sour cream, yogurt, sugar,
Sour Cream	1 qt.		and liqueur.
Powdered Sugar	1 c.		Over first cake layer, dribble
Plain Yogurt	1/2 c.		1/4 of coffee/marsala, then
Liqueur (amaretto or brandy)	3 Tbsp.		spread 1/4 of the cheese mixture. Repeat with re-
Coffee	1 c. triple strength, or 1 c. espresso		maining layers. Top w/cocoa.
Marsala Wine	1/4 liter (250 ml.)		3. Freeze entire dessert, then cut into shapes to fit 1-gal.
Unsweetened cocoa	2 Tbsp. Powdered or 2 oz. shaved solid		freezer sacks; label "Nite 6 Dessert."

CHECKLISTS – nITE 6

PB #6:

		Label all Nite 6.
❏ Antipasto jug (if won't fit, pack in pantry box)	1	
❏ Bread Mix Sacks	3 sacks flour mixture	
❏ Spaghetti	2 lbs.	
❏ Honeybear, optional	1 8-oz. bottle, opt.	
❏ Kosher Salt, optional	1/4 cup, optional	
❏ Parchment Sheets	2 sheets for D.O.	

The Cooler nite 6:

		Nothing from Cooler for this meal.

Freezer nite 6:

		Label all Nite 6.
❏ Pasta Meat Sauce	3 sacks	
❏ Parmigiano Pkt.	2 c. pkt.	
❏ Pesto (optional)	1 pint, optional	
❏ Butter for Bread◆	3 cubes	
❏ Tiramisu	2 or more gallon zips	

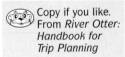 Copy if you like.
From *River Otter:*
Handbook for
Trip Planning

TABLE APPENDIX 2B-8: **RIVER DAY #7 – FINAL CAMP NIGHT**

"**River Day #7**"_____/_____/ Last Night Camp _____– mi.___

B: Kielbasa Sausages, Oatmeal, Leftover Tiramisu

L: Tuna, Red Onion, Mayo, Thawed Tortilla Wraps

D: "**Irish Eyes**": Pilot Biscuits/Smoked Fish, Heavenly Ham, Mashers, 3-Bean Salad, Cherry Fudge D.O. Cake

→ INGREDIENTS ARE IN LUNCH COOLER, THE FREEZER, AND PB#7.

"Oh lads 'n' coleens, 'tis heavenly, 'tis!"

INGREDIENTS – NITE 7

(♣ = Advance Prep.)	Amounts for 12:	Amount for (_____):	DIRECTIONS IN CAMP:
Briquets (*"Glowin' turf or lumps o' coal," me dear Mah woulda said.*)	34		Light them. Use butter papers from potato project to grease D.O. for cake. Place parchment circle on bottom and magic can on center.
Ham, precooked, presliced (loads o' rashers for all)	6 lbs. (What river elf wouldn't like the sugar-cured kind?)		Use the cake briquets heating up for warming ham: place ham in foil on a griddle, then cover w/a foil tent.
Potatoes, mashed ♣ (*"Oh those grand spudatoes...makes me heart so glad!"* – Dah)	2 lbs. Potato flakes (about 20 cups dry = 12 svgs. 1 2/3 c. each)		Heat 1 gallon + 1 qt. (20 c.) water to boiling; add to freezer bags of flakes.
Milk, instant ♣	2/3 c. in 1 1/2 c. water		Mix up dry milk w/water. When potatoes are done, stir in milk.
Butter ♦	2 sticks (1 cup)		From The Freezer. Cut butter into pats, stir into potatoes.
Gravy ♣	5 packets, instant, in a gallon freezer bag.		Slowly add 5 c. boiling water to bag. Whisk and avoid a messy pot. Set out w/spoon for self-service.
Smoked Fish Appetizer	5 cans (oysters, clams, herring)		Open; serve w/biscuits, crackers.
Pilot Biscuits	18		Set sack for self-serve.
Little People Bean Salad: Green Beans, cut	1 can (1 lb., 2 cups)		Open cans, drain into pre-wash bucket, and put beans into an available 2 qt. bowl/pan. Toss w/vinaigrette and serve wid a wee fond memory of childhood picnics.
Garbanzo Beans	" (same)		
Kidney Beans	" (same)		
Vinaigrette ♣	Homemade		

(♣ = Advance Prep.)	Amounts for 12:	Amount for (_____):	DIRECTIONS IN CAMP:
Cherry Fudge Cake:			
Mushy Mix (Pkt. 1) ♣	In PB #7		Put Pkt. 1 Mushy Mix into mixing bowl.
Eggs (Pkt.2, freezer)♣	6 frozen, now thawed		Add Pkt. 2 (eggs), water + Pkt. 3 (dry milk), and sour cream.
Water	1 cup		Mix well with whisk. Slowly fold in Pkt. 4 Dry Mix (some lumps ok).
Instant Milk (Pkt.3) ♣	1/3 c. in PB #7		
Sour Cream ♦ (in freezer)	2 cups (1 pint), thaw		Oil center can and D.O.; pour mix around can; sprinkle cherries and chips (Pkt. 5) on top.
Dry Mix (Pkt. 4) ♣	In PB #7		
Dried Cherries + Chocolate Chips (Pkt.5)	In PB #7		Bake 45" w/22 coals on top, 12 under. Rotate 3 times, then put bottom coals on lid and bake 15" more.
Fudge Frosting Mix	1 can pre-made		Frost in D.O.
			STAND BACK! *Here comes the whole blessed Irish Army!*

♣♣♣ ADVANCE PREP. NITE 7 DETAILS ♣♣♣

Ingredients:	Amounts for 12:	Amount for (_____):	DIRECTIONS:
Potato Milk, instant			
Potatoes, instant	2 lb. sack divided into two 1-gal. bags		Label "Nite 7 Potatoes; save sacks for mixing" on the bags.
Gravy, instant	5 packets sealed in a 1-gal. freezer zip bag		Label "Nite 7 Gravy; save sack for mixing" on the bag.
Milk, instant	2/3 cup		Pack in 1/2 pint zipper bag; label "Nite 7 Potato Milk (add 1 and 1/2 cups cold water to mix up)"
Vinaigrette			
Vinegar, balsamic	1/4 c.		Bottle together in a tight-lidded plastic bottle/jar; put in zip bag; label "Nite 7 for Bean Salad."
Oil, olive	3/4 c.		
Garlic Powder	1 tsp.		
Salt	1 tsp.		
Pepper	1/2 tsp.		

CONTINUED

♣♣♣ ADVANCE PREP. NITE 7 DETAILS (CONTINUED) ♣♣♣

Ingredients:	Amounts for 12:	Amount for (____):	DIRECTIONS:
Cherry Fudge Cake			
Mushy Mix Pkt. 1: Butter Cooking Oil Vanilla Sugar	1/2 c. (1 stick) 3/4 c. oil 2 tsp. 31/3 c.		Put butter + sugar into 1-gal. zipper bag; massage until mostly mixed; add oil and vanilla. Triple bag. Label "Nite 7 Dessert, Pkt. 1."
Eggs Pkt. 2 (in Freezer)	6, w/o shells! Frozen in a zip bag.		Break eggs into bowl and beat; pour into 1-pint (or larger) baggie; double bag; label "Nite 7 Dessert Pkt. 2 Eggs for Cake"; freeze.
Milk, instant Pkt. 3	1/3 c.		In 1/2 pint baggie, label "Nite 7 Dessert, Pkt. 3."
Dry Mix Pkt. 4: Flour Cocoa, unsweetened Baking Soda Salt	4 c. 11/3 c. powdered 2 tsp. 2 tsp.		Sift all ingredients into a 1-gal. zipper bag; Double bag; label "Nite 7 Dessert Pkt. 4."
Cherries 'n' Chips Pkt.5: Dried Cherries Chocolate Chips	 1 cup 2 cups		Combine in a 1-qt. (or larger) zipper bag; label "Nite 7 Dessert, Pkt. 5."

CHECKLISTS – NITE 7

PB #7:   Label all "Nite 7."
❑ Potatoes, instant — 2 lb. sack
❑ Milk, instant for spuds — 2/3 c. in baggie
❑ Gravy Packets — 5 packets
❑ Smoked fish — 5 cans: herring, smoked clams, oysters
❑ Pilot Biscuits — 18
Bean Cans:
    ❑ Green — 1 can
    ❑ Garbanzo — 1 can
    ❑ Kidney — 1 can
❑ Vinaigrette — 1 plastic container
❑ Dessert Pkt. 1 — Mushy Mix
❑ Dessert Pkt. 3 — Milk, instant 1/3 c.
❑ Dessert Pkt. 4 — Dry Cake Mix
❑ Dessert Pkt. 5 — Cherries 'n' Chips
❑ Frosting — 1 can

Copy if you like.
From River Otter: Handbook for Trip Planning

The Freezer Nite 7:   Label each item "Nite 7."
❑ Ham, sugar-cured — 1 big, heavenly type
❑ Butter for Potatoes — 2 cubes
❑ Dessert Pkt. 2 (Eggs) — 6 frozen "for Cake"
❑ Sour Cream — 1 pint "for Cake"

TABLE APPENDIX 2B-9: **BLANK SAMPLE SHEETS TO COPY**

INGREDIENTS

(♣ = Advance Prep.)	Amount for (_____):	DIRECTIONS IN CAMP:

(Blank sample to copy)

♣♣♣ ADVANCE PREP. nITE ___ DETAILS ♣♣♣

INGREDIENTS:	Amount for (_____):	DIRECTIONS:

(Blank sample to copy)

CHECKLISTS – nITE ____

ITEMS:	Amount for (____):	PACKING DIRECTIONS:
PB #____		
❏		
❏		
❏		
❏		
❏		
❏		
❏		
Cooler:		
❏		
❏		
❏		
❏		
❏		
❏		
❏		
Freezer:		
❏		
❏		
❏		
❏		
❏		
❏		
❏		
❏		
❏		
❏		

TABLE APPENDIX 23-1: **ADVANCE FOOD PREP ASSIGNMENTS**

Please sign up for items to prepare in advance for the trip meals...we'll provide you with instructions.

PERSON(S):	ITEMS:	Guru check-off & location* column:
	Pre-bake Potatoes & Marinate Steaks for Day 0 (Launch Camp)	
	Bottle up 3 salad dressings for Days 0, 4, and 7	
	Moroccan Chicken, Rice Seasoning Packet, Tabouli Oil for Day 1	
	Chocolate Chip Pan Cookies for Days 2, 4	
	Pemmican for Day 2	
	MRE's for Day 2	
	Salisbury Steaks for Day 3, and **Potatoes, Milk, Gravy Mix** Days 3 and 7	
	Chutney Salad for Day 3	
	Appley Coffee Cake Mix Bags for Nite 3	
	Lasagne Meat Filling for Day 4	
	Cheesecake Packet Assembly for Day 4	
	Monkey Bread Caramel Mix for Day 4	
	Chorizo Meat Mix for Arroz Vasco for Day 5	
	Chocolate Fudge for Day 5	
	Antipasto for Day 6	
	Panne Bread Mix for Day 6	
	Pasta Marinara Meat Sauce for Day 6	
	Tiramisu for Day 6	
	Chocolate Yogurt Cake Mix for Day 7	
	Cut **ten sheets of parchment** for the Dutch	
	Make 12 **team assignment work cards**	Copy if you like. From *River Otter: Handbook for Trip Planning*

*Location where the item will be stored until packing day so it can be easily found (not left in somebody's freezer).

TABLE APPENDIX 23-1: **BLANK SAMPLE TO COPY**

Please sign up for items to prepare in advance for the trip meals.

ADVANCE FOOD PREP ASSIGNMENTS

PERSON(S):	ITEMS:	Guru check-off & location* column:
	Day 1:	
	Day 2:	
	Day 3:	
	Day 4:	
	Day 5:	
	Day 6:	
	Day 7:	
	Day 8:	

*Location where the item will be stored until packing day so it can be easily found (not left in somebody's freezer).

Table App. 2C-1 to 2C-6: Shopping Lists

TABLE APPENDIX 2C-1: **CANS 'N' BOTTLES**

♣ = ADVANCE PREP. ITEM (If the item is prepared in advance, DON'T buy this amount.)

♦ = DEDICATED ITEM (This item or portion of an item is necessary for a recipe. Since it's apt to be used at another time – innocent mistakes happen – label and pack with care.)

X = VARIABLE USE ITEM (some mustard, mayo, cocoa mix, etc., used daily)

1. If your trip number is different than twelve (12), calculate amounts in the last column.

2. Check on all ♣ Advance Prep. items. If some are missing on packing day, you can highlight the ♣ ingredients needed to make them at the last minute.

3. Make a back-up photocopy of this list and use as reference in packing.

4. Highlight all remaining items to be purchased and give the list to the shopper so they can make purchases.

ITEMS:	RIVER DAY								AMOUNTS	
	Day 0	Day 1	Day 2	Day 3	Day 4	Day 5	Day 6	Day 7	Total Amt. for 12	Your Amt. ___#
Cans 'n' Bottles:										
Antipasto (about 1 gallon): ♣							All♣ below		All ♣ below	
Artichoke Hearts, 8 oz. jars♣							2 jars		2 jars	
Pepperonici, 1 pt. jar♣							1 pint		1 pint	
Black Olives, medium, pitted♣							1 can		1 can	
Green Olives, stuffed♣							1 can		1 can	
Pickled Onions, 8 oz.♣							1 jar		1 jar	
Gardiniera (pkld. cauli., carrots, etc.), 12 oz.♣							1 jar		1 jar	
Any other veggies your Italian heart desires ♣							1 jar		1 jar	
Bacon Bits, sm. bottle	1/2				1/2				1 jar	
Beans:										
Garbanzo (15-16 oz.)								1 can	1 can	
Green, cut (15-16 oz.)								1 can	1 can	
Kidney (15-16 oz.)								1 can	1 can	
1 can Beer: (trip decision for more) Pale Ale ♦ Guinness Stout (to freeze) ♦							♦ 3 can ♦12		3 12	
Canned Fish: Clams, smoked Herring, snacks Oysters, smoked	1 2 2							1 2 2	Cans: 2 4 4	

ITEMS:	Day 0	Day 1	Day 2	Day 3	Day 4	Day 5	Day 6	Day 7	Total Amt. for 12	Your Amt. ___#
	RIVER DAY								**AMOUNTS**	
Doodle-berry jams, 6-8 oz.			1		1				2	
Honey, bears, 8 oz.			1				♦ 1		2	
Lemon Juice, plastic lemon		1							1	
Lemon Zest (1 Tbsp.fresh)♣					♣1T.				♣1T.	
Mayo, squeeze-bottles		x	x	x	x	x	x	x	2 pint	
Milk, can sweetened condensed ♣						♣ 2			♣ 2	
Mushrooms, chopped, 8 oz. ♣				♣ 2					♣ 2 cans	
Mustard, Deli, squeeze-bottle		x	x	x	x	x	x	x	1 pint	
Olive Oil, liter (about ¹/₂ for ♣/♦ menu items, remainder for the pantry D.O., frying, etc.)	♣3/4 c.	♦3/4 c.			♣3/4 c.		♣1 c.	♣3/4 c.	♣ 1 liter; Buy 1 Liter	
Olives, Spanish stuffed (Manzanillas) ♣ and BUY 1	1 can					♣1 can			♣1 Buy 1 can	
Peanut Butter: 4 lbs. 1 creamy jar, 1 crunchy jar		x	x	x	x	x	x	x	2 jars	
Pesto, opt. (homemade donor or spring for expensive stuff)					1 pint		1 pint		2 pint opt.	
Pie Filling (thickened), blueberry, lg. can (#2¹/₂)						2 can			2 can	
Pineapple, crushed, lg. can ♣				♣ 1					♣1 can	
Salsa, good stuff, not too hot						1 qt.			1 qt.	
Seven-Up ♦						♦2 ca			2 can	
Tomatoes, crushed, lg. cans (#2¹/₂) ♣					2 can		2 ♣		♣2 ca Buy2	
Tomatoes, dried, optional (homemade are cheap!)					1 cup				1 c. opt.	
Tomato Paste, 8 oz. can ♣							1 ♣		♣1 ca	
Tuna, in water, foil packets								12	12	
Vinegar, balsamic, bottle (abt. ¹/₂ for ♣/♦ menu items, remainder for seasoning)	♣1/4 c.				♣1/4 c.		♣1/2 c.	♣1/4 c.	♣8 oz. Buy 8 oz.	

TABLE APPENDIX 2C-2: **DRY GOODS + BULK BIN STUFF**

♣ = ADVANCE PREP. ITEM (If the item is prepared in advance, DON'T buy this amount.)

♦ = DEDICATED ITEM (This item or portion of an item is necessary for a recipe. Since it's apt to be used at another time – innocent mistakes happen – label and pack with care.)

X = VARIABLE USE ITEM (some mustard, mayo, cocoa mix, etc., used daily)

1. If your trip number is different than twelve (12), calculate amounts in the last column.

2. Check on all ♣ Advance Prep. items. If some are missing on packing day, you can highlight the ♣ ingredients needed to make them at the last minute.

3. Make a back-up photocopy of this list and use as reference in packing.

4. Highlight all remaining items to be purchased and give the list to the shopper so they can make purchases.

ITEMS:	Day 0	Day 1	Day 2	Day 3	Day 4	Day 5	Day 6	Day 7	Total Amt. for 12	Your Amt. ___#
			RIVER DAY						AMOUNTS	
Dry Goods + BulkBinStuff:										
Beans, dried refried mix (svg. size = ½ c. dry = 3 oz.)						6 c.			2.3 lb (6 c.)	
Biscuits, Pilot (bulk bin)								18	18	
Cake Mixes:										
Pound Cake, Betty Crocker♣							♣ 2 box		♣ 2 box	
Cheesecake, Jello No-Bake♣					♣ 2 box				♣ 2 box	
Yellow Cake, Duncan Hines						2 box			Buy 2 box	
Candy:										
Chocolate Bars			12						12	
Halvah, 8 oz. bricks		2							2	
Sesame 'n' honey, wrapped		36							36	
Chocolate Chips ♣			♣ 12oz.			♣ 36oz.		♣ 12 oz.	♣4 lbs.	
Cocoa, unsweetened powder (1 c. = 4 oz.)	X	X	X	X	X	X	X	1⅓ c. ♣	Buy 1.5 lbs 1⅓ c. ♣	
(Note: See Appendix 9 for homemade cocoa recipe)										
Drink Mixes:	X	X	X	X	X	X	X			
Coffee (2 c. strong/pers/day)									4 lbs.	
Coffee, decaf									1 lb.	
Gatorade Powder, Lemon-lime (1 can = 1 lb. 2oz. [32 svgs.])									3 lbs.	
Gatorade Pwd., other flavors									3 lbs.	
Lemonade, instant									2 lbs.	
Orange Breakfast Drink									2 lbs.	
Teas, assorted bags, (¾ herbal)									60	

ITEMS:	RIVER DAY Day 0	Day 1	Day 2	Day 3	Day 4	Day 5	Day 6	Day 7	AMOUNTS Total Amt. for 12	Your Amt. ___#
Dried Fruit (♣ *for Adv. Prep. recipes*):									All ♣	
Apples ♣			♣2 c.						1/2 lb.	
Apricots ♣			♣2 c.						1/2 lb.	
Cherries ♣								♣1 c.	1/4 lb.	
Figs, Black ♣			♣2 c.						1/2 lb.	
Figs, Yellow (Calmyra)♣			♣2 c.						1/2 lb.	
Prunes ♣			♣1 c.						1/4 lb.	
Raisins, Black ♣			♣2 c.	♣3.5	♣2 c.				2.8 lb.	
Raisins, Yellow (Sultanas) ♣		♣2 c.	♣2 c.						1 lb.	
Dried Fruit (*brkfst, lunch, snax*):		x	x	x	x	x	x	x	BUY	
Apples									1 lb.	
Apricots									1 lb.	
Banana Chips									2 lbs.	
Cranberries									1 lb.	
Figs, Black									1 lb.	
Figs, Yellow									1 lb.	
Peaches									1 lb.	
Prunes									1/2 lb.	
Raisins, Black									1 lb.	
Raisins, Yellow									1 lb.	
Flour, Adv. Prep. Recipes ♣ (4 cups = 1 lb.)			♣4.5 c.	♣8 c.				♣4 c.	♣16.5 c. ~4 lb	
Flour, homemade self-rising: ♣									♣	
White Flour ♣ plus							♣6 c.		6 c.	
Baking Powder ♣							♣3 T.		3 T.	
Frosting, instant, fudge								1 can	1 can	
Gravy Mix, 10 packets beef♣				5 pkt ♣			5 pkt ♣		♣10 pkt	
Hummus Mix, lunches			x	x	x	x	x	x	2 lbs.	
Milk, instant Adv.Prep ♣ ~5 cups, about 1 lb. (1 c. dry = 3 oz.) ♣				♣ 2 2/3 c.	♣ 1 2/3 c.			♣ 1 c.	♣ ~1 lb. 5.3 c.	
Milk, instant for Oatmeal and Hot Cocoa (svg. size 1/3 c dry = 1 oz. for 1 cup liquid)		x	x	x	x	x	x	x	4.5 lb. (24 c.)	
M & Ms:		x	x	x	x	x	x	x		
Plain									2 lbs.	
Peanut									2 lbs.	

CONTINUED

DRY GOODS + BULK BIN STUFF (CONTINUED)

	RIVER DAY								AMOUNTS	
ITEMS:	Day 0	Day 1	Day 2	Day 3	Day 4	Day 5	Day 6	Day 7	Total Amt. for 12	Your Amt. ___#
Noodles:										
Lasagne, (20 += 1.5 lb.)					1.5lb				1.5 lb	
Spaghetti or Linguine, 2 lbs.						2 lbs			2 lbs	
Nuts, All ♣:			♣						♣	
Peanuts, roasted, unsalted ♣			6 c.						2 lbs	
Cashews, roasted, unsalted ♣			♣ 2 c.						♣ 1 lb	
Pecans, roasted, chopped♣				♣ 2 c.					♣ 1 lb.	
Walnuts, roasted, chopped ♣			♣ 1 c.	♣ 3/4 c.					♣ 1 lb	
Oatmeal, Regular (svg. size = 1/2 c dry = 2 oz.)	x	x	x	x	x	x	x	x	5 lb. (20c)	
Potatoes, instant flakes (svg. size 1.7 c. dry. = 2 oz.)			2 lbs.				2 lbs.		4 lbs.	
Rice, Basmati (svg. size 1/3 c dry = 2.7 oz.)		4 c.				4 c.			4 lb (8 c.)	
Salt, Kosher, optional ♦							♦1/4 c.		1/4 c.	
Sugars in Adv. Prep: ♣			♣		♣				♣	
Brown (2 1/3 c. = 1 lb.)			2 c.		3 c.				5 c. (2 lb)	
White (2 1/8 c. = 1 lb.)			♣ 1 c.	♣ 4 c.	2/3 c.		♣ 1/2 c.	♣ 3.3 c.	9.5 c. (4.5)	
Powdered (4 c. = 1 lb.)			♣ 2 c.				♣ 1 c.		3 c. (.75)	
Sugar for oatmeal, coffee:									BUY	
Brown		x	x	x	x	x	x	x	2 lbs.	
White		x	x	x	x	x	x	x	2 lbs.	
Tabouli Mix, w/spices included		4 c.							4 c.	
Trail Mixes (Gorp), 4 kinds	x	x	x	x	x	x	x	x	8 lbs.	

TABLE APPENDIX 2C-3: **BREAD + SWEET STUFF**

♣ = ADVANCE PREP. ITEM (If the item is prepared in advance, DON'T buy this amount.)

♦ = DEDICATED ITEM (This item or portion of an item is necessary for a recipe. Since it's apt to be used at another time – innocent mistakes happen – label and pack with care.)

X = VARIABLE USE ITEM (some mustard, mayo, cocoa mix, etc., used daily)

1. If your trip number is different than twelve (12), calculate amounts in the last column.

2. Check on all ♣ Advance Prep. items. If some are missing on packing day, you can highlight the ♣ ingredients needed to make them at the last minute.

3. Make a back-up photocopy of this list and use as reference in packing.

4. Highlight all remaining items to be purchased and give the list to the shopper so they can make purchases.

ITEMS:	RIVER DAY								AMOUNTS	
	Day 0	Day 1	Day 2	Day 3	Day 4	Day 5	Day 6	Day 7	Total Amt. for 12	Your Amt. ___#
Bread + Sweet Stuff:										
Bagels: Breakfast (plain, raisin) Lunch (garlic, mixed types)			18 B 12 L		12L		12L		18 36L	
Cliff Bars (2 per person)									24	
Cookies, Oreo, large box		1							1	
Crackers, WheatThins/ Other for snacks		x	x	x	x	x	x		3 box	
Croissant Dough, frozen bags of 2 doz. small ones *OR* Crescent Rolls Dough (8 large ones per can)					2 bag OR 4 can				2 bag OR 4 can	
English Muffins (some lunch)					12 B	12 L			24	
Fruitcake (homemade best)				1					1	
Muffins, large breakfast ones		12B							12	
Pies, Big 'n' Luscious	2								2	
Pita Breads: (mostly lunch) White Whole Wheat		10D 10D	10 10	10 10		10 10			40 40	
Potato/Corn Chips, Sacks	2								2	
Potato Chips, Pringles cans		x	x	x	x	x	x	x	7 can	
Power Bars (4/person)		x	x	x	x	x	x	x	48	
Tortillas: (mostly lunch) Flour, 12" Whole Wheat, 8"		10 10				30D 10D	10	10 10	50 40	

TABLE APPENDIX 2C-4: **VEGGIES + FRUIT**

♣ = ADVANCE PREP. ITEM (If the item is prepared in advance, DON'T buy this amount.)

♦ = DEDICATED ITEM (This item or portion of an item is necessary for a recipe. Since it's apt to be used at another time – innocent mistakes happen – label and pack with care.)

X = VARIABLE USE ITEM (some mustard, mayo, cocoa mix, etc., used daily)

1. If your trip number is different than twelve (12), calculate amounts in the last column.
2. Check on all ♣ Advance Prep. items. If some are missing on packing day, you can highlight the ♣ ingredients needed to make them at the last minute.
3. Make a back-up photocopy of this list and use as reference in packing.
4. Highlight all remaining items to be purchased and give the list to the shopper so they can make purchases.

ITEMS:	RIVER DAY								AMOUNTS	
	Day 0	Day 1	Day 2	Day 3	Day 4	Day 5	Day 6	Day 7	Total Amt. for 12	Your Amt. ___#
Veggies + Fruits:										
Apple, Green (Coffeecake)			♦1						♦1	
Cabbage, Green				1					1	
Carrots, Baby, 2 lb. sacks		1	1			1			3	
Carrots, Large for ♣ Salad				♣12					♣12	
Cucumbers (♦tabouli, and lunches)		♦2	2						4	
Garlic Cloves, fresh ♣					♣4	♣8	♣4		♣16 clove	
Lettuce, equiv. 2 heads	2 hd.								2 hd.	
Melons: Cantaloupe Seedless Watermelon	1	2							2 1	
Onions, Green bunches for ♦tabouli		♦2							2	
Onions, Red for salad and lunches	1	1			1			1	4	
Onions, White or Yellow ♣ (♦1 is dedicated for burritos condiments – buy)				♣1	♣2	♣2 ♦1	♣3		♣8 BUY 1	
Peas, frozen 2 lb. sack				2 lbs.					2 lb.	
Peppers, Anaheim ♣						♣4			♣4	
Peppers, Green for lunches		2	2						4	
Peppers, Red for lunches		1	2	1					4	
Potatoes, Bakers	12								12	
Radicchio				1					1	

ITEMS:	RIVER DAY								AMOUNTS	
	Day 0	Day 1	Day 2	Day 3	Day 4	Day 5	Day 6	Day 7	Total Amt. for 12	Your Amt. ___#
Spinach, frozen, box					2				2	
Spinach, fresh lg. sack for lunches		1							1	
Tomatoes, Cherry, pt. basket	2	1							3	
Tomatoes, lunch slicers		3							3	

TABLE APPENDIX 2C-5: **DAIRY + MEAT CASE**

[Note: consider avoiding pre-sliced meats and cheeses –
they go bad quickly and are much more expensive.]

♣ = ADVANCE PREP. ITEM (If the item is prepared in advance, DON'T buy this amount.)

♦ = DEDICATED ITEM (This item or portion of an item is necessary for a recipe. Since it's apt to be used at another time – innocent mistakes happen – label and pack with care.)

X = VARIABLE USE ITEM (some mustard, mayo, cocoa mix, etc., used daily)

1. If your trip number is different than twelve (12), calculate amounts in the last column.

2. Check on all ♣ Advance Prep. items. If some are missing on packing day, you can highlight the ♣ ingredients needed to make them at the last minute.

3. Make a back-up photocopy of this list and use as reference in packing.

4. Highlight all remaining items to be purchased and give the list to the shopper so they can make purchases.

| ITEMS: | RIVER DAY | | | | | | | | AMOUNTS | |
	Day 0	Day 1	Day 2	Day 3	Day 4	Day 5	Day 6	Day 7	Total Amt. for 12	Your Amt. ___#
Dairy + Meat Case:										
Butter, sticks (1/2 c. = 1/4 lb.) for Adv. Prep. recipes ♣			♣4	♣4	♣2, ♣2			♣1	3 1/4 ♣lbs.	
Butter, sticks (1/2 c.ea): some dedicated for recipes, extra for potatoes, muffins	2			♦2		♦1	♦3	♦2	BUY 2 1/2 lbs.	
Canadian Bacon, 2 lbs.						2 lbs.			2 lbs.	
Cheese: (mostly lunches)										
Cheddar, 2 lb. bricks			2 lb.			♦2 lb.			4 lbs.	
Mascarpone, 8 oz. ♣							♣8 oz		♣8 oz.	
Monterey Jack, 2 lb. bricks		2 lb.			2 lb.				4 lbs.	
Mozzarella, 2 lb. bricks					♦2 lb.		2 lb.		4 lbs.	
Parmesan, grated (good stuff)					1.5 c.		2 c.		3.5 c.	
Ricotta, 1 qt.					1 qt.				1 qt.	
Other Cheeses: Pepper, etc.					1 lb.		2 lb.		3 lbs.	
Chorizo, Dry, 1 lb. "Amaias" ♦Dedicated to Breakfast extra for lunch thereafter					♦2 lb.				2 lb.	
Cream Cheese, breakfasts + lunches, 8 oz. containers ♦2			♦2		♦2				2 lbs.	
Eggs, fresh for scrambling						22			22	
Eggs, in Adv. Prep.♣ recipes Salisbury steaks and Pan Cookies			♣4	♣4					♣8	

ITEMS:	Day 0	Day 1	Day 2	Day 3	Day 4	Day 5	Day 6	Day 7	Total Amt. for 12	Your Amt. ___#
Eggs, frozen in packets for ♣ In-Camp use			♣4 froz				♣6 froz		♣10	
Guacamole Dip (good kind w/Avocado as #1 ingredient)	1 pt.				2 pts.				3 pts.	
Hams:										
Black Forest, 4 lb whole			4 lbs.						4 lbs.	
Sugar-cured, circular-sliced								8 lbs.	8 lbs.	
Turkey, 2 lb. unsliced						2 lbs.			2 lbs.	
Kielbasa Sausages (brkfsts)		5			4			4	13	
Major Meats: All Adv. Prep♣									All ♣	
London Broil Steak	♣6 lb								6 lbs.	
ChickenBreasts, no bone/skin		♣12							12	
Ground Beef				♣ 6 lb	♣2 lb	♣	♣3 lb.		11 lb.	
Cacique Chorizo, 12 oz. pkgs						3 pks			3 pks	
Chorizo Sausage, uncooked						♣6			6	
Salami, dry (Gallo, 1 lb. not pre-sliced.)			1	3		1			5	
Sausages, link, frozen, pre-cooked							36		36	
Sour Cream, pints (label) ♣ Adv. Prep recipe ♦ Dedicated for in-camp use	♦1				♦1	♦2	♣2	♦1	♣2 pt BUY 5 pt.	
Summer Sausages, whole for breakfasts and lunches			♦2			♦2			4	
Turkey Breast, whole (unsliced), pre-cooked, smoked		4 lbs							4 lbs	
Yogurt, plain (Nancy's Lo-fat, 2 lb. container for breakfasts)									2 lbs.	

TABLE APPENDIX 2C-6: **BLANK SAMPLE SHOPPING LIST TO COPY**

♣ = Advance Prep.	RIVER DAY								AMTS.
ITEMS:	Day 0	Day 1	Day 2	Day 3	Day 4	Day 5	Day 6	Day 7	Total Amt.

APPENDIX 2D

Table App. 2D-1 to 2D-4:
Cooler Packing Lists

What exotic river calls your name, tempting you to plan another trip?

Photo: Keith Taylor

TABLE APPENDIX 2D-1: **LAUNCH CAMP COOLERS**

Launch Camp Cooler #1 (when empty, fill w/trash, open vent, leave in shuttle vehicle)

Check-off:	Item:	Amount for 12:	Amount for ___#
	Chips 'n' dip (guacamole)	2 sacks 'n' 1 pint	
	Spanish Olives	1 can	
	Steaks London Broil ♣	6 lbs.	
	Potatoes – Bakers ♣	12	
	Butter for Spuds	2 cubes ($1/2$ lb.)	
	Sour Cream for Spuds	1 pint	
	Bacon Bits for Spuds	$1/2$ jar	
	Garden Salad ♣	2 heads lettuce equiv.	
	Tomatoes, Cherry	2 baskets	
	Other salad veggies	Broccoli, red onion	
	Salad Dressing ♣	Homemade, 1 cup	
	Pies	2 large bakery pies	
	Kielbasa Sausages for Breakfast	5	

*Don't forget the Watermelon, Beverages, Canned Fish 'n' Crackers, Breakfast Muffins 'n Melons!

Launch Camp Cooler #2 (use for overflow from Cooler #1 and label "**Lunch Cooler**" from now on)

Check-off:	Item:	Amount for 12:	Amount for ___#
	Breakfasts: Butter	2 sticks	
	Breakfast Cream Cheese	2 - 8 oz. containers	
	Bagels	18, frozen	
	Summer Sausage (Day 2)	2	
	Chorizo"Amaia"Sausage (Day 3)	2	
	Lunch Day 1: Tortillas	20	
	Monterey Jack Cheese	2 lbs.	
	Turkey Breast	1 - 4 lb.	
	Mayo + Mustard	1 bottle each	
	Carrot babies, Spinach + Peppers	2 lbs. /Lg. sack /4 peps.	
	Tomatoes, slicing	3	
	Dinner Nite 1: Chicken Breasts	12, frozen, cut-up	
	Pita Breads	4 pkgs. of 5 each	
	Cucumbers	4 large (extra for lunch)	
	Green Onions	2 bunches	
	Cherry Tomatoes	1 pint box	
	Peppers	2 red, 2 green (snacking)	
	Lunch Day 2 and 3: Bagels	12	
	Cheddar Cheese	2 lbs.	
	BlackForest Ham + Gallo Salami	4 lb. ham/1 lb. salami	
	Pita Breads	8 pkgs. of 5 each	
	Dinner Nite 2: Carrots, baby	2 lbs.	

TABLE APPENDIX 2D-2: **THE MAIN TRIP COOLER (FLOWN INTO RE-SUPPLY POINT, DAY 3. CONTAINS DAYS 3-5)**

"The Cooler" (Remember: Pack items in reverse order. "Day 5 is First in = Last out!")

Check-off:	Item:	Amount for 12:	Amt. for __#
	Day 3 Dinner:		
	Salisbury Steaks	24	
	Butter for Potatoes	2 sticks	
	Peas	2 lbs., frozen, 1-gal.sack	
	Chutney Salad	1 sack, frozen	
	Eggs for CoffeeCake (Day 4 am)	4 beaten, frozen in pkt.	
	Day 4 Breakfast:		
	English Muffins (leftovers for L)	24	
	Kielbasa Sausages	4	
	Day 4 Lunch:		
	Monterey Jack	2 lbs.	
	Other Cheese	1 lb.	
	Salami	3	
	Bagels	12	
	Pancookies (2nd installment)	12 squares	
	Cream Cheese	2 - 8 oz. containers	
	Day 4 Dinner:		
	Ground Beef	2 gallon sacks	
	Pesto, optional	1 pint	
	Spinach	2 boxes, frozen	
	Ricotta Cheese	1 quart (2 pts.)	
	Mozzarella Cheese	2 lbs. (labeled Lasagne)	
	Parmesan Cheese	1 1/2 cups	
	Cabbage (wrap to avoid iceburn)	1 head	
	Radicchio (wrap to avoid iceburn)	1 head	
	Sour Cream	1 pint	
	Croissant Dough OR Crescent Roll Dough for Day 5 Breakfast	2 pkgs., freeze, then allow to thaw OR 4 cans, same treatment	
	Day 5 Breakfast:		
	Canadian Bacon	2 lbs.	
	Eggs, scrambled, frozen	22 in freezer sack	
	Day 5 Lunch:		
	Pitas	20	
	Summer Sausages	2	
	Turkey Ham	1	
	Carrots, baby	3rd sack (if needed)	
	Day 5 Dinner: (more in Freezer)		
	Guacamole	2 pints	
	Cheddar Cheese	2 lbs. (labeled Burritos)	
	Sour Cream	2 pints	

TABLE APPENDIX 2D-3: **THE TRIP FREEZER** (FLOWN INTO RE-SUPPLY POINT, DAY 3. CONTAINS DAYS 5-7)

"The Freezer" (Remember: Pack items in reverse order. "Day 7 is First in = Last out!")

Check-off:	Item:	Amount for 12:	Amt. for __#
	Day 5 Dinner:		
	Chorizo Meat for *Arroz Vasco*	2 pkgs.	
	Mexican Fudge	2 qt. sacks	
	Tortillas	40	
	Butter for D.O.	1 stick ($1/2$ c.)	
	Day 6 Breakfast:		
	Sausages, link	36	
	Day 6 Lunch:		
	Mozzarella Cheese	2 lbs.	
	Other Cheese	2 lbs.	
	Tortillas	10	
	Bagels, whole wheat	12	
	Day 6 Dinner:		
	Pasta Meat Sauce	3 sacks	
	Parmigiano Pkt	2 c. pkt	
	Pesto, optional	1 pint	
	Tiramisu	Gallon baggies	
	Butter	3 cubes	
	Day 7 Breakfast:		
	Kielbasa Sausages	4	
	Day 7 Lunch:		
	Tortillas for Tuna Wraps	20	
	Day 7 Dinner:		
	Ham	1 big, heavenly type	
	Butter for potatoes	2 cubes	
	Dessert Pkt. 2 (6 Eggs)	6 in frozen pkt. (cake)	
	Sour Cream	1 pint (for cake)	
	Frozen Cans Guiness Stout	12	

TABLE APPENDIX 2D-4:
BLANK SAMPLE COOLER PACKING LIST TO COPY

Cooler Name _____

Check-off:	Item:	Amount:

River Food Management: Principles and Methods

Whitewater boaters I know are a thrifty bunch when it comes to buying food. They also hate carrying extra pounds in their craft (especially true for self-contained kayak trips). Heavy, hard-to-maneuver craft can make the mildest-mannered boater cranky. If you've been in low water and watched a friend "Flintstoning" a cataraft through rock gardens, you'll know what I mean. And, no one can surf worth beans in a heavy boat.

So, how can you plan the right amount of food to fuel hungry boaters without unnecessary weight or waste to pack out?

BEGIN BY THINKING ABOUT FOOD SAFETY.

I have a bias toward food that can be prepared easily, and often in advance. Remember the rule "Keep Hot Foods Hot and Cold Foods Cold." It's a good motto for your kitchen crews, but often difficult to follow on a summer river trip and in a river camp.

Sheila Mills relates in *Rocky Mountain Kettle Cuisine* that J.T. Brock studied cooler temperatures in July on the Middle Fork. On the fourth day the inside of the cooler bottom was 34° and yet the top approached 70°! Food safety experts with the Department of Agriculture recommend two to three hours is the maximum time food should remain at 60°-125°. For that reason, my preference is against bringing thawed, uncooked fish and poultry, or egg items like homemade mayo or potato salad. Preventing food infections (*Salmonella*) and food toxins (*Staphylococcus* or *Clostridium*) is way easier than treating boaters with vomiting and diarrhea caused by poor camp cooking technique.

NEXT, FIND AND ADJUST FAVORITE CAMP RECIPES.

Be sure to discuss food preferences and ask for recipes at your trip meetings. Everyone has a beloved recipe or snack, yet adjusting for changing group sizes may stymie even the most experienced cook. Don't lose patience when someone's favorite calls for a pound of ham and you wonder if that's enough meat in the scalloped potato recipe for eight. Figuring out weights in terms of cups helps assure the amount in each serving. For large trips, you need to quickly estimate food pounds/volume, size of cooking/serving containers required, and the number of rafts necessary to carry the weight. How?

One alternative to enlarging or decreasing recipes is to guess on quantities and cross your fingers. We've all been there – too much salt in the biscuits, not enough cornstarch in the gravy, etc – and food gets tossed out in the garbage. There must be a better way, I thought.

I went to the U.S. Department of Ag's Human Nutrition Information Service. They recommend calculating *an adjusting factor* for each ingredient (take the number of servings needed in the new recipe and divide that by the old recipe number of servings, producing a factor you can use to multiply all quantities). Example: you have a church recipe for coffeecake for four dozen people and want to decrease it for your river trip of 18.

$$18/48 = .375 \text{ (factor)}$$

The math gets interesting as you then try to multiply $1\frac{2}{3}$ cups, $2\frac{1}{4}$ teaspoons, or other fractional quantities by the decimal fraction factor. Or, consider the reverse case, your mom's three-bean salad for six that needs to be increased for your trip of fifteen boaters.

$$16/6 = 2.67 \text{ (factor)}$$

Yes, it works, but would be much easier if American cooking practice worked on the metric system. We're stuck with teaspoons, tablespoons, cups, pints, quarts, ounces and pounds and the headache of trying to remember "three teaspoons in a tablespoon…two cups to a pint, etc."

Wouldn't it be easier to look it up on a table? I asked years ago and began making up tables. Soon I had one for lasagna for 8, 12, and 16 and another for my grandmother's coffeecake. Our group size varied from 9 to 18 and finally 23. I was tired of recopying and checked the Net. *Bingo!* There actually are services (especially for the Grand Canyon boaters) that will take one of your daily menus and for a fee, turn it into shopping, packing and meal prep details, then put it all together for you. Some even sell software packages that could blow the entire budget of a modest private trip. Our gang's pretty penny-pinching, so I went back to making conversion tables like Table App. 3-1:

TABLE APPENDIX 3-1:
CONVERSION EXAMPLE USING DEHYDRATED REFRIED BEANS

# Pers.	2	4	6	8	10	12	14	16	18	20	22	24
Beans	$1\frac{1}{2}$ c	3 c	$4\frac{1}{2}$ c	6 c	$7\frac{1}{2}$ c	9 c	$10\frac{1}{2}$ c	12 c	$13\frac{1}{2}$ c	15 c	$16\frac{1}{2}$ c	18 c
Water	2 c	4 c	6 c	8 c	10 c	12 c	14 c	16 c	18 c	20 c	22 c	24 c

Cute as these tables are, no one in their right mind wants to make them for every new recipe. So I hit the old-fashioned public library. In Treat and Richards' Quantity Cooking, first published in 1922 and now out-of-print, there was a partial "enlarging table" that fascinated me. Adapting their information and adding my own, I put together my solutions for river meal planners: the **River Trip Table of Quantities and Measures** and the **Recipe-Adjusting Table**. These two helpful tables (Appendix 4 and 5, respectively) will give you courage to forge ahead and modify any recipe. You'll be a happy camper, quickly converting quantities to fit your trip size. Try using them for your own recipes or in conjunction with the recipes described in the "Meal Planning Guru" section.

APPENDIX FOUR

River Trip Food
Quantities and Measures

TABLE APPENDIX 4-1: **TABLE OF FOOD QUANTITIES AND MEASURES**

(# = pound = 16 oz.)

Apples, dried $^{1}/_{2}$ #	= 2 cups (a handful is ~ $^{3}/_{4}$ c. and weighs ~ 2 oz.)
Butter 1#	= 2 cups (stick is $^{1}/_{4}$ # = $^{1}/_{2}$ cup)
Bacon 1#	= 20-28 slices
Cabbage 1 head (5$^{1}/_{2}$ inch diameter)	= 5$^{1}/_{2}$ cups shredded, 4$^{1}/_{2}$ cups chopped
Carrots 1#	= 3$^{1}/_{2}$ chopped
Cocoa Powder, unsweetened 1#	= 4 cups
Coffee 1#	= 5 cups (makes 2 gallons; 48 servings of $^{2}/_{3}$ cup each; 24 servings 1$^{1}/_{3}$ c.)
Eggs 1 dozen	= 24 oz. (12 large eggs = 3 cups)
Flour 1 #	= 4 cups
Ham 1#	= 4 cups
Lettuce 1#	= 1$^{1}/_{2}$ quarts
Milk 1# instant skim powder	= 6$^{2}/_{3}$ cups powder (makes 5 quarts liquid)
2.4 - 3 oz. dry milk powder	= 1 cup
$^{1}/_{3}$ cup dry milk + $^{7}/_{8}$ cup water to make a cup of liquid milk	
Oatmeal 1#	= 5 c. dry = 2$^{1}/_{3}$ qts. cooked = 8$^{1}/_{3}$ cups
Oil 1#	= 2$^{1}/_{5}$ cups
Pasta 1#	= 5 cups dry (1# when cooked = 3# 11oz. = 2$^{5}/_{8}$ quarts = 8$^{5}/_{8}$ cups)
	(1 # spaghetti = 8 servings = 10 cups cooked in 5 qt. water and 1 Tbsp. salt)
Peanut Butter	= 1$^{2}/_{3}$ cups (about 13 servings of 2 tablespoons each)
Peas 1# frozen	= 2$^{7}/_{8}$ cups
Potatoes 1# fresh	= 3 cups cooked or uncooked
Potatoes 1# instant	= 16 cups mashed/cooked
Raisins 1#	= 3 cups
Rice 1#	= 2$^{1}/_{8}$ cups dry (1# when cooked = 3# 6 oz. = 2 quarts = 8 cups)
Sugar 1# white	= 2$^{1}/_{8}$ cups (a 5 # bag = 10$^{5}/_{8}$ cups)
Sugar 1# brown	= 2$^{3}/_{4}$ cups
Tuna 1#	= 2 cups
Water, Milk, Juice, etc. 1#	= 2 cups (1 pint.) [So a gallon weighs 8 pounds!]

An 8 oz. can of tomatoes, fruit, etc. = 1 cup
A No. 2 can (20 oz. tomatoes, fruit, etc.) = 2$^{1}/_{2}$ cups
A No. 2$^{1}/_{2}$ can (28 oz.) = 3$^{1}/_{2}$ cups

Why Use the Table of Quantities and Measures?

Spend a moment with Table App. 4-1 and notice the added weight of pre-cooked (water-laden) foods. Two cups of cooked rice, for example, weighs about a pound and will only feed two people. However, a pound of dry rice will feed eight. What about pre-cooking your pasta? This is extreme, but if you have 24 pasta-for-every-dinner boaters on a seven-night trip, you'll need about 21 pounds of dry pasta. If these pasta-lovers want their pasta pre-cooked, this means you'll carry along 56.4 unnecessary pounds of water weight (7 gallons!) and needless bulk in your cooler.

APPENDIX FIVE

Recipe-Adjusting Table

Try Table App. 5-1 out on your favorite recipe. Say you normally make it for six people, but you want sixteen. Simply look up the quantities of each item in the recipe under the "6" column [e.g., 2¼ teaspoons] and follow the row for each quantity to the "16" column. There are your conversion amounts carefully translated into the proper amount (e.g., 2 tablespoons, not 6 teaspoons, which would need an additional calculation!).

For vegetarians, simply substitute an equal quantity of soy chicken/beef burger or tofu for meat items in the sample menus. For metric cooks, just make the conversions using Table App. 6-1 in the next appendix.

TABLE APPENDIX 5-1: RECIPE ADJUSTING TABLE

SERVINGS

1	2	3	4	6	8	10	12	14	16	18	20	22	24
pinch	1/8 t	1/5 t	1/4 t	3/8 t	1/2 t	5/8 t	3/4 t	7/8 t	1 t	1 1/8 t	1 1/4 t	1 3/8 t	1 1/2 t
1/8 t	1/4 t	3/8 t	1/2 t	3/4 t	1 t	1 1/4 t	1 1/2 t	1 3/4 t	2 t	2 1/4 t	2 1/2 t	2 3/4 t	1 T
1/4 t	1/2 t	3/4 t	1 t	1 1/2 t	2 t	2 1/2 t	1 T	1 T, 1/2 t	1 T, 1 t	1 1/2 T	1 T, 2 t	1 T, 2 1/2 t	2 T
3/8 t	3/4 t	1 1/8 t	1 1/2 t	2 1/4 t	1 T	1 T, 3/4 t	1 1/2 T	1 T, 2 1/4 t	2 T	2 T, 3/4 t	2 1/2 T	2 T, 2 1/4 t	3 T
1/2 t	1 t	1 1/2 t	2 t	1 T	1 T, 1 t	1 T, 2 t	2 T	2 T, 1 t	2 T, 2 t	3 T	3 T, 1 t	3 T, 2 t	1/4 C
3/4 t	1 1/2 t	2 1/4 t	1 T	1 1/2 T	2 T	2 1/2 T	3 T	3 1/2 T	1/4 C	1/4 C, 1/2 T	1/4 C, 1 T	1/4 C, 1 1/2 T	3/8 C
1 t	2 t	1 T	1 T, 1 t	2 T	2 T, 2 t	3 T, 1 t	1/4 C	1/4 C, 2 t	1/4 C, 1 T, 1 t	3/8 C	3/8 C, 2 t	3/8 C, 1 T, 1 t	1/2 C
1/2 T	1 T	1 1/2 T	2 T	3 T	1/4 C	1/4 C, 1 T	3/8 C	3/8 C, 1 T	1/2 C	1/2 C, 1 T	5/8 C	5/8 C, 1 T	3/4 C
1 T	2 T	3 T	1/4 C	3/8 C	1/2 C	5/8 C	3/4 C	7/8 C	1 C	1 1/8 C	1 1/4 C	1 3/8 C	1 1/2 C
1 1/2 T	3 T	1/4 C, 1/2 T	3/8 C	1/2 C, 1 T	3/4 C	7/8 C, 1 T	1 1/8 C	1 1/4 C, 1 T	1 1/2 C	1 5/8 C, 1 T	1 7/8 C	2 C, 1 T	2 1/4 C
1/8 C	1/4 C	3/8 C	1/2 C	3/4 C	1 C	1 1/4 C	1 1/2 C	1 3/4 C	2 C	2 1/4 C	2 1/2 C	2 3/4 C	3 C
1/6 C	1/3 C	1/2 C	2/3 C	1 C	1 1/3 C	1 2/3 C	2 C	2 1/3 C	2 2/3 C	3 C	3 1/3 C	3 2/3 C	4 C
1/4 C	1/2 C	3/4 C	1 C	1 1/2 C	2 C	2 1/2 C	3 C	3 1/2 C	4 C	4 1/2 C	5 C	5 1/2 C	6 C
1/3 C	2/3 C	1 C	1 1/3 C	2 C	2 2/3 C	3 1/3 C	4 C	4 2/3 C	5 1/3 C	6 C	6 2/3 C	7 1/3 C	8 C
3/8 C	3/4 C	1 1/8 C	1 1/2 C	2 1/4 C	3 C	3 3/4 C	4 1/2 C	5 1/4 C	6 C	6 3/4 C	7 1/2 C	8 1/4 C	9 C
1/2 C	1 C	1 1/2 C	2 C	3 C	4 C	5 C	6 C	7 C	8 C	9 C	10 C	11 C	12 C
3/4 C	1 1/2 C	2 1/4 C	3 C	4 1/2 C	6 C	7 1/2 C	9 C	10 1/2 C	12 C	13 1/2 C	15 C	16 1/2 C	18 C
1 C	2 C (1 pt.)	3 C	4 C (1 qt.)	6 C	8 C (2 qts.)	10 C	12 C (3 qts.)	14 C	16 C (1 gal.)	18 C	20 C (1 gal., 1 qt.)	22 C	24 C (1 gal., 2 qt.)

APPENDIX SIX

Metric Conversions

TABLE APPENDIX 6-1: **METRIC CONVERSIONS**

1 inch (in.)			= 2.54 centimeters (cm)
1 ounce (oz.)			= 28.35 grams (g)
16 ounces	= 1 pound (lb.)		= 453.6 grams (g)
2.2 pounds (lbs.)			= 1 kilogram (kg)
1 teaspoon (t. or tsp.)	= 1/6 fluid oz.		= 5 milliliters (ml)
1 tablespoon (T. or Tbsp.)	= 3 teaspoons		= 15 milliliters (ml)
1 fluid ounce (fl. oz.)	= 6 teaspoons	= 1/8 cup	= 30 milliliters (ml)
1 cup (c.)	= 16 tablespoons	= 8 fluid oz.	= 237 milliliters (ml)
1 pint (pt.)	= 2 cups =	16 fluid oz.	= 0.5 liter (L)
1 quart (qt.)	= 2 pints =	32 fluid oz.	= 0.9 liter (L)
1 gallon (gal.)	= 4 quarts =	64 fluid oz.	= 3.8 liter (L)

NOTE: Camp cooking is fun, not pharmacology, so round your measurements and use these conventions for converting to and from metric.

APPENDIX SEVEN

Hints for the Meal Planning Guru

Hints for the Meal Planning Guru :

- Discard as much packing material/cardboard as possible before placing food items in the buckets (e.g., tear off the recipe on the cake box, tape it to the plastic sack, and pitch the cardboard). Yes, you can burn trash in your firepan, but why make polluting smoke and excess ash?
- To cut down on camp clean-up, pre-measure and pre-mix certain items, bagging in zipper plastic bag, and labeling them appropriately (e.g., for a cake: pre-mix flour, sugar, leavening, salt; for a stir-fry dish, pre-mix spices, soy sauce, and cornstarch).
- Use dried milk, dried fruits, dehydrated vegetables, and other weight-saving items (try to find substitutions that can have water added later, like tomato paste instead of sauce).
- Butter for cooking doesn't need to be refrigerated and travels well in zipper bags right along with pre-measured flour and sugar, or the package of cake mix for your "dump cake."
- Use items with short lives early in the trip (tomatoes, cucumbers, lettuce, broccoli, etc.).
- Avoid fish with shells, skin and bones if you want to cut down on weight and garbage odors (many trips put garbage into plastic bags and store in an empty cooler – but the smells always escape on a hot day).
- For eggs needed for late in the trip, break and freeze them in plastic, store in your frozen cooler.
- Bread items like English muffins, tortillas, pita breads, and bagels travel much better than loaves of pre-sliced bread.
- The coldest part of a cooler is the bottom – on a sunny day the top layer may not be cool enough to preserve your food.
- Leave frozen foods for late in the trip in a taped "freezer" cooler because every time a cooler is opened it heats up.
- Supply each trip member with an emergency day ration packet (energy bar, jerky, etc.) so they won't rifle through packed rafts between lunch and dinner.
- Encourage all trip members to watch out for hydration and electrolyte imbalance by setting out dry mixes of Gatorade® in the morning and at lunch for personal water bottle refreshment.
- Many boaters enjoy extra calories and fat to hold them until lunch, so set out peanut butter or summer sausage along with cereals for breakfast.
- Remember that commercial mayonnaise actually keeps well because of its additives and preservatives (homemade, not so). Keep in cooler though!
- Pre-sliced cheeses and meats are not only more expensive, but have greater surface area for contamination.
- Whenever possible consider pre-cooking hamburger or chicken, bagging, and freezing (the clean-up crew will love you for cutting down on the grease in dishwater).
- And smile....

APPENDIX EIGHT
Details on Fuel Estimates

CHARCOAL BRIQUETS: Twenty pounds of regular Kingsford brand charcoal briquets fit nicely in one 5-gallon bucket with space for a small can of lighter fluid. This gives you approximately 334 briquets (I counted them) – enough for ten Dutch uses of 32 briquets each.

Use a "chimney" made from an old coffee can to start charcoal: cut the ends out of a 4 lb. can and make vents by using a church-key can opener to cut little triangles all around the bottom rim. Bring a few extra pounds to make up for breakage or windy weather or a spontaneous barbecue breakfast.

Of course, you can use "Match Light" briquets for easy starting. The bags are eight pounds and the cost per briquet is almost double regular charcoal.

Photo: Todd Swanson

Double-stacking 12" and 16" Dutch ovens on a fireproof blanket. Note long-handled fire tongs and use of aluminum foil wrapping over menu items on the grill to preserve heat.

Not worth the vapor smells in my opinion, when compared to a chimney and a cheap bottle of lighter fluid, especially considering wastage and dust, which seem to be proportionately more with the Match Light variety. Plus, if you ever have a flip and a bucket of these breaks open in the river, creating a smell like the wreck of an oil tanker, you'll never forget it.

Apply "2/3 rule" with charcoal Dutch oven cooking. Cook for two-thirds of the recommended time; remove Dutch from bottom coals; put those on top for the last third of the cooking time. Always sniff for doneness and burning, especially with baked goods.

The International Dutch Oven Society (yes, there really is such a group!) suggests a general rule for determining number of briquets needed: first, put briquets on the top and bottom equal to the inches in the diameter, then move two or three from the bottom to the top (move even more when baking, less when stewing or boiling). Aluminum is lighter than cast iron, but cools quicker and develops hot spots. To remedy this make a windbreak and don't forget to rotate the oven a quarter turn one way and the lid a quarter turn the other way every ten minutes.

Hints on hotness: if you can hold your hand at cooking level over the briquets for 2 sec., they're hot, 3 sec. medium hot, 4 sec. medium, and 5 sec. low heat. Also put a tsp. of flour on a small square of aluminum foil in the heating oven with lid on: if flour turns dark brown in 3 minutes, your oven's too hot for cooking; if it turns light brown in 5 minutes, you have approx. 350° in the oven and are set to go (dark brown is 450° and no color is 300° or less). One extra briquet top and bottom adds 25° inside. A 16" Dutch is equivalent to two 12" ovens in total capacity, but servings and briquets vary as shown in Table App. 8-1.

PROPANE: Propane is the fuel of choice for most river runners because it is clean burning, easy to use, and safe when handled appropriately. Refillable tanks (4 - 40 lb. size) have been required since a 1998 law to be equipped with an Overflow Prevention Device (OPD) for added safety. Table App. 8-2 shows amounts needed based on *minimal* use – calculate propane accordingly.

Remember an old-timer's trick for monitoring the level of propane in your tank: look for the dew-line every morning. If the climate is neither extremely dry nor wet and your tank is upright, condensate will appear on the lower portion of the tank holding the liquid propane.

Some commercial trips use a device called "The Blaster," which sells for under $200 and can bring 5 gallons of water to a boil in minutes (ref. Clavey River Equipment [info@clavey.com]). However, when a commercial trip guide demonstrated it for me on the river, it sounded like a hot air balloon just lit down in camp. Loud. He also reported it sucked propane like lemonade on a hot day, so it didn't seem economically profitable for a private trip.

TABLE APPENDIX 8-1: **ABOUT CHARCOAL BRIQUETS**

Ovens:	12" Dutch Oven	14" Dutch Oven	16" Dutch Oven
Capacity	6qts. *(4" sides)*	8qts. *(4.75" sides)*	12qts. *(4.5" sides)*
Main Dish Serving OR Side Dish Serving	6-18 OR 20 (20 cups) *(+1qt. headroom)*	8-25 OR 28 (28 cups) *(+1qt. headroom)*	12-38 OR 36 (36 cups) *(+2 qt. headroom)*

Briquet Use:

# Briquets on Top	14-15	16-17	18-19
# Briquets Bottom	10-9	12-11	14-13
Total briquets (lbs.)	24 *(24 oz. = 1.5 lbs.)*	28 *(28 oz. = 1.75 lbs.)*	32 *(32 oz. = 2 lbs.)*
Lbs. Total/trip Min. *(assume 7 oven uses)*	10.5 lbs.	12.25 lbs.	14 lbs.
Lbs. Total/trip with "Margin of Error"	14 lbs.	17 lbs.	20 lbs.

KEY:

Each briquet weighs about 1 oz.; 16 briquets = ~1 pound; 334 briquets = 20 lb. bag.
20 lbs. of briquets fit in one 5-gallon bucket; enough for 9-10 uses of a 16" Dutch.

TABLE APPENDIX 8-2: **PROPANE FOR A SIX-DAY SUMMER TRIP**

(a 2.5 gallon cylinder is 11 lbs. and a 4.7 gallon cylinder is 20 lbs.)

Propane Needed by Trip Size	12 People	15 People	20 People	24 People
"Minimal" Propane Use (rate = .028 gal.* per person/day)	2.02 gallons	A 2.5 gallon cylinder (Mills)	3.36 gallons	4.03 gallons

*This is an accepted minimal use rate based on fifteen people on a six-day trip when the stove is used for one-half of the cooking jobs and there's no heating water for dishwashing or camp lantern usage (ref. Sheila Mills, 1997). However, with careful use (e.g., keep hot coffee in a carafe, not on the flame) and adding one-two Dutch oven dishes per day, our trips are able to use these minimal amounts to also heat water for dishwashing and for one to two nights of camp lantern use. Remember, if your trip needs to boil drinking water or is a winter trip, you will need more propane.

APPENDIX NINE
Bulk-Bin Staples for a River Kitchen

Here are seven lightweight, easy-to-prepare, economical staples from your bulk-bin grocer. Pesky conversion problems are solved for your convenience.

BEANS: Refried Bean Mix (dried, instant, including spices) is a great burrito filling or fast chili.

> 1 full quart bag = 4 - 5 c. bean mix (1.25 - 1.5 lbs.) = 5 - 6 one-cup servings rehydrated
>
> 1 full gallon bag = 18 c. bean mix = 24 one-cup servings rehydrated

To make 1 one-cup serving: use 3/4 c. (3.75 oz.) dried bean mix, add 1 c. boiling water, stir, cover, and let sit for 5 minutes. For richer flavor add 1 Tbsp. oil per serving.

To make 12 one-cup servings: pack 9 cups refried bean mix in a gallon freezer-weight plastic zip bag. In camp add 12 cups boiling water, stir, cover, and let sit for 5 minutes as above.

COCOA BEVERAGE MIX, INSTANT HOMEMADE: About half the price, this mix is cheaper than popular "add-hot-water" cocoa mixes. It uses dry skim milk, not dried whey, and you can control the sugar-cocoa ratio. For a basic 6-cup batch of mix (makes 15 one-cup servings of cocoa):

> 1 cup (3.75 - 4 oz.) – Cocoa, dry, unsweetened powder, bulk-bin
>
> 1 - 2 cups (7 - 14 oz.) – Sugar
>
> 3 cups (about 9 oz.) – Milk, instant skim milk powder
>
> 1/2 cup (about 2 oz.) – Coffee creamer, optional (for a richer cocoa)

To make 1 one-cup serving: use 1/3 - 1/2 cup cocoa mix, add 1/4 cup boiling water or coffee, stir to dissolve, then add remaining 3/4 cup water or coffee.

To make 15 one-cup servings: pack this recipe (6 cups cocoa mix) in a plastic zip bag. In camp add 15 cups boiling water or coffee according to individual tastes and *voilà* – a protein-rich instant breakfast! Two gallons of dry mix is plenty for an 8-day trip of 12, where about half are cocoa drinkers.

COUSCOUS: This handy bulk-bin pasta is a nice alternative to rice or potatoes – and quick!

> 1 full quart bag = ~4 cups dry coucous (24 oz. or 1.5 pounds) = 12 three-quarter cup svgs.
>
> 1 half-gallon bag = ~8 cups dry coucous (48 oz. or 3 pounds) = 24 three-quarter cup svgs.

To make 1 three-quarter cup serving: use 1/3 cup dry couscous (2 oz.), add 1/2 cup boiling water, mix, cover, let sit for 5 minutes, then fluff with a fork. Salt, butter or oil to taste.

To make 12 three-quarter cup servings: pack 4 cups dry couscous (1.5 pounds) in a gallon freezer-weight plastic zip bag. In camp add 6 cups boiling water, mix, cover, let sit for 5 minutes, then fluff with a fork. Salt, butter or oil to taste.

MILK: Instant skim powder is a lightweight protein source and great emergency ration.

>1 full quart bag = ~4 cups instant milk (about 12 ounces), makes 3 quarts liquid milk
>
>1 full gallon bag = ~16 cups instant milk (about 3 pounds), makes 3 gallons liquid milk

To make 1 one-cup serving: use 1/3 cup (1 oz.) instant milk, add 7/8 cup cold water.

To make 12 one-cup servings: use 4 cups (12 oz.) instant milk, add 10.5 cups cold water.

To make enough milk for 12 people to use on oatmeal for 4 days (48 half-cup servings milk = 6 qts.), pack 1.5 lbs. (about 8 cups) instant milk powder.

OATMEAL: Regular oatmeal doesn't get creamy-pasty like the instant kind and only needs a minute or two more to soak in boiling water. It makes excellent back-up fuel on a cold morning.

>1 full quart bulk-bin bag = ~4 cups oatmeal (about 1 pound) = 8 one-cup cooked servings
>
>1 full gallon bulk-bin bag = ~16 cups (about 4 pounds) = 32 one-cup cooked servings

To make 1 one-cup serving: use 1/2 cup dry oatmeal, add about 1 cup boiling water.

To make 12 one-cup servings: use 6 cups dry oatmeal, add 12 cups boiling water.

To make enough oatmeal for 12 people for 3 days (36 one-cup servings), pack 4 1/2 pounds (18 cups dry) oatmeal. Don't forget about two pounds of brown sugar (5 1/2 cups = 44 one-eighth cup servings) and packets of dried fruit like raisins, apricots, apples, and cranberries (9 - 18 cups of dried fruit weigh roughly 3 - 6 pounds = 36 servings of 1/4 - 1/2 cup).

POLENTA (ITALIAN CORNMEAL): Use fine or medium ground cornmeal for this hearty main or side dish. Cook it until firm, spread on a plate, and cut into pieces like bread or pie. Or, cook it soft and serve like mashed potatoes. Add cheese, sausage, red sauce, or pesto for unique flavors.

To make one side-dish serving: Boil 1 cup water with 1/2 tsp. salt and 2 tsp. oil.

Sprinkle in 1/3 cup dry polenta = 2 ounces, stirring constantly with whisk or spoon.

Lower heat and continue boiling 2 minutes, or until it reaches desired consistency.

For 12: Boil 3 qts. water with 2 Tbsp. salt and 6 Tbsp. oil. Add 4 c. (1.5 lbs.) polenta.

TEXTURIZED VEGETABLE PROTEIN (TVP): This soy product substitutes well for meat, is light-weight, and is a great protein enhancer for your vegan dishes. It can be used wherever ground meat is used and makes exceptional chili.

>1 cup dry TVP = 3.7 ounces
>
>1 quart bulk-bin bag = 3 1/2 cups TVP (about 13 ounces)

To use as a substitute for cooked ground meat in chili recipes, hydrate per product instructions and pair 2 cups moist TVP with every 4 cups cooked beans.

Keep on hand in your river pantry for emergency rations and for thickening sauces in main course dishes.

APPENDIX TEN

Additional River Recipes

This appendix includes recipe alternatives formatted like recipe sheets in Appendix 2. However, the advance prep and shopping lists now come first as in traditional recipes.

[A] "Eat Dessert First" are Dutch oven family favorites that work as breakfast treats or desserts:

- Banana (or –) Bread from Grosmuder's Dutch Oven
- Scones, County Mayo
- Pineapple Upside-down Cake
- Caramel Apple Pudding-Pie

[B] These dinner recipes offer additional variety to the red meat-based menus in Appendix 2.

- Salad, Munchy Quick
- Cornbread for the Dutch
- Chili 'n' Cornbread, Easy, Meatless
- Tuna 'n' Noodles, Speedy
- Curry-nut Stew, Vegan's Delight
- Vegetarian Posole
- Enchiladas Verdes

TABLE APPENDIX 10[A]-1:

BANANA (OR –) BREAD, FROM GROSMUDER'S DUTCH OVEN

♣♣♣ ADVANCE PREP. NITE __ DETAILS ♣♣♣

Ingredients for: (also shopping list)	Amounts for 12:	Amount for (_____):	DIRECTIONS: (don't forget to add Trip Day # to all packets)
Banana (or –) Bread:			
PACKET #1: ♣ Butter Cooking Oil Sugar	1/2 cup 1/2 cup 2 cups		Combine butter, oil, and sugar in zip bag. Double bag and label "Bread Pkt. #1."
PACKET #2: ♣ Eggs, beaten	4, frozen		Beat eggs; put in freezer-weight zip bag; label "Bread Pkt. # 2"; freeze.
PACKET #3: ♣ Flour Baking Soda Cinnamon, Mace, Cardamom	4 cups 2 tsp. 1 tsp. of each spice		Sift together flour, baking soda, and spices. Put in a zip bag and label "Bread Pkt. #3."
PACKET #4: ♣ Bananas (or Carrots, Zucchini, Peaches, Cranberries, Pumpkin, etc.) Nuts (walnuts, almonds, pecans, cashews, etc.)	4 cups mashed (or grated or chopped or cooked to a pulp) 1/2 cup, chopped		Here's where the cook can be creative: Prepare 4 c. fruit or vegetable (add 1-2 c. more of sugar if your choice isn't sweet. Use ascorbic acid prep dip if browning is a problem: 1/4 tsp. or 2 crushed vitamin C tabs in 2 c. water for dipping 4 c. fruit). Then bag the fruit (or veggies) and nuts; label "Bread Pkt. #4." Freeze.

In CAMP

Banana (or −) Bread:			Directions In Camp:
Briquets	30 for a 14" D.O. If doubling or half-againing this recipe, use a 16" D.O. or two 14" and if halving it use a 12" D.O. Use briquets per Appendix on Fuel Estimates.		Light briquets; grease 14" D. O. Place parchment sheets on bottom and greased magic can in center (the donut effect eliminates a doughy center!).
PACKET #1: ♣ Butter Cooking Oil Sugar	Double bagged.		Pour Pkt. #1 in mixing bowl or tall plastic bag (s).
PACKET #2: Eggs ♣	4 frozen, thaw first.		Stir in the eggs Pkt. #2 (lumps are okay).
PACKET #3: ♣ Flour Baking Soda Cinnamon, Mace, Cardamom	Flour packet.		Mix in Pkt. #3. You may need a pastry cutter because it'll be thick.
PACKET #4: ♣ Fruit (Veggies)/ Nuts	Frozen packet; thaw.		Mix thawed Pkt. #4 into batter. Pour batter around can in D.O.
Dutch Oven			If your coals are super hot, let them get ashy or lay a sheet or two of parchment on top of the dough. Put lid on with 18 coals top, 12 under-neath; bake 50" rotating lid ¼ turn clockwise and bottom ¼ turn counter-clockwise every 10". At 30" put bottom coals on top of D.O. (Two-thirds Rule). When done, remove coals, cool w/ lid off at least 5" before cutting.

CHECKLISTS – nITE __

PickleBucket or Drybox: ❑ Bread Mix Pkts. 1, 3	2 sacks		Label all by river day.
Frozen Cooler: ❑ Bread Mix Pkts. 2, 4	2 sacks		Label all by river day.

TABLE APPENDIX 10[A]-2: **Scones, county Mayo**

♣♣♣ ADVANCE PREP. nite ___ DETAILS ♣♣♣			
Ingredients for: (also shopping list)	**Amounts for 12:**	**Amount for (___):**	**DIRECTIONS:** (don't forget to add Trip Day # to all packets)
County Mayo Scones:			
PACKET #1: ♣Sultana (Yellow) Raisins	1 cup		Package in zip bag; label "Scones Pkt. #1."
PACKET #2: ♣ Flour Sugar Salt Baking Powder	6 cups 6 Tbsp. 2 tsp. 2 Tbsp.		Sift together; package in zip bag; label "Scones Pkt. 2."
PACKET #3: ♣ Butter Eggs (OR Mayo, yes!) Plain Yogurt (or Milk) Orange Zest	$2/3$ cup 2 eggs (OR $1/2$ c. Mayonnaise) 2 cups 1 Tbsp. (1 grated orange rind)		This packet can be mixed up and frozen in advance. It can also be made up in camp by adding lunch cooler mayonnaise, dry milk and water to a pkt. of butter and zest. Your choice! Label whatever Adv. Prep you make "Scones Pkt. #3." Freeze if Pkt. #3 contains eggs or yogurt or liquid milk.

In CAMP

County Mayo Scones:			Directions In Camp:
Briquets	30 for a 14" D.O. If doubling or half-againing this recipe, use a 16" D.O. or two 14" and if halving it use a 12" D.O. Use briquets per Appendix on Fuel Estimates.		Light briquets; grease 14" D.O. Place parchment sheets on bottom and greased magic can in center (the donut effect eliminates a doughy center!).
PACKET #1: ♣ Sultana (Yellow) Raisins	1 cup		Hydrate the raisins in 1½ c. water overnight or for 1 hr. in hot water.
PACKET #2: ♣ Flour Sugar Salt Baking Powder	6 cups 6 Tbsp. 2 tsp. 2 Tbsp.		Put these ingredients into a bowl.
PACKET #3: ♣ Butter Eggs (or Mayo, yes!) Plain Yogurt (or Milk) Orange Zest	²/₃ cup 2 eggs (or ½ c. Mayo) 2 cups 1 Tbsp. (1 grated orange rind)		Cut Pkt. #3 into flour mixture in the bowl — pastry cutter is handy. Mix like pie crust; divide in two; knead 1 min. Pat out first layer in D.O.; spread on drained raisins; pat on second layer; pinch edges closed. Lay sheet of parchment on top of dough to keep top from burning.
Dutch Oven			Put lid on with 18 hot coals on top, 12 underneath; bake 20" rotating lid ¼ turn clockwise and bottom ¼ turn counter-clockwise every 5". At 13" put bottom coals on top of D.O. (Two-thirds Rule). When done, remove coals, cool w/ lid off at least 5" before cutting.

CHECKLISTS – nITE __

PickleBucket or Drybox: ❑ Bread Mix Pkts. 1, 2	2 sacks		Label all by river day.
Frozen Cooler: ❑ Bread Mix Pkt. 3	1 sack		Label all by river day.

TABLE APPENDIX 10[A]-3: **PINEAPPLE UPSIDE-DOWN CAKE**

	♣♣♣ ADVANCE PREP. NITE ___ DETAILS ♣♣♣		
Ingredients for: (also shopping list)	Amounts for 12:	Amount for (_____):	DIRECTIONS: (don't forget to add Trip Day # to all packets)
Pineapple Upside-down Cake:			
PACKET #1: ♣ Butter Brown Sugar Karo Syrup Cherries, maraschino	1 cup ³/₄ cup ³/₄ cup 8 oz., drained		Mix and package butter, sugar, syrup, and cherries in zip bag; double bag; label "Pineapple Cake Pkt. #1."
PACKET #2: ♣ Sugar Butter Flour Baking Powder	2 cups 1 cup 4 cups 4 tsp.		Mix with pastry cutter and package in zip bag; label "Pineapple Cake Pkt. 2."
PACKET #3: ♣ Dry Milk	²/₃ cup		Package in zip bag; label "Pineapple Cake Pkt. #3."
PACKET #4: ♣ Eggs, beaten	2, frozen, then thawed		Beat eggs; package in zip bag; label "Pineapple Cake Pkt. #4." Freeze.
Also Purchase: Pineapple, crushed Pineapple, slices	1 No.2 can (2¹/₂ cup) 1 No.2 can (2¹/₂ cup)		Label cans of pineapple "for Pineapple Cake."

In CAMP

Pineapple Cake:			Directions In Camp:
Briquets	30 for a 14" D.O. If doubling or half-againing this recipe, use a 16" D.O. or two 14" and if halving it use a 12" D.O. Use briquets per Appendix on Fuel Estimates.		Light briquets; grease 14" D.O. and grease magic can in center (the donut effect eliminates a doughy center!).
PACKET #1: ♣ Butter Brown Sugar Karo Syrup Cherries Pineapple, crushed Pineapple, slices	1 cup ³/₄ cup ³/₄ cup 8 oz., drained 1 No.2 can (2¹/₂ cup) 1 No.2 can (2¹/₂ cup)		Empty Pkt. #1 into D.O. and heat with all coals under; stir in crushed pineapple; mix well. Drain the pineapple rings (juice makes a great Mai-Tai), arrange them evenly with cherries in sugar mixture; simmer while you make the cake batter.
PACKET #2: ♣ Flour/sugar/butter mix			Empty Pkt. #2 into mixing bowl or tall plastic bag(s).
PACKET #3: ♣ Dry Milk	²/₃ cup		Add 2 cups water to dry milk.
PACKET #4: ♣ Eggs, beaten, frozen	2 thawed		Beat eggs into milk; then add to Pkt. #2; stir (some lumps okay).
Dutch Oven			Pour batter around can in D.O. Put lid on with 18 hot coals on top, 12 underneath; bake 50" rotating lid ¹/₄ turn clockwise and bottom ¹/₄ turn counter-clockwise every 10". At 30" put bottom coals on top of D.O. (Two-thirds Rule). When done, remove coals, cool w/ lid off at least 5" before cutting.

CHECKLISTS – nITE __

PickleBucket or Drybox:			Label all by river day.
❏ Cake Mix Pkts. 1,2,3	3 sacks		
❏ Pineapple, crushed	1 can		
❏ Pineapple, slices	1 can		
Frozen Cooler:			Label all by river day.
❏ Cake Mix Pkt. 4	1 sack		

TABLE APPENDIX 10[A]-4: **CARAMEL APPLE PUDDING-PIE**

	♣♣♣ ADVANCE PREP. NITE ___ DETAILS ♣♣♣		
Ingredients for: (also shopping list)	Amounts for 12:	Amount for (____):	DIRECTIONS: (don't forget to add Trip Day # to all packets)
Pudding-Pie:			
PACKET #1: ♣ Flour Sugar Baking Powder Salt	4 cups 2 cups 2 Tbsp. 2 tsp.		Sift together; package in plastic zip bag; label "Pudding-Pie Pkt. #1."
PACKET #2: ♣ Dry Milk	2/3 cup		Package in zip bag; label "Pudding-Pie Pkt. #2."
PACKET #3: ♣ Brown Sugar Butter Nutmeg, Cinnamon	4 cups 1/4 cup 1 tsp. each spice		Mix and package in freezer-weight gallon zip bag; double bag; label "Pudding-Pie Pkt. #3."
PACKET #4 (Topping Sauce): ♣ Sugar Cornstarch Butter Lemon Zest	1 1/2 cups 3 Tbsp. 3 Tbsp. 1 Tbsp. (1 lemon rind, grated)		Mix sugar and cornstarch well, then mash in butter and lemon zest with fork; put in freezer-weight zip bag; label "Pudding-Pie Pkt. #4 (Sauce)."
Also Purchase: Apples, fresh or dried	8 (about 8c. fresh slices or 2c. dried)		Label "Apples for Pudding-Pie."

In CAMP

Pudding-Pie:			Directions In Camp:
Briquets	30 for a 14" D.O. If doubling or half-againing this recipe, use a 16" D.O. or two 14" and if halving it use a 12" D.O. Use briquets per Appendix on Fuel Estimates.		Light briquets; grease 14" D.O. and grease magic can in center (the donut effect eliminates a doughy center!).
PACKET #1: ♣ Flour/sugar mix			Empty Pkt. #1 into mixing bowl or tall plastic bag(s).
PACKET #2: ♣ Dry Milk	²/₃ cup		Add 2 cups water to dry milk and combine with Pkt. #1; mix well.
Apples, fresh or dried	8 (about 8 c. fresh slices or 2c. dried)		Rehydrate dried apples if necessary. Fold apple slices into batter; pour around can in greased D.O.
Water **PACKET #3** ♣	8 cups		Boil and add to Pkt. #3 sack of brown sugar, butter, and spices; stir to mix, then pour over batter in D.O.
Dutch Oven			Put lid on with 18 hot coals on top, 12 underneath; bake 50" rotating lid ¼ turn clockwise and bottom ¼ turn counter-clockwise every 10". At 30" put bottom coals on top of D.O. (Two-thirds Rule).
Water **PACKET #4** (Topping Sauce) ♣	3 cups		While the pudding-pie is cooking, bring water to a boil and stir in Pkt. #4; simmer until thick, then serve warm sauce on top of pudding-pie.

CHECKLISTS – nITE __

PickleBucket or Drybox:			Label all by river day.
❏ Pudding-Pie Pkts. 1, 2, 3, 4	3 sacks		
❏ Apples	8 fresh or 2 c. dried		

TABLE APPENDIX 10[B]-1: **SALAD, MUNCHY QUICK**

♣♣♣ ADVANCE PREP. NITE ___ DETAILS ♣♣♣			
Ingredients for: (also shopping list)	**Amounts for 12:**	**Amount for (____):**	**DIRECTIONS:** (don't forget to add Trip Day # to all packets)
Quick Munchy Salad			
Cauliflower ♣	1 head		Rinse all veggies, tossing
Broccoli ♣	1 head		unneeded stems and leaves.
Cucumbers ♣	3		Package in zip bags; label
Peppers, green ♣	5		"Munchy Salad."
Chili Powder ♣	¼ cup in shaker		Package each in a separate
Curry Powder ♣	⅛ cup in a shaker		container; label "Munchy Salad."

IN CAMP		
Quick Munchy Salad		**Directions In Camp:**
Cauliflower ♣		Rinse all veggies. Break or
Broccoli ♣		cut into bit-sized pieces.
Cucumbers ♣		Arrange on or in serving con-
Peppers, green ♣		tainer. Since this is "al mano" service, remind all munchers to wash hands well first.
Chili Powder ♣	¼ cup in shaker	Sprinkle with spice of choice
Curry Powder ♣	⅛ cup in a shaker	and munch away!

CHECKLISTS – NITE ___		
PickleBucket or Drybox: ❏ Chili Powder Shaker ❏ Curry Powder Shaker		Label all by river day.
Cooler: "Crunchy Salad": ❏ Cauliflower ❏ Broccoli ❏ Cucumbers ❏ Peppers, green		Label all by river day.

TABLE APPENDIX 10[B]-2: **CORNBREAD FOR THE DUTCH**

♣♣♣ ADVANCE PREP. NITE ___ DETAILS ♣♣♣

Ingredients for: (also shopping list)	Amounts for 12:	Amount for (___):	DIRECTIONS: (don't forget to add Trip Day # to all packets)
Dutch Cornbread:			
Cornbread Combo: ♣	2 sacks:		Mix all dry ingredients well in two gallon freezer-weight zip bags; label each "Cornbread Combo."
1. Cornbread Mix (add-water type like Marie Callender's)	2 one-pound cans (each 3 c., total 6 c.)		
2. Flour	2 cups		
3. Cornmeal, fine	2 cups		

IN CAMP

Dutch Cornbread:			Directions In Camp:
Briquets	30 for a 14" D.O. If doubling or half-againing this recipe, use a 16" D.O. or two 14" and if halving it use a 12" D.O. Use briquets per Appendix on Fuel Estimates.		Light briquets; grease 14" D.O. Place parchment sheets on bottom and greased magic can in center (the donut effect eliminates a doughy center!).
Cornbread Combo ♣	2 sacks		Add water to dry ingredients in the heavy plastic bags – 2 1/2 cups each; mix only until moistened.
Water	5 cups		
Dutch Oven			Pour into greased D.O. around the greased center can. Put lid on with 18 hot coals on top, 12 underneath; bake 20-25" rotating lid 1/4 turn clockwise and bottom 1/4 turn counter-clockwise every 5". At 15" put bottom coals on top of D.O. (Two-thirds Rule)

CHECKLISTS – NITE ___

Pickle Bucket or Drybox:			Label all by river day.
❑ Cornmeal Combo	2 sacks mix		

TABLE APPENDIX 10[B]-3: **CHILI 'N' CORNBREAD, EASY MEATLESS**

♣♣♣ ADVANCE PREP. NITE ___ DETAILS ♣♣♣			
Ingredients for: (also shopping list)	Amounts for 12:	Amount for (_____):	DIRECTIONS: (don't forget to add Trip Day # to all packets)
Chili 'n' Cornbread:			
Beans, refried, dried mix♣ PKT. #1:	9 cups		Package in gallon freezer-weight zip bag; label "Pkt. #1 Chili."
Cornbread Mix: ♣ PKT. #2: 1. Cornbread Mix (add-water type like Marie Callender's) 2. Flour 3. Cornmeal, fine	1 sack: 1 one-pound can (each 3 c.) 1 cup 1 cup		Mix all dry ingredients well in a gallon freezer-weight zip bag; label "Pkt. #2 Chili."
Also Purchase; Green Chiles, chopped Tomatoes, crushed Salsa	1 can (8 oz.) 1 No. 2½ can (28 oz., about 3½ c.) 1 No. 2 can (2½ c.)		Label "for Chili-Cornbread."
In CAMP			
Chili 'n' Cornbread:			**Directions In Camp:**
Briquets	30 for a 14" D.O. If doubling or half-againing this recipe, use a 16" D.O. or two 14" and if halving it use a 12" D.O.		Light briquets; grease 14" D. O. and magic can in center (the donut effect eliminates a doughy center!).
PKT. #1: ♣ Refried Beans Water Green Chiles Tomatoes, Crushed	9 cups 1 can 1 can		Boil 12 cups (3 quarts) water and add to contents of bean sack; mix and pour around can in D.O. Add chiles and tomatoes and stir; bring to boil over coals.
PKT. #2: ♣ Cornbread Mix Water	1 sack 2½ cups		Add water to dry ingredients in plastic bag; mix only until moistened. Pour over hot beans.
Dutch Oven Salsa	1 can		Put lid on with 18 hot coals on top, 12 underneath; bake 25-30" rotating lid ¼ turn clockwise and bottom ¼ turn counter-clockwise every 10". At 18" put bottom coals on top of D.O. (Two-thirds Rule) Serve with Salsa!

CONTINUED

CHILI 'N' CORNBREAD, EASY MEATLESS CONTINUED

CHECKLISTS – NITE __

Picklebucket or Drybox:			Label all items by river day.
Chili Pkt. #1	1 sack		
Chili Pkt. #2	1 sack		
Green Chiles	1 can		
Tomatoes, Crushed	1 can		
Salsa	1 can		

TABLE APPENDIX 10[B]-4: TUNA 'N' NOODLES, SPEEDY

♣♣♣ ADVANCE PREP. NITE __ DETAILS ♣♣♣

Ingredients for: (also shopping list)	Amounts for 12:	Amount for (____):	DIRECTIONS: (don't forget to add Trip Day # to all packets)
Purchase:			Label all "Tuna 'n' Noodles."
Ramen Noodles	6 packages		
Tuna	6 cans, ea. 6 oz. (2/3 c.)		
Mushroom Soup	3 cans		
Peas	1 No. 2 can (2 1/2 c.) [or 1 lb. frozen]		
Parmesan Cheese	1/2 cup		

IN CAMP

Tuna 'n' Noodles:			Directions In Camp:
Water, boiling Ramen Noodles	9 cups		Add noodles to boiling water; cover on low heat until noodles soft.
Tuna, drained	6 cans, ea. 5 oz. (2/3 c.)		Stir in these ingredients; heat well, adding more water if needed. Serve hot.
Mushroom Soup	3 cans		
Peas	1 can		
Parmesan Cheese	1/2 cup		

CHECKLISTS – NITE __

Picklebucket or Drybox:			Label all items by river day.
❑ Ramen Noodles	6 packages		
❑ Tuna	6 cans		
❑ Mushroom Soup	3 cans		
❑ Peas	1 can		
❑ Parmesan Cheese	1/2 cup		

TABLE APPENDIX 10[B]-5: **CURRY-NUT STEW – VEGAN'S DELIGHT**

Rice or noodle component could be added for additional carbohydrate, but not necessary.

♣♣♣ ADVANCE PREP. NITE ___ DETAILS ♣♣♣			
Ingredients for: (also shopping list)	Amounts for 12:	Amount for (_____):	DIRECTIONS: (don't forget to add Trip Day # to all packets)
Curry-nut Stew: Svg. Size ~ 1²/₃ cups			
1. ROOT VEGGIES:			Boil root veggies until tender. Drain half the liquid and reserve for sauce in step two.
Potatoes, large, diced	4 (unpeeled)		
Carrots, large, peeled	6 cut in 1" pieces		
Parsnips, med.	4 cut in 1" pieces		
Water	~ 4 c. (cover veggies)		
2. FLAVOR VEGGIES:			Heat oil and mustard seeds until they turn gray. Add veggies and sauté in oil until onion is transparent; reduce heat. Mix curry powder and cornstarch with the reserved liquid from step one; simmer until sauce thickens and add root veggies.
Onion, large, diced	2		
Celery Stalks	6 cut in 2" pieces		
Garlic Cloves	6 minced		
Canola Oil	¼ cup		
Black Mustard Seed	2 tsp.		
Curry Powder	½ cup		
Cornstarch	2 Tbsp.		
3. MORE TREATS:			Add these items to the simmering mix of root and flavor veggies. Simmer 5 minutes.
Broccoli, bite-sized	2 cups		
Peas, frozen or can	2 cups		
Apples, diced	2 whole, unpeeled		
Raisins or Currants	½ cup		
Tamari Sauce	2 Tbsp.		
Ginger Root, minced	2 Tbsp. (or 2 tsp. dry)		
4. NUTTY SAUCE:			Mix these items into the simmering mixture until well blended. Cool and double-bag in quart freezer-weight zip bags. Label "Curry-nut Stew" and freeze flat.
Chunky Peanut Butter	2 cups		
Sesame Oil	½ cup		
Hot Sauce	6 shakes or more		
Whole Nuts	2 c. cashews or peanuts		

In CAMP

Curry-nut Stew:			Directions In Camp:
Method #1: Hot Water Bath for Curry-nut Bags♣ (thawed, of course)	1 gallon in a 2-gal. pot		This method is great if you don't want to wash oily pots. Heat large pot of river water to rolling boil for at least a minute and remove pot from heat. Sink 4 or more layers of paper towel (or hot pad you don't mind getting wet) on bottom before adding plastic bags to warm up. Camp stoves melt baggies when they sit directly on the hot metal pot bottom. Cover with lid or plate until contents of zip bags are nice 'n' hot.
Method #2: Dutch Oven for Curry-nut Stew Bags ♣ (thawed, of course)	Heated with 12 coals Dump in bags and heat them up.		This method does leave you with a dirty D.O., but has advantage over Method #1 of conserving propane. Stir to keep from sticking.

CHECKLISTS – nITE __

Frozen Cooler:			Label all items by river day.
❏ Curry-nut Stew Quart Bags	Your number_____		

TABLE APPENDIX 10[B]-6: **VEGETARIAN POSOLE BY GARY PAYNE**

Meat that could be added for non-vegetarians would be 4-6 oz. barbecued pork loin per person, says our kayak mentor and camp chef Gary Payne.

♣♣♣ ADVANCE PREP. NITE __ DETAILS ♣♣♣			
Ingredients for: (also shopping list)	**Amounts for 12:**	**Amount for (____):**	**DIRECTIONS:** (don't forget to add Trip Day # to all packets)
Vegetarian Posole:			
Onion ♣ Garlic Cloves ♣	1 4		Pack these items together and label "Veggie Posole."
Veggie Pieces: ♣ Mushrooms, fresh Carrots, peeled, sliced Green Beans, fresh Squash (Tatuma or Zucchini), chopped	2 cups, quartered 7 large or 9 small 3 cups 4½ cups		Depending on your anticipated time to cook in camp, these items could be cut up before packing or done in camp. Canned produce is an option, but not as tasty. Label zip bags of veggies "Veggie Posole" and decide when in trip this meal will be, then put Cooler or Freezer.
Tomatoes, canned ♣ or fresh + water Hominy, canned ♣	4½ c. (2 No. 2 cans) OR 10 fresh tomatoes plus 3¾ c. water 3 29-oz. cans, drained		Label these items "Veggie Posole." You can save weight by draining the hominy at home and putting it in zip bags in cooler or freezer.
Cilantro, fresh ♣ or dried Lime, fresh ♣	4½ Tbsp. chopped OR 2 Tbsp. dried 2 sliced for squeezing		These garnishes add to the flavor. Label "Veggie Posole Garnish." Store in cooler.
Spice Packet: ♣ Cumin Powder Oregano Powder Salt Pepper	1½ tsp. 1½ tsp. ¾ tsp. ½ tsp.		Label the spice packet "Veggie Posole: Cumin, Oregano, Salt & Pepper."

In CAMP

Vegetarian Posole:			Directions In Camp:
Onion & Garlics ♣ Oil	Chopped		Chop onions and garlic, then brown in pan or D.O. using a small amount of oil.
Veggie Pieces ♣	Bagged veggies.		Stir in all the veggie pieces.
Tomatoes ♣	2 cans (OR 10 fresh plus 3³/₄ c. water)		Add to vegetables and cook until they begin to soften (about 12 minutes).
Spice Packet ♣	Bagged and labeled.		Add to simmering veggies.
Hominy ♣	3 cans		Cook until everything is soft (12 minutes).
Cilantro ♣ Limes			Stir in right before serving or use as a garnish and serve with delight!

CHECKLISTS – nITE __

Picklebucket or Drybox:			Label all items by river day. (Some variability of location depending on decisions to use fresh or canned items and cooler or freezer location depending on when meal is expected to be served.)
❑ Onion and Garlics	1 and 4		
❑ Tomatoes, canned	2 cans		
❑ Spice Packet	1 packet		
❑ Hominy, canned	3 cans		
Cooler or Freezer:			As above.
❑ Veggie Sacks	2 + sacks		
❑ Cilantro	1 sack		
❑ Limes	2		

TABLE APPENDIX 10[B]-7: **ENCHILADAS VERDES**

This river recipe uses layering instead of the usual method of rolling the filling up in tortillas. For vegetarians, leave out the chicken and it'll still be packed with protein.

♣♣♣ ADVANCE PREP. NITE ___ DETAILS ♣♣♣			
Ingredients for: (also shopping list)	Amounts for 12:	Amount for (_____):	DIRECTIONS: (don't forget to add Trip Day # to all packets)
Enchiladas Verdes:			
Enchilada Filling: ♣			Boil the chicken in enough water to cover it for 20 min. Cool and shred the cooked chicken into a bowl. Chop the onions into fine pieces. (Hint: wear swimming goggles.) Add onions and cheese to chicken. Mix well. (Hint: wear gloves and do it by hand.) Package in zip bags, flatten, and label: "Enchiladas Verdes."
Chicken Breasts	9 (boneless, skinless is easier, but pricey)		
Onions, large	2		
Cream Cheese	3 8-ounce packets		
Enchilada Sauce: ♣			In a blender mix all ingredients to a thick sauce. If this recipe is to be served in the first few days of a trip, storing the sauce in a plastic bottle in the cooler is fine. However, if it is for later, or the cooler's not sure to be cold, freeze the sauce in E-Z-fill zipper bag(s) or qt. bottles. Leave headroom for expansion.
Green Tomatoes OR Tomatillos	2 cups, chopped		
Green Chilis	1 7-ounce can		
Milk	4 cups		
Eggs	4		
Coriander Seed	1 tsp.		
Salt	1 tsp.		
Flour Tortillas ♣	16		Label these ingredients "Enchiladas Verdes," and store appropriately, freezing or cooling as necessary.
Monterey Jack Cheese♣	2 lbs.(shred at home or in camp)		
Salsa(Red or Green)♣	1 quart		

In CAMP

Enchiladas Verdes:		Directions In Camp:
Briquets	30 for a 14" D.O. If doubling or half-againing this recipe, use a 16" D.O. or two 14" and if halving it use a 12" D.O.	Light briquets; grease 14" D.O. and magic can in center (the donut effect eliminates an uncooked center center!).
Enchilada Sauce ♣	Thawed	Pour about ¼ of the sauce in the D.O.
Flour Tortillas ♣ Enchilada Filling ♣	16 Packaged and labeled.	Make a layer of tortillas in the sauce around the center can. Then make a filling layer and cover with more tortillas and tortillas pieces. Press the layer down and pour on a sauce layer. Continue until filling and tortillas are used up, then top with shredded Monterey Jack cheese.
Monterey Jack Cheese♣		
Dutch Oven		Put lid on with 18 hot coals on top, 12 underneath; bake 25-30" rotating lid ¼ turn clockwise and bottom ¼ turn counter-clockwise every 10". At 18 minutes put bottom coals on top of D.O. (Two-thirds Rule). Allow to cool for 5-10" to set up. Serve with Salsa.
Salsa	1 quart	

CHECKLISTS – nITE

Picklebucket or Drybox:		Label all items by river day.
❏ Salsa	1 quart	
Cooler OR Freezer:		Label all items by river day. (Some variability of location depending on decisions to use cooled or frozen items depending on when meal is expected to be served.)
❏ Enchilada Sauce ♣	1 2-qt. bottle (or bags)	
❏ Flour Tortillas ♣	16	
❏ Enchilada Filling ♣	Quart sacks	
❏ Monterey Jack Cheese♣	2 lbs.	

Contacts for River Trip Permits

ALSEK – Kluane National Park and Reserve, Yukon, Canada
http://parkscan.harbour.com/kluane/adventure/rafting/water1.htm

CARSON (EAST) – Toiyabe National Forest, Nevada
http://www.fs.fed.us/htnf/raftcarson.htm

COLORADO (GRAND CANYON, LITTLE COLORADO, DIAMOND CREEK) – Arizona
http://www.nps.gov/grca/river/non_commercial_general_info.htm
Additional Info: Grand Canyon Private Boaters Association: http://www.gcpba.org.

COLORADO (WESTWATER) – Moab, Utah
http://www.blm.gov/utah/moab/riverec.html

GREEN (DESOLATION-GRAY CANYONS SECTION) – Price, Utah
http://www.blm.gov/utah/price/riverinf.htm

GREEN (DINOSAUR) – Dinosaur, Colorado
http://www.nps.gov/dino/river/RiverDoc/

ILLINOIS – Siskiyou National Forest, Oregon
http://svinet2.fs.fed.us/r6/siskiyou/illinriv.htm

MAIN SALMON – North Fork, Idaho
http://www.fs.fed.us/r4/sc/recreation/4rivers/index.htm

MIDDLE FORK OF THE SALMON – Challis, Idaho
http://www.fs.fed.us/r4/sc/recreation/4rivers/index.htm

PLATTE – Medicine Bow-Routt National Forests, Laramie, Wyoming
http://www.fs.fed.us/r2/mbr/rd-parks/platteriver.shtml
(currently only necessary for commercial permits)

RIO CHAMA AND RIO GRANDE – Taos, New Mexico
http://www.nm.blm.gov

ROGUE – Roseburg, Oregon
http://www.umpcoos.com/rogue (Tioga Resources, Inc. Lottery Contact)
Additional Info: http://www.fs.fed.us/r6/siskiyou/rogurivr.htm

SALT – Tonto National Forest, Globe, Arizona
http://www.fs.fed.us/r3/tonto/recreation/watersports/tribalpermit.htm
(Ft. Apache area)
http://www.fs.fed.us/r3/tonto/recreation/watersports/vispermit.htm
(Wilderness area)

SAN JUAN — Monticello, Utah
http://www.blm.gov/utah/monticello/rec_fr.htm

SELWAY — Darby, Montana
http://www.fs.fed.us/r4/sc/recreation/4rivers/index.htm

SMITH — Great Falls, Montana
http://fwp.state.mt.us/parks (then search "Smith River Float")

SNAKE (HELLS CANYON) — Clarkston, Washington
http://www.fs.fed.us/r4/sc/recreation/4rivers/index.htm

SNAKE — Bridger-Teton National Forest, Jackson, Wyoming
http://www.fs.fed.us/btnf/teton/ngcuse.html (currently only necessary for > 15 people)

TATSHENSHINI-ALSEK — Glacier Bay National Park and Reserve, Yakutat, Alaska
http://www.nps.gov/glba/visit/activities/wilderness/raft.htm

TUOLUME — Stanislaus National Forest, Groveland, California
http://www.r5.fs.fed.us/stanislaus/groveland/tcover.htm

UMPQUA, NORTH — Glide, Oregon
http://www.fs.fed.us/r6/umpqua/rec/rafting/nu_boating.html
(currently only necessary for commercial permits)

YAMPA — Dinosaur, Colorado
http://www.nps.gov/dino/river/RiverDoc

ADDITIONAL PERMIT ASSISTANCE:

RIVER MANAGEMENT SOCIETY: http://river-management.org — check out their links for comprehensive connections to all major sources — governmental in U.S. and Canada, national and international guide services, and conservation/preservation organizations. See their listing of all rivers with limited, required permits (they defer to American Whitewater's listing for all others.)

AMERICAN WHITEWATER: http://www.americanwhitewater.org — check out their annual "Permit Schedule" for dates and group size for the whole gamut of registrations: statewide, simple, high water, on-site, lottery, lottery with limited daily launches, and required pre-registrations.

NATIONAL RIVERS INVENTORY (NRI): http://www.ncrc.nps.gov/programs/rtca/nri — check out more than 3400 free-flowing river segments by state on an interactive map server. Or, order their free CD-ROM compiled by the National Park Service.

Resource Contacts:
Conservation, Education/Training,
Maps, Water-user Links

CONSERVATION

NATIONAL ORGANIZATIONS AND REGIONAL CONTACTS
Use this list as a starting point for locating groups to increase your fund of river knowledge. (Descriptions excerpted from each organization's website, March 2003.)

American Canoe Association
7432 Alban Station Blvd. Suite B-232,
Springfield, VA 22150
703/451-0141
http://acanet.org

Founded in 1880 by a group of avid canoeists, the ACA has grown into the nation's largest and most active nonprofit paddle sports organization. Today the ACA is dedicated to promoting canoeing, kayaking, and rafting as wholesome lifetime recreational activities. We accomplish this mission by providing a variety of worthwhile programs and public services in such areas as: event sponsorship, safety education, instructor certification, waterway conservation, paddler's rights and protection, and public information campaigns.

Appalachian Mountain Club
5 Joy Street, Boston, MA 02108
617/523-0636; fax 617/523-0722
http://www.outdoors.org

Since 1876, the Appalachian Mountain Club has promoted the protection, enjoyment, and wise use of the mountains, rivers, and trails of the Northeast. The AMC believes that successful, long-term conservation depends on first-hand experience and enjoyment of the outdoors. A nonprofit organization, AMC's membership of more than 72,000 enjoy hiking, canoeing, skiing, walking, rock climbing, bicycling, camping, kayaking, and backpacking, while − at the same time − help to safeguard the environment. All AMC programs and facilities are open to the public.

American Rivers
1025 Vermont Ave., N.W. Suite 720,
Washington, DC 20005
202/347-7550; fax 202/347-9240
amrivers@amrivers.org
http://americanrivers.org

American Rivers is a national non-profit conservation organization dedicated to protecting and restoring healthy national rivers and the variety of life they sustain for people, fish, and wildlife.

California Field Office (water resources):
6 School Street, Suite 200,
Fairfax, CA 94930-1650
415/482-8150; fax 415-482-8151
msamet@amrivers.org

California Field Office (dams and hydro):
PO Box 559, Nevada City, CA 95959
530/478-5672
srothert@amrivers.org

Mid-Atlantic Field Office:
600 North 2nd Street, Suite 403,
Harrisburg, PA 17101
717/232-8355; fax 717/232-8309
snicholas@amrivers.org

Montana Field Office:
215 Woodland Estates,
Great Falls, MT 59404
406/454-2076; fax 406/454-2530
malbers@amrivers.org

Nebraska Field Office:
Mill Towne Bldg., 650 J St, Ste. 400,
Lincoln, NE 68508
402/477-7910; fax 402/477-2565
csmith@amrivers.org

Northeast Field Office:
20 Bayberry Road,
Glastonbury, CT 06033
860/652-9911; fax 860/652-9922
lwildman@amrivers.org

Northwest Field Office (Portland):
320 SW Stark Street, Suite 418,
Portland, OR 97204
503/827-8648; fax 503/827-8654
arnw@amrivers.org

Northwest Field Office (Seattle):
150 Nickerson Street, Suite 311,
Seattle, WA 98109
206/213-0330; fax 206/213-0334
arnw@amrivers.org

South Dakota Field Office:
PO Box 1029, Aberdeen, SD 57402
605/229-4978; fax 605/229-6306
pcarrels@amrivers.org

Southeast Field Office:
500-A Fortwood Place,
Chattanooga, TN 37403
423/265-7505; fax 423/265-7506
dsligh@amrivers.org

American Whitewater
1424 Fenwick Lane,
Silver Springs, MD 20910
866/262-8429 (866/BOAT4AW);
fax 301/565-6714
info@americanwhitewater.org
http://www.americanwhitewater.org

The mission of American Whitewater is to
conserve and restore America's whitewater resources and to enhance opportunities to enjoy them safely. (American
Whitewater maintains links with affiliate

padling clubs throughout the U.S. and
publishes *The Safety Code of American
Whitewater*, a "collection of guidelines"
booklet, revised in 1998, that includes
diagrams of the universal river signals and
the text of the international scale of river
difficulty, classes I-VI. This is available as
an internet download, or in booklet
format.)

*Regional Coordinators for American
Whitewater* (alphabetical by state):

Lonnie Carden, Montgomery, AL
(334/272-0952)

Steve Gowins, Birmingham, AL
(205/967-9592)

Michael Bean, Coloma, CA
(mike@rivervilla.com)

Keith Beck, Redendo Beach, CA
(213/546-1780;
kbeck999@earthlink.net)

Mike Fentress & Hilde Schweitzer, Lotus,
CA (mikefen@innercite.com)

Paul Martzen, Fresno, CA
(pamartzen@cvip.net)

Aida Parkinson, McKinleyville, CA
(Aida_parkinson@nps.gov)

Ronald Rogers, Redding, CA
(rrogerskayaker@juno.com)

Ric Alesch, Lakewood, CO
(ralesch@worldnet.att.net)

Pope Barrow, Washington, DC
(pbarrow@holc.house.gov)

Don Piper, Savannah, GA
(912/201-2390; donpiper@att.net)

Michael Terry, Atlanta, GA
(terry@bondurant-mixson.com)

Russell Partain, Marietta, GA
(russellhp@mindspring.com;
770/579-8879)

Mark Rist, Bonner's Ferry, ID
(riverm@coldreams.com)

Erik Sprenne, Highland, IN
(sprenne@netnitco.net)

James Stapleton, Elkhorn City, KY
(surfin@kymtnnet.org)

Steven Taylor, Potomac, MD
(potomacsurf@worldnet.att.net;
301/794-5256)

Mac Thornton, Cabin John, MD
(potomacgorge@compuserve.com)

**American Whitewater, Regional
Coordinators** *(continued)*

Jesse Whittemore, Friendsville, MD
(301/746-5389)

Steve Demetriou, Windham, ME
(207/892-4268)

John Frachella, Bangor, ME
(johncf@midmaine.com)

John Tansil, Cape Girardeau, MO
(jetcape@yahoo.com)

Doug Ammons, Missoula, MT
(bammons@compuserve.com)

Triel Culver, Missoula, MT
(tculver@dmllaw.com)

Rich Hoffman, Carrrboro, NC
(RRHoff@email.unc.edu)

Glen Banks, Placitas, NM
(glenbanks@aol.com)

Marshall Seddon, New Paltz, NY
(imkayaknut@hotmail.com;
845/256-1647)

Jerry Hargrave, Rochester, NY
(k1c1c2@aol.com)

Pete Skinner, West Sand Lake, NY
(skinnp@rpi.edu)

Nancy Weal, Watertown, NY
(fishinsp@hotmail.com)

Matt Muir, Akron, OH
(rivieraratt@aol.com; 330/668-2329)

Keith Jensen, Portland, OR
(acks@teleport.com)

Britt Gentry, Portland, OR
(bgentry@gri.com)

Mark Antonik, Johnstown, PA
(mantonik@surfshop.net;
814/288-6112)

Charlene Coleman, Columbia, SC
(cheetahtric@hotmail.com)

Jason Darby, Knoxville, TN
(wepaddle@usit.net)

Dale Robinson, Knoxville, TN
(tn_riverdog@att.net)

Bob Tonnies, Gray, TN
(btonnies@eastman.com)

Steve Daniel, College Station, TX
(sdaniel@philosophy.tamu.edu;
979/846-4649)

Charlie Vincent, Salt Lake City, UT
(charliev@xmission.com;
801/243-4892)

John Heffernan, Bristol, VA
(johnheff@bvunet.net; 540/669-9597)

Paul Delaney, Spokane, WA
(riverruner@icehouse.net)

Gary Korb, Port Orchard, WA
(360/876-6780)

Judy Theodorsen, Spokane, WA
(jtheodorson@arch.wsu.edu;
509/327-4517)

Thomas O'Keefe, Seattle, WA
(okeefe@u.washington.edu;
206/527-7947)

Steve Morgan, White Salmon, WA
(sjmorgan@gorge.net; 509/493-2832)

Mike Sklavos, Whitewater, WI
(msklavos@wiscnet.net; 608/883-2260)

Tim Daly, Scott Depot, WV
(timdaly@prodigy.net)

Canadian River Heritage System
Secretary CHRB,
Ottawa, Ontario, K1A OM5
819/994-2913
http://collections.ic.gc.ca/rivers

Established in 1984 by federal, provincial,
and territorial governments to conserve
and protect the best example of Canada's
rivers. (Excellent links.)

**Grand Canyon Private Boaters
Association**
P.O. Box 2133, Flagstaff, AZ 86003-2133
928/214-8676
http://www.gcpba.org

Formed in 1996 to provide the self-
outfitted public an advocate and voice to
achieve fair access for the noncommercial
river runner in the Grand Canyon. (An
excellent information source on statistics,
history, waiting lists, and reference books.)

Idaho Rivers United
PO Box 633
Boise, ID 83701
408/343-7481; fax 208/343-9376
iru@idahorivers.org
http://www.idahorivers.org

Since 1990 Idaho Rivers United has been
saving rivers including the Payette, the
Salmon, the Priest, the Bear, the Snake,
and the high desert rivers of the Owyhee
uplands. We defend your rivers from
unnecessary new dams, diversions and
and over-development. We are building a
legacy for future generations: the
opportunity to fish, boat, and be
personally rejuvenated by Idaho's free-
flowing rivers.

**Leave No Trace Center for
Outdoor Ethics**
PO Box 997, Boulder, CO 80306
800/332-4100
ben@LNT.org
http://www.LNT.org

The Leave No Trace educational program
promotes skills and ethics to support the
sustainable use of wildlands and natural
areas. The concept originated in the US as
a way to help recreationists minimize their
impacts while enjoying the outdoors. In
1991, the US Forest Service teamed with
the National Outdoor Leadership School
(NOLS) and the Bureau of Land Management as partners in the Leave No Trace
educational program. NOL, a recognized
leader in minimum-impact camping
practices, became involved as the first
provider of Leave No Trace materials and
training. Today, the nonprofit organization
Leave No Trace Center for Outdoor Ethics,
established in 1994, manages the national program. Leave No Trace unites
four federal land management agencies
(the US Forest Service, National Park
Service, Bureau of Land Management,
and US Fish and Wildlife Service) with
manufacturers, outdoor retailers, user
groups, educators, and individuals who
share a commitment to maintain and
protect our wildlands and natural areas
for future enjoyment.

National Wild and Scenic Rivers System
http://www.nps.gov/rivers/index.html

This site provides information and links to
many sources, including the four principle
governmental agencies managing US
rivers:

Bureau of Land Management (BLM):
http://www.blm.gov
National Park Service (NPS):
http://www.nps.gov
US Fish and Wildlife Service (FWS):
http://www.fws.gov
US Forest Service (FS):
http://www.fs.fed.us

River Management Society
PO Box 9048,
Missoula, MT 59807-9048
406/549-0514; fax 406/542-6208
rms@river-management.org
http://www.river-management.org

The River Management Society is a nonprofit professional society dedicated to
the protection and management of North
America's river resources. Its mission is to
protect and conserve our nation's river
resources. The RMS develops and promotes professional river management
techniques, positively influences public
policy on river management issues,
educates decision makers and the public,
serves as a forum for information sharing,
and promotes and encourages professional development opportunities for
members. (They maintain a current list of
rivers with limited, required permits and
publish *Rivers Digest*, full of useful
information about river conditions and
permitting.)

EDUCATION AND TRAINING:

PADDLING, FIRST AID, WILDERNESS MEDICINE, RESCUE, AND OUTDOOR LEADERSHIP SCHOOLS
This list is for your research and carries no recommendations: ask about their instructor certification and always get references. Don't forget that your local college or university outdoor activities center and YMCA can be good sources of training as well.

Ace Paddling Center
PO Box 1168, Oak Hill, WV 25901
800/787-3982
ace@aceraft.com
http://www. KayakWV.com;
http://www.aceraft.com

Adventures Abound
1500 Oak Ridge Ct., O'Fallon, IL 62269
618/628-3902
riverruner5@aol.com
http://www.adventuresabound.com

American Red Cross
431 18th St., NW, Washington, DC 20006
202/639-3520
http://www.redcross.org

Appalachian Mountain Club
5 Joy St., Boston, MA 02108
617/523-0636; fax 617/523-0722
http://www.outdoors.org

Barry Smith's Mountain Sports
Kayak School
PO Box 1986,
Steamboat Springs, CO 80488
970/879-8794
MrKayakSteamboat@c.s.com
http://www.mtsportkayak.com

Bear Paw Outdoor Adventure Resort
N3494 Highway 55,
White Lake, WI 54491
715/882-3502
bearpaw@newnorth.net
http://www.bearpawinn.com

Bob Foote
Route 1, Box 183, Cleveland, Oklahoma
74020-9712
281/844-6854
bobfoote1@aol.com
http://www.bobfoote.com/instruction.htm

California Canoe & Kayak
Jack London Square, 409 Water St.,
Oakland, CA 94607
510/893-7833; fax 510/893-2617
calkayak@aol.com
http://www.calkayak.com

Camp Mondamin for Boys & Camp Green
Cove for Girls
PO Box 8, Tuxedo, NC 28784
800/688-5789
http://www.mondamin.com;
http://www.greencove.com

Canyon Voyages Adventure Co. Kayak
School
211 North Main, Moab, UT 84532
800/733-6007
info@canyonvoyages.com
http://www.canyonvoyages.com

Cascade Kayak School
7050 Hwy 55, RIO,
Horseshoe Bend, Idaho 83629
800/292-RAFT or 208/793-2221
http://www.cascaderaft.com

Charles River Recreation
2401 Commonwealth Ave.,
Newton, MA 02466
617/965-5110; fax 617/965-7696
http://www.ski-paddle.com

Confluence Kayaks, LLC
1537 Platte Street, Denver, CO 80202
303/433-3676; fax: 303/455-4583
http://www.confluencekayaks.com

Canyon Canoeing Adventures
PO Box 775363,
Steamboat Springs, CO 80477
Ph/fax: 888/922-2663
Douglas@canyonadventures.com
http://www.canyonadventures.com

Endless River Adventures
14157 Hwy 19 West, PO Box 246,
Bryson City, NC 28713
828/488-6199
EndRivAdv@cs.com
http://www.endlessriveradventures.com

Four Corners Riversports
PO Box 379 Durango, CO 81301
800/426-7637 (800/4CORNERS)
http://www.riversports.com

Hanging Rock Outdoor Center
Store: 232C Moores Springs Rd.,
Westfield, NC 27053
336/593-8283
Office: 30 Glenwood St.,
Winston-Salem, NC 27106
336/765-4477
http://www.hroconline.com

Jackson Hole Kayak School
PO Box 9201, Jackson, WY 83002
800/733-2471
JacksonHoleKayak@wyoming.com
http://jhkayakschool.com

Kayak & Canoe Institute
Univ. of Minn., Duluth; Outdoor Program;
121 SpHC, 10
University Drive, Duluth, MN 55812
218/726-6533
outdoor@d.umn.edu
http://www.d.umn.edu/umdoutdoors

Liquid Skills Kayak School
#9 Jamieson Lane, RR#1,
Beachburg, Ontario K0J 1C0 Canada
613/582-3340
http://www.liquidskills.com

Madawaska Kanu Centre
247 River Rd, Barry's Bay, Ontario K0J
1B0 Canada
Summer: 613/756-3620;
Winter: 613/594-5268
http://www.mkc.ca

Mountain & River Adventures
PO Box 858, Kernville, CA 93238
800/561-6553
mtnriver@mtnriver.com
http://www.mtnriver.com

National Outdoor Leadership School
(NOLS)
284 Lincoln St., Lander, WY 82520-2848
800/710-NOLS; fax 307/332-1220
admissions@nols.edu
http://www.nols.edu

Nantahala Outdoor Center
13077 Hwy 19 West
Bryson City, NC 28713-9114
800/232-7238, ext. 600
programs@noc.com
http://www.noc.com

National Association for Search
and Rescue
4500 Southgate Place, Ste 100, Chantilly,
VA 20151-1714
703/222-6277; fax 703/222-6283
info@nasar.org
http://www.nasar.org

New England Outdoor Center
PO Box 669, Old Medway Rd.,
Millinocket, ME 04462
800/766-7238; 207/723-5438
info@neoc.com
http://www.neoc.com

North American River Runners
PO Box 81, Hico, WV, 25854
800/950-2585; fax 304/658-4212
narr@narr.com
http://www.narr.com

Ottawa Kayak School
PO Box 89, Beachburg,
Ontario K0J 1C0 Canada
800/267-9166
http://www.ottawakayak.com

Otter Bar
Box 210, Forks of Salmon, CA 96031
530/462-4772
otterbar@aol.com
http://www.otterbar.com

Pisgah Whitewater
828/883-4026
mail@pisgahwhitewater.com
http://www.pisgahwhitewater.com

Education and Training (continued):

Potomoc Outdoors
7687 MacArthur Blvd.,
Cabin John, MD 20818
301/320-1544
http://www.potomacoutdoors.com

Potomac Paddlesports Center
Potomac, MD
877/529-2542
info@potomacpaddlesports.com
http://www.potomacpaddlesports.com

Riversport School of Paddling
PO Box 95, 355 River Rd.,
Confluence, PA 15424
800/216-6991
whiteh2o@qcol.net
http://www.riversportonline.com

RiverRun Paddling Centre
PO Box 179, Beachburg,
Ontario K0J 1C0 Canada
800/267-8504; 613/646-2501
riverrun@renc.igs.net
http://www.riverrunners.com

Rocky Mountain Adventures, Inc.
PO Box 1989, Fort Collins, CO 80522
800/858-6808; 970/493-4005
classes@shoprma.com
http://www.shoprma.com

Rocky Mountain Outdoor Center
228 N. F St., Salida, CO 81201
800/255-5784
rmoc@romc.com
http://www.rmoc.com

Saco Bound
PO Box 119, Center Conway, NH 03813
603/447-2177
rivers@sacobound.com
http://neoutdoors.com/sacobound

School of Wilderness Arts & Technology
RR#1 Box 79, Palmer Rapids, ON,
Canada K0J 2E0
613/758-1092 (voice and fax)
info@madawaska.com
http://www.mv.igs.net/ ~ wildtek/white.htm

Sierra South Mountain Sports
Box 1909, Kernville, CA 93238
800/376-7303
http://www.sierrasouth.com

Stonehearth Open Learning Opportunties
(SOLO)
PO Box 3150, Conway, NH 03818
603/447-6711
info@soloschools.com
http://www.stonehearth.com

Summit Kayak School/Colorado
Kayak Supply
131 Blue River Parkway,
Silverthorne, CO 80435
or PO Box 1, Nathrop, CO 81236
sks@amigo.net
http://www.coloradokayak.com

Summit Whitewater Expeditions
PO Box 22, Hendersonville, NC 28793
828/606-4477
jamie@summitwhitewater.com
http://www.sumitwhitewater.com

Sundance River Center
344 Thornridge Lane, Merlin, OR 97532
888/777-7557; 541/479-8508
info@sundanceriver.com
http://www.sundanceriver.com

Tarkio Kayak Adventures
PO Box 3025, Missoula, MT 59806
406/543-4583
kayak@teamtarkio.com
http://www.teamtarkio.com

Voyageur Outward Bound School
800/311-3919
vobs@vobs.com
http://www.vobs.org

Wilderness Medical Associates
189 Dudley Rd., Bryant Pond, ME 04219
888/WILDMED; fax 207/655-2747
office@wildmed.com
http://www.wildmed.com

Wilderness Medicine Institute, NOLS
284 Lincoln St., Lander, WY 82520-2848
800/710-NOLS; fax 307/322-7800
wmi@nols.edu
http://www.NOLS.edu

Wild Waters Outdoor Center
1123 State Rte 28 The Glen,
Warrensburg, NY 12885
800/867-2335
paddler@WildWaters.net
http://www.WildWaters.net

Whitewater Challengers Outdoor
Adventure Center
PO Box 8, White Haven, PA 18661
800/443-RAFT
info@wc-rafting.com
http://www.wc-rafting.com

World Class Kayak Academy
PO Box 1557, Missoula, MT 59806
800/538-6716; 406/829-8071
http://www.worldclassacademy.com

Zoar Outdoor Paddling School
Mohawk Trail, Charlemont, MA 01339
800/532-7483
info@zoaroutdoor.com
http://www.zoaroutdoor.com

MAPS:

FOR UNITED STATES AND CANADA

Use publications and topographic maps to improve your planning process and increase your river knowledge and trip safety.

Maps à la Carte, Inc.
Web Store: http://www.topozone.com

National Geographic Society
Phone orders US/Can: 800/437-5521
Web Store:
http://shop.nationalgeographic.com

Canada:

Centre for Topographic Information, NRC
615 Booth Street, Room 711, Ottawa
Ontario Canada K1A 0E9
800/465-6277; fax 613/947-7948
topo.maps@NRCan.gc.ca
http://www.maps.NRCan.gc.ca

Canadian River Heritage System
Secretary CHRB, Ottawa, Ontario, K1A OM5
819/994-2913
http://collections.ic.gc.ca/rivers

United States:

US Geological Survey Information Services
12201 Sunrise Valley Drive, Reston VA 20192
888/275-8747 (888/ASK-USGS)
ask@usgs.gov
http://ask.usgs.gov

National Park Service (NPS):
Maps and River Mileage Classifications for Components of Wild and Scenic Rivers System:
http://nps.gov/rivers/publications/rivers-table.pdf

Bureau of Land Management (BLM):
http://www.blm.gov/nhp/index.htm

US Fish and Wildlife Service (FWS):
http://www.fws.gov

US Forest Service (FS):
http://www.fs.fed.us

WATER-USER LINKS:

USE THESE WEBSITES TO FIND MORE INFORMATION TO PLAN YOUR RIVER TRIP:

http://www.usbr.gov/rsmg/links/waterspots.html

This Bureau of Reclamation website is a goldmine. It contains 181 useful category links like: Meteorology, Storage and Flows for Rivers, Snowpack-data, current and by past years, and many more. Follow the links and bookmark rivers of interest to you. You can then see how flows are and what to expect in the future for planning a trip today, in a few days, or in a few months.

http://www.boatertalk.com

This site bills itself as "The International Information Site for the Whitewater Paddler." It links with more than 500 member pages, has book reviews, gear information, river reports, and is fun.

http://www.webpak.net/ ~ rafter

Known as "Vince's Idaho Whitewater Page," this site is a gem of a site focusing on Idaho rivers.

http://www.publiclands.org

"Your one-stop source for recreation information" says the site headline, and it is. Sponsored by the Public Lands Interpretive Association (PLIA), this nonprofit educational partnership between the Bureau of Land Management and the USDA Forest Service links you to national parks and forests, wildlife refuges, state lands, and lakes and reservoirs. Free books and maps available for the cost of postage.

Bibliography

Alloway, David. *Wilderness 911*. Seattle, WA: The Mountaineers Books, 2000.

American Red Cross. *Health and Safety Fact Sheet, sect. x, 60*. Washington, DC: March, 2000.

Auerbach, Paul S. *Field Guide to Wilderness Medicine*. St. Louis, MO: Mosby, 1999.

Bechdel, Les, and Slim Ray. *River Rescue: A Manual for Whitewater Safety*. Boston, MA: Appalachian Mountain Club Books, 1997.

Bennett, Jeff. *The Complete Whitewater Rafter*. Camden, ME: Ragged Mountain Press, 1996.

Burt, William H., and Richard P. Grossenheider (Roger Tory Petersen, ed.). *A Field Guide to the Mammals*. Boston: Houghton Mifflin Co., 1964.

Cooper, Mike. "Boater's Fruit Pemmican." *On the Eddy Line* (Idaho Whitewater Association) 124: 1-2 (December 1999).

Curtis, Rick. *OA Guide to Planning a Safe River Trip*. This copyrighted, eight-page monograph and four-page decision tree emphasizes personal and group safety and is published on the Princeton University Outdoor Action website: princeton.edu/ ~ oa/paddle/rivplan.shtml.

Davidson, James W., and John Rugge. *The Complete Wilderness Paddler*. NY: Knopf, 1983.

Delaney, Tim. "'CFS': What Does It Mean?" *On the Eddy Line* (Idaho Whitewater Association) 102: 5 (May 1997).

Fiedler, Fred, Martin Chemers, and Linda Mahar. *Improving Leadership Effectiveness: The Leader Match Concept*. New York: John Wiley & Sons, 1977.

Fulton, Lois, Carolee Davis, and Evelyn Matthews. *Recipes for Quantity Food Service*. U.S.D.A. Home Economics Research Report #47, 1984.

Gill, Paul. *Wilderness First Aid*. Camden, ME: Ragged Mountain Press, 2001.

Gookin, John. *Defining and Developing Judgment*. This excerpt from the NOLS Leadership Education Toolbox, 1998, is published on the website for the National Outdoor Leadership School: http://www.nols.idu/Publications/Toolbox/Judgment.html.

Graham, John. *Outdoor Leadership: Technique, Common Sense, & Self-Confidence*. Seattle, WA: The Mountaineers Books, 2002.

Hermann, Eric. "River Trip Planning." *Paddler Magazine* 20 (2): 67 (March-April 2000).

Huser, Verne. *River Running*, Seattle. WA: The Mountaineers Books, 2001.

Jacobson, Cliff. *Expedition Canoeing: A Guide to Canoeing Wild Rivers in North America*. Globe Pequot Press, 2000.

Johnson, Jimmie. *Whitewater Rafting: Manual of Tactics and Techniques for Great River Adventures*. Stackpole Books, 1994.

Kellogg, Zip. *Whole Paddler's Catalog*. Camden, ME: Ragged Mountain Press, 1997.

Kesselheim, Alan. *Camp Cook's Companion*. Camden, ME: Ragged Mountain Press, 2002.

Kesselheim, Alan. *The Wilderness Paddler's Handbook*. Camden, ME: Ragged Mountain Press, 2001.

Leave No Trace Center for Outdoor Ethics. *Western River Corridors, Skills and Ethics*. Boulder, CO: Leave No Trace Center for Outdoor Ethics, 2001. Website: http://www.LNT.org.

Marrone, Teresa. *The Back-Country Kitchen*. Minneapolis, MN: Northern Trails Press, 1996.

Mason, Bill. *Song of the Paddle*. Toronto: Key Porter Books, 1997.

McGinnis, William. *The Guide's Guide*. El Sobrante, CA: Whitewater Voyages, 1981.

McGinnis, William. *Whitewater Rafting*. NY: Quadrangle/ The New York Times Book Co., 1975.

Miller, Dorcas. *Backcountry Cooking*. Seattle, WA: The Mountaineers, 1998.

Mills, Sheila. *Rocky Mountain Kettle Cuisine, II*. Boise, ID: Sheila's Good Taste, Inc., 1990.

Nealy, William. *Kayak*. Birmingham: Menasha Ridge Press, 1986.

O'Bannon, Allen, and Mike Clelland. *Allen & Mike's Really Cool Backpackin' Book: Traveling & Camping Skills for a Wilderness Environment*. Guilford, CT: Globe Pequot, 2001.

Petzoldt, Paul. *The Wilderness Handbook*. New York: Norton, 1974.

Treat, Nola, and Lenore Richards. *Quantity Cooking*. NY: Little Brown, and Co., 1966.

Walbridge, Charles, and Wayne Sundermacher. *Rescue Manual: New Techniques for Canoeists, Kayakers, and Rafters*. Camden, MA: Ragged Mountain Press, 1995.

Watters, Ron. *The White-water River Book: A Guide to Techniques, Equipment, Camping, and Safety*. Seattle, WA: Pacific Search Press, 1982. Also, Ron Watters' Idaho State University website publishes "Planning Multiday Rafting or Kayaking Trips" at http://www.isu.edu/outdoor/.

Wilkerson, James A. *Medicine for Mountaineering & Other Wilderness Activities*. Seattle, WA: The Mountaineers Books, 1992.

Wyler, Susan. *Cooking for a Crowd*. New York: Harmon Books, 1988.

Yeager, Jeffrey A. "Paddle Sport Recreation in the United States," in *Outdoor Recreation in Amercian Life* (the final summary findings report of the National Survey on Recreation and the Environment), ed. H. Ken Cordell. Champaign, IL: Sagamore Publishing, 1999.

Yeamans, David. *Critical Incident Stress Syndrome*. Grand Canyon Private Boaters Association website, Summer, 2001: http://www.gcpba.org/pubs/.

Index

Acknowledgments

Believe me, my young friend, there is *nothing* – absolutely nothing – half so much worth doing as simply messing about in boats.*

– KENNETH GRAHAME, *THE WIND IN THE WILLOWS*

Without Keith Taylor's and Mike Norell's friendly prodding, this book wouldn't exist. My lists, menus, and planning ideas would still be on 3-by-5 cards and in e-mails to our friends and family. Special thanks to these first-descent kayakers for their mentoring, and to Gary Payne for sharing his paddling and river trip skills with me. These boaters have passed on their genuine love of "messing about in boats" to me and countless other younger paddlers. To my most constant partner, my husband Barry, thanks for the love and years of fun. True to his years of faithful stern-paddling our Grummans, he boosted my lagging resolve when he promised to write the chapters on leadership and safety. Kate Krakker, RN, FPN, KB (Kayaking Buddy) graciously contributed her up-to-date wisdom to the first aid section. Thanks also to my readers and peer advisors at the Log Cabin Literary Center for their editing assistance: Judy Barker-Frederick, Joyce Davis, Coston Frederick, Liz Goins, Kelly Jones, Frank Marvin, Byron Meredith. And, to our wonderful children, Christian, Eric and his wife Andrea – always eager with paddles in hand and plates held out for seconds – thanks coming on so many of our adventures in the past and for helping edit this one! From toddlerhood "the boys" joyfully participated in their parents craziness. Now competent kayakers, they are great trip members, willingly assuming trip leadership positions and taking the team approach into the next generation of successful river trippers. I'm indebted to many boaters of all ages who've allowed me to use photos of them in this book and to provide memorable antics for my river poems. Special thanks to contributing artist Joshua Hindson and photographer Todd Swanson for sharing their talents with the paddlesport community. Finally, my technical advisors, Gail LeBow, Bill and

---

Maryl Sedivy, Katie Watts, Clare Woods and Margaret Parker – they have my sincere appreciation for the help in navigating the publishing world.

For permissions to reprint from copyrighted material, I gratefully acknowledge being able to quote from those on the copyright page and these additional generous sources:

Ron Myers, Editor, *On the Eddyline* Idaho Whitewater Association Newsletter: "Boater's Fruit Pemmican" (124:1-2, Dec. 1999) and "CFS : What Does It Mean?" (102:5, May 1997). Thanks to Mike Cooper for sharing the Boater's Fruit Pemmican recipe.

Frederick Reimers, Managing Editor, *Paddler* and Eric Hermann, author: "River Trip Planning" (20:2, Mar.-Apr. 2000, 67).

From A FIELD GUIDE TO THE MAMMALS, 3/e. Copyright 1952, © 1964, 1976 by William Henry Burt and the Estate of Richard Phillip Grossenheider. Reprinted by permission of Houghton Mifflin Company. All right reserved.

Quotations from Leave No Trace Center for Outdoor Ethics, *Skills & Ethics Series, Western River Corridors.* Copyright 2001. Reprinted from pages 5, 7, 9 by permission. For more information, call 800/332-4100 or use their website http://www.LNT.org.

From *River Rescue*, by Les Bechdel and Slim Ray. Copyright 1997. Reprinted from pages xiv and 237 by permission of Appalachian Mountain Club Books, 5 Joy St., Boston, MA 02108.

From *Improving Leadership Effectiveness*, by Fred Fiedler, Martin Chemers, and Linda Mahar, Wiley & Sons, 1977. Reprinted from page 12 by permission of Fred Fiedler and Martin Chemers.

About the Author and Contributors

A river runner for the past thirty-four years, Maria was first a canoeist, then kayaker. Her passion for well-planned river trips comes from whitewater adventures with friends and family in New York, Maine, Oklahoma, Arkansas, Colorado, California, Oregon, Montana, Wyoming, and Idaho. She credits her husband and two sons as invaluable assistants in helping her learn the essentials of river trip planning. She also thanks a host of friends who shared their wisdom and let her experiment with them. Her background as a registered nurse and former professor of public health makes *River Otter* not only a practical handbook, but one with a solid base in human behavior, health theory, and research. A lifelong member of the Sierra Club and former board member of Idaho Rivers United and Idaho Whitewater Association, Maria resides in Boise, Idaho, where she serves on the board of the Log Cabin Literary Center.

Maria and Barry Eschen and sons Christian and Eric

BARRY ESCHEN, MD, PHD: LEADERSHIP AND SAFETY SECTIONS; APPENDIX RIVER SAFETY TALK.

A 23-year veteran stern-paddler of the Eschens' beloved Grumman canoes. Hung up the single-blade paddle to join Maria kayaking twelve years ago. Years of river camping and a career in public health/preventive medicine make his contributions authoritative and useful.

KATE KRAKKER, RN, MN, FAMILY NURSE PRACTITIONER: MEDICAL/FIRST AID COORDINATOR SECTION.

Nurse practitioner in an emergency room in Boise. Accomplished kayaker and outdoors woman. Whitewater or desert, it's all fun. Mother and wife to an enjoyable rafting family: Joe, JJ, and Lauren.

Kate Krakker

JOSHUA HINDSON, SWM, ARTIST.

Earned a degree in graphic design and interactive multimedia before working as an art director for three years in Boulder, Colorado. A novice rafter, but no kayaker and not a strong swimmer, Josh has been on one expedition with the Eschens. He attributes his surviving to be a testament to The Eschen know-how. He's currently promoting his clothing company and designing on a freelance basis out of the home office in Boise, Idaho.

Joshua Hindson

ANOTTER PRESS, LLC

See reverse side for quick order form.

QUICK ORDER FORM
(to copy)

WEB SITE ORDERS: http://www.anotterpress.com

E-MAIL ORDERS: Orders@anotterpress.com

FAX ORDERS: 208-344-9930. Send this form.

POSTAL ORDERS: Send this form to...
Anotter Press, LLC
115 Provident Drive, Ste. 200
Boise, ID 83706-4017 USA

Please send book(s) to...   (PLEASE PRINT CLEARLY)

NAME

ADDRESS

CITY   STATE/PROV.   ZIP

TELEPHONE OR E-MAIL
(Will be used only if problems with your order)

River Otter: Handbook

(# copies) x $24.95 U.S.   =

(# copies) x $39.95 Can.   =

SALES TAX, IDAHO BUYERS ONLY: =
(6% for each book is $1.50)

SHIPPING:
UNITED STATES: $4 for first book, $2 ea. add'l.   =

INTERNATIONAL: $9 for first, $5 ea. add'l.   =

TOTAL $

Payment

❏ Check (make it to Anotter Press, LLC)

❏ Credit Card:

  ❏ Visa ❏ MasterCard ❏ Discover ❏ American Express

  ❏ Other:

CARD NUMBER   EXP. DATE (MO./YR.)

NAME ON CARD (PRINT)

SIGNATURE AS IT APPEARS ON CARD